MW00444794

GRACE AND GRATITUDE

FOR DAWN

Without whom this book would
not have been written

GRACE AND GRATITUDE

THE EUCHARISTIC THEOLOGY
OF JOHN CALVIN

B. A. Gerrish

Wipf and Stock Publishers
150 West Broadway • Eugene OR 97401

Wipf and Stock Publishers
150 West Broadway
Eugene, Oregon 97401

Grace and Gratitude
The Eucharistic Theology of John Calvin
By Gerrish, B.A.
©1993 Augsburg Fortress
ISBN: 1-59244-013-4
Publication date: August, 2002
Previously published by Fortress Press, 1993.

CONTENTS

The same thought keeps coming back to me: that there is a risk of my doing an injustice to the mercy of God by laboring so painstakingly to assert it— as if it were doubtful or obscure! But because we are so grudging that we never concede to God what belongs to him unless very strongly constrained, I shall have to insist on it at a little greater length.

I have now said repeatedly that he is treated with the honor he deserves when he is recognized as the author of all good things. It follows that our receiving them all from his hand should be attended with continual thanksgiving.

The Supper itself is a gift of God that ought to have been received with thanksgiving.

John Calvin

PREFACE _____

My purpose in writing this study of John Calvin is indicated in the title and subtitle I have given it. I certainly wish to make my contribution to the vexed question how he understood the Sacrament of the Lord's Supper. But I am even more concerned to show that the theme of grace and gratitude, presented in the words and actions of the Eucharist, shapes his entire theology and makes it from beginning to end a eucharistic theology. All six chapters began, under a slightly different title, as a broadly conceived interpretation of Calvin's theology for my Cunningham Lectures (1990) at the University of Edinburgh. My warmest thanks are due to the Cunningham Council for the invitation to deliver the lectures, and to the Principal and Professors of New College, Edinburgh, for their generous hospitality throughout the autumn term, 1990. I am deeply aware of the honor, as well as the challenge, that such an old and distinguished lectureship laid upon me. And I must add that my sense of indebtedness grows from strong roots. The lectureship gave me an occasion to acknowledge, and I hope in some measure to repay, two debts of very long standing.

There is, first, my debt to the host country, which in 1990 celebrated the three-hundredth anniversary of the establishment of Presbyterianism. Those who know me will attest how genuine a debt this is. Some four decades ago, I entered the theological college of what was then called (a little immodestly) the Presbyterian Church of England. The wisdom and learning my generation of students borrowed from Scotland was immense. We were brought up on the writings of H.R. Mackintosh, James Stewart, the Baillie brothers, and all those Scottish missionaries who brought the living word to us south of the border:

John Oman, John Skinner, J.Y. Campbell, and others. (I name only a few among many.) Especially important for my own development was the fact that my years at Cambridge (1949–55) coincided with the new Calvin studies of Thomas Torrance (*Calvin's Doctrine of Man*, 1949) and Ronald Wallace (*Calvin's Doctrine of the Word and Sacrament*, 1953). It will be clear from this book how permanently both of these distinguished scholars influenced my reading of Calvin and his theology. I studied their writings all the more avidly because I was not myself born into the Calvinist or Presbyterian tradition, though I am certain I was foreordained to it.

When I moved from Britain to America in 1955, I found the Scottish connection equally strong at Union Theological Seminary in New York, and in my two academic homes in Chicago: McCormick Theological Seminary and the University of Chicago. An announcement made one year by my colleague Joseph Haroutunian perfectly expressed my continuing sense of indebtedness to Scottish theology. He had decided to teach a course in which one of the required texts was to be Friedrich Schleiermacher's *The Christian Faith*, published in English by a team of brave Scottish translators in 1928. With an unconscious depth of meaning, the announcement read: "The Christian Faith is being imported from Scotland."

My second long-standing debt is, of course, to the subject of my lectures and of this book: John Calvin. The year of my matriculation at Queens' College, Cambridge, coincided with the reprinting of Calvin's *Institutes* in the old translation by Henry Beveridge. Although my field then was classics, not theology, I purchased the two-volume set, bound in dark green, and began eagerly to read it. I had not foreseen how much more difficult serious theology would prove to be than Sunday sermons and church-school lessons. And yet, I was wholly captivated by Calvin's vision of a world filled or to be filled in every corner with the glory of God—a sovereign God, who yet watches unresting over his children with a father's loving care. Calvin was installed immediately as my favorite theologian. I have read a number of theological books since, but Calvin's place in my thinking has remained secure and will no doubt continue to do so, unless, or until, I run across someone else who can call up that fundamental religious vision for me more compellingly than he does. Naturally, while I am grateful for the occasion that was given me in the lectures to acknowledge my debt to Calvin, I do not think of him as above criticism, or as the founder of an unchangeable Reformed *theologia perennis*. Indeed, one good friend whose Calvinism is less fluid than mine described me, upon reading my *Tradition and the Modern World*

(1978), as "a master of Reformed deviations." In these chapters I try to understand Calvin, to interpret him with deference and even affection, but also to indicate some respects in which I deviate from him.

My particular interest in Calvin's doctrine of the Eucharist goes back to my very first year as a teacher, when I rashly announced my intention to write a comparative study of the eucharistic theologies of Luther and Calvin. At about the same time, I was commissioned to put together a source book on the sixteenth-century eucharistic debates for the Library of Protestant Thought, published by Oxford University Press. The Library, alas, died from lack of purchasers. But the comparative study, though it took second place to other tasks, did yield some fragments from time to time, several of which have appeared as articles and reviews published between 1959 and 1988—a time span of nearly thirty years. In my Cunningham Lectures I tried to bring the pieces together and to cast them in a form more suited to a series of public addresses than to individual research papers. I ventured to inquire, in particular, how Calvin's doctrine of the Lord's Supper fits into his total theological project, as far as I am able to grasp it. Though the genesis of *Grace and Gratitude* is accordingly quite different, I should like this book to be viewed as a long overdue sequel to my youthful dissertation on Luther, *Grace and Reason* (1962). As in the earlier study, here too I attempt to shed light on a particular theological theme by setting it in the framework of the author's most fundamental thoughts, which, admittedly is a much more hazardous task than merely assembling the things he said about the Lord's Supper. In short, my purpose, is not just to offer another study of the Real Presence and to ask whether the elusive John Calvin, in his heart, really believed in it, but rather to display the eucharistic shape of Calvin's entire theology.

Not that I would wish to claim too much originality for him in this, or indeed in any other, respect. Originality is not the greatest of theological virtues; it is not to be ranked as highly as faithfulness to tradition. Calvin belonged self-consciously within the tradition of St. Augustine, for whom true religion was gratitude for our justification, expressed in the *Sursum corda* of the liturgy (see Augustine's *On the Spirit and the Letter*, chaps. 18–19). Some years ago, I found myself travelling on a train from Lancaster to London in the company of a young scholar I had just met at a conference. A recent convert to Roman Catholicism, he was amazed to learn that I actually do read the *Institutes*, and he asked me what I could possibly find worth reading in Calvin. Though a little disconcerted, I tried valiantly to answer as best I could, and when I was done he commented disdainfully:

"There's nothing peculiar to Calvin about that: it's just plain Christianity." And I said: "I know." If my audience heard nothing but plain Christianity in these lectures, I have good reason to be happy. But I also wanted to convince them, if possible, that John Calvin was a good interpreter of plain Christianity.

In reviewing the manuscript for publication, I have thought it best to retain the style of the spoken word. I have restored several passages that had to be left out when the lectures were delivered. But since my hope is that the book will have some value as an introduction to Calvin's theology, I have checked the obsessive urge to insert more and more refinements that would hold up the argument and perhaps conceal it. It would be easy, particularly in the final chapter, to lose a reader in details that have been lovingly dissected over the last four hundred years. Still, they are not trivial details and should not be simply ignored; historians of ideas and ecumenical theologians, myself among them, continue to find them irresistible. I have solved the resulting problem by leaving the lectures intact and accessible, relegating further scrutiny of the old, disputed questions to the footnotes, in which I make the case for my interpretations and try to open the way to further reflection and conversation.

Most of my academic debts are acknowledged in my references to the secondary literature. But I must add a special word of thanks to three friends for their encouragement and comments during the writing of these pages. Bruce McCormack, now of Princeton Theological Seminary, heard the lectures, responded to them publicly, and was my partner in a number of conversations, which I recall with deep apppreciation. He made the interesting remark (without disapproval, I am happy to add) that what I presented at Edinburgh was "a Schleiermacherian's Calvin." He was right. My interest in Schleiermacher has undoubtedly led me to notice things in Calvin I might otherwise have missed. But I must add that an even longer interest in Martin Luther seems to me to have done much the same for me, and I was glad that my Lutheran colleague Jerald Brauer, who read the manuscript for me, stressed its ecumenical possibilities. John Burkhart, of McCormick Theological Seminary, who also read the manuscript, rightly urged me to take fuller account of liturgical texts and offered some helpful comments on the cardinal term *pietas*. Besides these three colleagues, I wish to thank my assistants, Paul Capetz and Mary Stimming, for help beyond the call of duty, and my secretary, Peggy Edwards, for patient work on the manuscript. I am especially indebted to Mary Stimming for preparing the index. Last but not least, my greatest debt is to the Calvin scholar named in the dedication.

ABBREVIATIONS

BC   *The Book of Concord: The Confessions of the Evangelical Lutheran Church.* Trans. and ed. Theodore G. Tappert et al. Philadelphia: Fortress Press, 1959.

BELK   *Die Bekenntnisschriften der evangelisch-lutherischen Kirche.* 4th ed. Göttingen: Vandenhoeck & Ruprecht, 1959.

CERP   *Collectio confessionum in ecclesiis reformatis publicatarum.* Ed. H[ermann] A. Niemeyer. Leipzig: Julius Klinkhardt, 1840.

CO   *Ioannis Calvini opera quae supersunt omnia.* Ed. Wilhelm Baum, Eduard Cunitz, and Eduard Reuss. 59 vols. *Corpus Reformatorum,* vols. 29–87. Brunswick: C. A. Schwetschke and Son (M. Bruhn), 1863–1900.

DTC   *Dictionnaire de théologie catholique.* 15 vols. in 23. Paris: Letouzey and Ané 1899-1950.

Inst.   John Calvin, *Institutio Christianae religionis.* Cited by edition (see Bibliography).

LCC   *The Library of Christian Classics.* Ed. John Baillie et al. 26 vols. London: SCM Press, 1953–66.

LCL   *The Loeb Classical Library.*

LW   *Luther's Works.* American Edition. Ed. Jaroslav Pelikan and Helmut T. Lehmann. 55 vols. St. Louis, MO: Concordia Publishing House; Philadelphia: Fortress Press, 1955–86.

LWZ   *The Latin Works of Huldreich Zwingli.* Ed. Samuel Macauley Jackson et al. 3 vols. Vol. 1, New York: G.P. Putnam's Sons, 1912. Vols. 2–3, Philadelphia: Heidelberg Press, 1922–29. Vol. 1 carried the title *The Latin Works and the Correspondence of Huldreich Zwingli,* etc. Vols. 2 and 3 have been reprinted with the titles *On Providence and Other Essays* and *Commentary on True and False Religion* (Durham, NC: Labyrinth Press, 1983, 1981).

MPG   J.-P. Migne. *Patrologiae cursus completus: Series Graeca.* 161 vols. Paris, 1857–66.

MPL   J.-P. Migne. *Patrologiae cursus completus: Series Latina.* 221 vols. Paris, 1844-1900.
NPNF   *A Select Library of the Nicene and Post-Nicene Fathers of the Christian Church.* Ed. Philip Schaff. 14 vols. New York, 1886–90. Reprinted, Grand Rapids, MI: Wm. B. Eerdmans Publishing Co., 1969–75.
OS   *Joannis Calvini opera selecta.* Ed. Peter Barth, Wilhelm Niesel, and Doris Scheuner. 5 vols. Munich: Chr. Kaiser Verlag, 1926–52.
RGG³   *Die Religion in Geschichte und Gegenwart.* 3d ed. Ed. Kurt Galling et al. 7 vols. Tübingen: J. C. B. Mohr (Paul Siebeck), 1957-65.
ST   Thomas Aquinas, *Summa theologiae.*
SW   *Huldreich Zwinglis sämtliche Werke.* Ed. Emil Egli et al. *Corpus Reformatorum,* vols. 88 ff. Berlin, 1905–. The early volumes were reprinted and the series resumed in 1984 by the Theologischer Verlag, Zurich.
SWZ   *Selected Works of Huldreich Zwingi (1484–1531), the Reformer of German Switzerland.* Ed. Samuel Macauley Jackson. Philadelphia: University of Pennsylvania (New York: Longmans, Green & Co.), 1901.
TT   *Calvin's Tracts and Treatises.* Trans. Henry Beveridge. 3 vols. Edinburgh, 1844-51. Reprinted, Grand Rapids, MI: Wm. B. Eerdmans Publishing Co., 1958. Included as vols. 1–3 in *Selected Works of John Calvin: Tracts and Letters.* 7 vols. Grand Rapids, MI: Baker Book House, 1983.
VG   *Versio Gallica.* French version of *Inst.* (1560).
WA   *D. Martin Luthers Werke: Kritische Gesamtausgabe.* Weimarer Ausgabe. Weimar, 1883–.
ZW   *Huldrych Zwingli: Writings.* Trans. E. J. Furcha and H. Wayne Pipkin. 2 vols. Allison Park, PA: Pickwick Publications, 1984. (Library of Congress data give the title as *Selected Writings of Huldrych Zwingli.*)

One ——————————————————————

THE HOLY BANQUET AND THE
SUM OF PIETY

The Supper should be like a constant nourishment with which
Christ spiritually feeds the family of those who believe in him.

After the death of John Calvin (1509–64), and especially after the
Synod of Dort (1618–19), "Calvinism," as everyone knows, became
almost synonymous with "the dogma of predestination." In seventeenth-century England, for example, it was predestination that the
Latitudinarians found most offensive in the Puritan creed, and they
identified it simply as "the dogma of Calvin." Henry More (1614–87)
recalled how, even as a schoolboy standing on the playing fields of
Eton, he disputed with "this fate or Calvinistic predestination as it is
called"; and his fellow Cambridge Platonist Ralph Cudworth (1617–
88) judged the *arbitrary* fatalism of the predestinarian divines no less
obnoxious than the new, *natural* fatalism of Thomas Hobbes (1588–
1679).[1] If the identification of Calvinism and predestinarianism has
persisted, the blame (or the credit) must go as much to Calvin's friends
as to his critics. Some two centuries after More and Cudworth, another
Cambridge man, Henry Cole, D.D., of Clare Hall, alarmed by the
apostasy of certain "illegitimate Calvinists," published a work in two
volumes entitled *Calvin's Calvinism* (1856–57). It consisted of two
treatises by Calvin in English translation: one on eternal predestination, and the other on the secret providence of God. Cole remarked, a
little regretfully perhaps, that these are "the *only* productions of
Calvin, which he devoted expressly, exclusively, and purposely, to
the exposition and defence of the sublime doctrines of electing,

---

[1]   Gerald R. Cragg, ed., *The Cambridge Platonists*, Library of Protestant Thought
(New York: Oxford University Press, 1968), 9–10.

1

predestinating, and persevering grace."[2] Cole was in good company when he equated these themes with Calvin's Calvinism, and still would be today.

The association of Calvin's name with the "terrible" decree of predestination, as he himself admitted it to be, really needs no documentation. Harder to recognize is that Calvinism actually began its existence in the Reformation era as a distinct variety of sacramental theology, more particularly as a distinct interpretation of the central Christian mystery of the Eucharist. This is not to say that the Lord's Supper, not predestination, must therefore have been Calvin's central dogma. (A theologian's "center" is not necessarily whatever distinguishes his or her thinking from the thinking of everyone else.) Much less is it to offer a theological explanation for the existence of the Reformed or Calvinistic churches. Political realities are much too complicated for that. The point is simply that it may require an effort at disengagement from established stereotypes if one is to ask—without prejudice—about Calvin's own Calvinism. And I hope to show that his understanding of the Eucharist, even if it was not his central dogma, is a better indication of Calvin's primary theme than is the double decree. Unfortunately, however, I have to begin by admitting that his understanding of the Eucharist has always been a matter of controversy.

CRYPTO-CATHOLIC OR SUBTLE SACRAMENTARIAN?

In Calvin's own estimation, his teaching on the Eucharist or Holy Supper was simple, edifying, and irenic. True, his liberality was not extended to the Roman Catholics and their mass. But he believed that what he taught on the Holy Supper should have won the assent of both the German and the Swiss Protestants, and by the time of his return to Geneva in 1541 he saw himself as a mediating figure between the followers of Martin Luther (1483–1546) and the successors of Ulrich

---

[2]   John Calvin, *Calvin's Calvinism*, trans. Henry Cole, 2 vols. (London: Wertheim & Macintosh, 1856–57), ix–x. The work was reprinted by Wm. B. Eerdmans in a single centennial volume (Grand Rapids, MI, 1956). The National Union Catalogue gives Cole's floruit as 1823–46, apparently an inference from the date of his Luther translations. On his own testimony, he translated Calvin at a time of "great bodily and mental afflictions."

Zwingli (1484–1531).[3] And he suffered the fate of many a well-intentioned mediator: both sides found fault with his position. Heinrich Bullinger (1504–75), on whose shoulders Zwingli's mantle had fallen, wrote bluntly to Calvin: "I do not see how your doctrine differs from the doctrine of the papists, who teach that the sacraments confer grace on all who take them."[4] But the Lutherans, on the other side, though the issue for them was not the same, could see no essential difference between Calvin and the Zwinglians. The Calvinists and their Lutheran sympathizers, the crypto-Calvinists, are the "subtle sacramentarians" condemned in the Lutheran *Formula of Concord* (1577)—the most harmful kind. For whereas the *crass* sacramentarians (that is, honest Zwinglians) assert in plain German what they believe in their hearts, the *subtle* sacramentarians (wily Calvinists) talk Lutheran language and under this pretense still hold to the crass opinion: namely, that in the Holy Supper nothing but bread and wine are present and received by mouth.[5]

There is a rich secondary literature on Calvin's doctrine of the Lord's Supper in several languages: Dutch, English, French, and German. But whether he was a crypto-Catholic or a subtle Zwinglian, or something in between, is a question that has never been quite resolved.[6] It is not my intention to explore the literature now in detail, but only to set up one or two provisional markers at this stage of the way. The most intriguing discussion of Calvin's eucharistic thought in English is still John Williamson Nevin's (1803–86) *The Mystical Presence: A Vindication of the Reformed or Calvinistic Doctrine of the Holy Eucharist*. First published in Philadelphia in 1846, it has never been as widely known, even in America, as it should be; on the whole, it has been seen as something of a curiosity. Nevin's Calvin, we might say,

---

[3]   Particularly interesting is his review of the eucharistic debate in his *Petit traicté de la saincte Cene de nostre Seigneur Iesus Christ* (1541), OS 1:526–30; TT 2:194–98. Throughout the present study I use the adjective "eucharistic" in both its dictionary senses, to mean "relating to the Eucharist" and "expressing thanksgiving." Whether the restrictive or the more general sense is intended will be clear from the context.

[4]   In his notes (1548) on Calvin's propositions concerning the sacraments (CO 7:693). All translations in this volume are mine, unless otherwise stated, although I give parallel references to existing English versions wherever possible. No attempt has been made to provide cross-references to other texts and translations besides those cited.

[5]   *Konkordienformel*, Epitome, chap. 7, secs. 3–5 (BELK, 796–97; BC, 482).

[6]   Among the more important studies are (in order of publication): August [J.H.A.] Ebrard (1845–46), John W. Nevin (1846), Joachim Beckmann (1926), Alexander Barclay (1927), Wilhelm Niesel (1930), Helmut Gollwitzer (1937), Hans Grass (1940), Willem Frederik Dankbaar (1941), Jean Cadier (1951), Ronald S. Wallace (1953), G.P. Hartvelt (1960), Joachim Rogge (1965), and Kilian McDonnell (1967). See Bibliography.

was the Catholicizing Calvin. Even the editor of the *Lutheran Observer*
dismissed Nevin's interpretation of the Eucharist as an exploded
superstition, semi-Romanism, and equal to Puseyism; it was mystical,
confused, and carnal. Nevin, in his turn, was equally shocked: he
found this indictment, coming as it did from a Lutheran, "bare-faced
ecclesiastical infidelity."[7]

What, then, was the doctrine of the Holy Eucharist that Nevin
professed to retrieve from Calvin, but which to the ear of one nineteenth-century American Lutheran sounded too Catholic? In the
Lord's Supper, Nevin explains, we do not merely recall what Christ
has done for us, or merely partake of the benefits he has won. We
communicate with the living savior himself in the fullness of his
glorified person, which means: not only with his Spirit or divine
nature, but with his flesh and blood.[8] Nevin finds the heart of Calvin's
doctrine precisely in the thought of Christ's life-giving flesh. He
writes: "The living energy, the vivific virtue, as Calvin styles it, of
Christ's flesh, is made to flow over into the communicant, making him
more and more one with Christ himself, and thus more and more an
heir of the same immortality that is brought to light in his person."[9] Or,
as Nevin puts it in his own words, there is an "efflux" from Christ that
lodges itself in the inmost core of our personality and becomes the
"seed" of our sanctification.[10] Moreover, he insists that in the true
Calvinistic doctrine the Sacrament carries with it an objective force;
the virtue it possesses is not put into it by the faith of the worshipper.
"The signs are bound to what they represent [the very body and blood
of Christ], not subjectively simply in the thought of the worshipper,
but objectively, by the force of a divine appointment."[11]

The Mystical Presence was sent for review to Charles Hodge (1797–
1878), the presumed doyen of American Calvinists. He found the book
so repellant that it rested on his table unreviewed for two years.[12] He
took offense at many things, not least the assertion that the Sacrament
"serves in itself to convey the life of Christ into our person." "We know
nothing in [Cardinal] Bellarmine," Hodge commented, "that goes
beyond that."[13] Still, he could not overlook the fact that Nevin's book

7   *Mystical Presence*, 106-7 n.
8   Ibid., 57-58.
9   Ibid., 61.
10   Ibid., 168.
11   Ibid., 61.
12   Hodge, "Doctrine of the Reformed Church on the Lord's Supper" (1848): 227.
13   Ibid., 275.

was crammed with direct quotations from Calvin's eucharistic writings. And so, the great Princeton "Calvinist" dismissed the merely private authority of Calvin, and he reassured readers of the *Princeton Review* that Calvin's own doctrine of the Lord's Supper is an uncongenial foreign element in Reformed theology, partly derived from Lutheran influence. In the Reformed church, Hodge insisted, the notion of a mysterious efficacy flowing from the glorified body of Christ in heaven almost immediately died out.[14] Hodge leaves us wondering whether it is possible to be both a Calvinist and a Presbyterian. But the important point, for now, is that he conceded Nevin's picture of what we are calling the "Catholicizing Calvin."

In more recent years, a somewhat similar interpretation of Calvin's eucharistic thinking has appeared in the learned Dutch study by G.P. Hartvelt, *Verum Corpus* (1960). Hartvelt gives no indication of ever having heard of the debate between Nevin and Hodge. But he, too, concludes—somewhat to his own surprise—that the strange notion of Christ's life-giving flesh (the *caro vivifica*) stood at the center of Calvin's doctrine of the Lord's Supper and cannot be explained away.[15] But, like Hodge, he considers it a perilous intrusion into Reformed theology. By an odd exchange of allies (a *renversement des alliances*), it substitutes for the normally Antiochene affinities of Reformed Christology the Alexandrian christological type: Calvin appeals to Cyril of Alexandria (ca. 370–444) to support his belief that Christ's flesh is like a rich and inexhaustible fountain that pours into us the life streaming into it from the Godhead.[16] Hartvelt's own view, as a Reformed theologian, is that we can speak of Christ's "life-giving flesh" only because in it the work of redemption was accomplished, not because the divine life itself flows out of it. But this, of course, is intended as a *correction* of Calvin. Hartvelt *interprets* Calvin much as Nevin did.[17]

How, then, are we to account for the other image of the Reformer—the "Zwinglianizing Calvin"? One answer lies close to the surface, even in Nevin's *The Mystical Presence*. He has to follow his striking, realistic-sounding declaration of Calvin's eucharistic doctrine with an important rider: participation in Christ's flesh and blood in the Lord's Supper is of course spiritual, in no sense corporal or material. We are

---

[14]   Ibid., 251–52. See further my *Tradition and the Modern World* (1978), 60- 65.
[15]   Hartvelt, *Verum Corpus* (1960), 96–97, 114, 165, 201.
[16]   Ibid., 203, 211. Cf. *Inst.* 1559, 4.17.9 (2:1369). This passage goes back to the second edition (1539).
[17]   Hartvelt, *Verum Corpus*, 224–25.

not to suppose that the material particles of Christ's body are carried over by some supernatural process into the person of the believer.[18] Certainly, what is said generally in the sixth chapter of the Fourth Gospel about receiving Christ must apply to the eucharistic communion in particular: his flesh is meat indeed, his blood drink indeed— ἀληθῶς, in reality. But the language is figurative; the communication is real, but it is not oral.[19]

Because Calvin employed eucharistic language figuratively, as Nevin admits, many interpreters hear him saying nothing essentially different from what Zwingli had said. Otto Ritschl (1860–1944), for example, acknowledged that Calvin's doctrine of the Lord's Supper, like Martin Bucer's (1491–1551), was of the mediating type, harmonizing the extremes of Luther's and Zwingli's views, but he added: "Nevertheless, Calvin remained essentially faithful to Zwingli's symbolic theory (dem Symbolismus Zwinglis)." Calvin deliberately employed such expressions as "Christ's flesh is given to us for nourishment," or "we are fed substantially with the flesh of Christ," to refer to a purely spiritual (or nonliteral) "eating," and he did not worry about the misunderstandings and doubts to which such slippery usage exposed him.[20] The problem was made all the greater, we may add, because the realistic-sounding expressions were not the only ones he used: he spoke at times rather of receiving "life," "virtue," "energy," or "vigor" from Christ's flesh, rather than of receiving the flesh itself or the substance of the flesh. His language is not only figurative but bewilderingly inconsistent. Hans Grass concludes that Calvin's realistic way of speaking is therefore to be taken cum grano salis, with a grain of salt. If we take into account the expressions that say we receive life and strength from the substance of the flesh, then, in Grass's judgment, the reproach raised against Calvin from both the Lutheran and the Catholic sides is understandable: that no reception of the flesh and blood happens at all, according to Calvin, but only a reception of the power, effects, merits, and fruits of the flesh.[21]

It would be overhasty to infer that if Calvin's language was admittedly figurative or symbolic, he must have held the same theory of symbolic meaning as Zwingli did. All we are entitled to conclude at this point is that the question of communion with the body of Christ,

[18]   Nevin, The Mystical Presence, 60–61.
[19]   Ibid., 237–43. The more commonly accepted readings in John 6:55 are adjectival: Christ's flesh is "real meat," his blood "real drink" (ἀληθής, not ἀληθῶς).
[20]   Ritschl, Die reformierte Theologie (1926), 239.
[21]   Grass, Die Abendmahlslehre bei Luther und Calvin (1954), 248–53.

or of "eating Christ's flesh," necessarily carries us over into fundamental questions about signs, signification, and sacramental causality. For what is the reality to which the signs point? What does it mean
to eat the flesh of Christ spiritually? And are the liturgical objects and
actions in the Lord's Supper, for Calvin, in any sense bearers of the
reality they picture or signify? Or is a sign for him, as for Zwingli,
merely a token, a reminder, of an absent reality—of a past redemptive
deed to which one has access only in memory and imagination?[22] In
this regard, the most recent Calvin studies have, if anything, height-
ened the problem of his sacramental theology by seeing it as the
outcome of later medieval stress on the radical freedom and tran-
scendence of God. Kilian McDonnell, for example, says that "the
Scotistic and Occamistic philosophies, together with the mystical
movement and the *devotio moderna* piety, are important for the general
background to Calvin's eucharistic doctrine," because "they manifest
themselves in a flight from secondary causality and . . . a reassertion
of the sovereignty of God as the only cause."[23] Calvin's thought, fully
in line with this trend, according to McDonnell, betrays a weakened
instrumentality: for him, God "does not in any sense remain bound to
objects even after having chosen them."[24] If this reading of Calvin is
sound, it certainly puts him close to Zwingli, who expressly rejected
secondary causes and tirelessly insisted that God's Spirit needs no
means. Here, then, you have the Zwinglianizing Calvin, whose sacramental language has a question mark over it because it is symbolic,
inconsistent, and apparently influenced by a weakened sense of
instrumentality.

The conclusion we must draw is clear. The modern scholarly
literature on Calvin, at which we have only glanced, mirrors sixteenth-
century disagreement over his place in the eucharistic debate. Calvin,
of course, had no part in the fateful Marburg Colloquy (1529) between
the Lutherans and the Zwinglians; it took place years before he made
his public appearance. But the shadow of Marburg has hung over him
nonetheless. The fifteenth (and last) of the articles drawn up by Luther
at the end of the colloquy admitted that there was one thing on which
the two parties had not been able to agree: "whether the true body and
blood of Christ are bodily in the bread and wine."[25] Later, after

---

[22]   The differences between Zwingli and Calvin on the nature of signs are discussed in chapter six, pp. 163-69.
[23]   McDonnell, *John Calvin, the Church, and the Eucharist* (1967), p. 37.
[24]   Ibid., p. 166.
[25]   *Die Marburger Artikel* (1529), WA 30³.170.5–8; LW 38:88.

Marburg, it was repeatedly argued that the point at issue between the Lutherans and the Reformed was no longer whether, but only how, the body and blood of Christ were present in the Sacrament. Calvin himself so argued.[26] But debate over the fact, not just the manner, of the Real Presence continually returned. The Reformed denial of a local presence, or an oral receiving, of Christ's body was heard by the Lutherans as tacit doubt whether the body was present to believers at all, except in their imaginations.[27]

Calvin was at no time a pure Zwinglian. From the very first, he was convinced that Zwingli was wrong about the principal agent in both Baptism and the Lord's Supper. A sacrament is first and foremost an act of God or Christ rather than of the candidate, the communicant, or the church. Zwingli had the priorities wrong. Indeed, he not only put first what can only be secondary but made it the whole sacrament; he imagined that a sacrament is only an act by which we attest our faith and not rather, as it truly is, a sign by which God strengthens our faith.[28] And yet, although he found Zwingli's understanding of a

[26]   See chapter six, p. 174. From Calvin's assessment of Marburg in his *De la Cene* (see n. 3 above) it can perhaps be inferred that it was more natural for him to speak of agreement on our partaking of Christ's body and blood rather than on their presence, and this is a point that assumes greater importance in Calvin's later controversy with Westphal. See especially *Secunda defensio piae et orthodoxae de sacramentis fidei contra Ioachimi Westphali calumnias* (1556): "Quod inter opiniones reiectitias alicubi posui, Christi corpus realiter et substantialiter adesse in coena, minime cum vera et reali communicatione pugnat." (CO 9:73; TT 2:281). But, for Calvin, this is a matter of defining the mode of presence, and he could use presence language, too, more particularly in the formula "present *to*." See, e.g., *Inst.* 1536, OS 1:142; *Institution,* 145. Cf. *Inst.* 1559, 4.17.18 (2:1381). I return to the question of the mode of Christ's presence in chapter six, pp. 173-82. Calvin was convinced from the first that with his view of the partaking (*corporis participatio*) he allowed just as genuine a nourishing of faith as those who "pulled Christ down from heaven" (*Inst.* 1536, OS 1:143; *Institution,* 146).

[27]   See, for instance, Calvin's disclaimers in his *Defensio sanae et orthodoxae doctrinae de sacramentis* (1555), OS 2:282-84; TT 2:238-40.

[28]   *Inst.* 1536, OS 1:118, 122, 127, 137; *Institution,* 118, 122-23, 128, 139. Cf. the anti-Donatist remarks in the section on Baptism: the "letter" is from God, no matter who the carrier may be (OS 1:133; *Institution,* 135). Calvin does not identify Zwingli or his followers by name, but his intention is clear. It may be objected that he is not quite fair to them when he says: "Non ferimus, quod posterius est in sacramentis, ab illis primum, *atque adeo unum* constitui" (OS 1:122, my emphasis; *Institution,* p. 123).   Zwingli himself, at any rate, sometimes conceded that the sacraments *also* support faith, albeit this was not his main thought and he voiced it only with qualifications (see pp. 105-6 and notes below). But if, as is likely, Calvin's judgment was formed by Zwingli's *Commentary on True and False Religion,* he would have had no reason to believe that Zwinglians found anything more in a sacrament than an act by which Christians attest their faith. Zwingli there states expressly that a sacrament is nothing but the taking of a pledge, like a military oath (*De vera et falsa religione commentarius* [1525], SW 3:758-59, 761; LWZ 3:180-81, 184) and he disdains the view that a sacrament serves to reassure the recipient or to confirm faith (SW 3:757, 761; LWZ 3:179, 184). Had Calvin been able to read

sacrament defective, Calvin thought him right about the meaning of Christ's ascension for what happens in the Lord's Supper: if the Lord's body has been taken up to heaven, it cannot be enclosed down here in the bread.[29] A literal eating of Christ's flesh is impossible; the elements and actions in the Eucharist, as Zwingli held, must be an analogy of a spiritual eating.[30] For all his criticisms of him, Calvin accepted Zwingli's arguments against a local presence, and for this reason he could not lay to rest the Lutherans' doubts about his own position. The interpretation of his eucharistic theology still to this day turns largely around the same doubts: whether, in particular, there really was, for him, a bodily presence of Christ to the communicant. And with the question of the Real Presence goes the second, companion question concerning the instrumental efficacy of sacred objects and actions: whether sacramental signs are genuine means of grace. The suspicion has never quite been laid to rest that even when Calvin's language appears to affirm a real presence and the efficacy of sacred signs, he could not honestly have meant it.

THE HOLY BANQUET AND THE
1536 INSTITUTES

What are we to make of these uncertainties in the interpretation of Calvin's eucharistic theology? We should not rule out the possibility that in the course of his career he may have changed his mind, or his emphasis, or at least his language. True, it is commonly said that his thinking preserved a remarkable consistency from the first edition of his *Institutes* till the last. But anyone who traces all his writings on the Lord's Supper in chronological sequence will be struck by the evidence of fresh thoughts in new contexts; and in the successive editions of the *Institutes* itself the revisions are by no means trivial.

The problem surfaces already in the famous "Prefatory Address to King Francis I of France," which Calvin prefixed to every edition of his *Institutes*. In one trenchant section of the address, he firmly repudiates

---

German, he would have found it explicitly affirmed in Zwingli's treatise on Baptism, published the same year, that no outward thing can strengthen faith: " Denn es nit möglich ist, das ein usserlich ding den glouben vesten mög; denn der gloub kumt nit von usserlichen dingen, sunder allein von dem ziehenden gott; darumb mag inn ghein usserlich ding bevesten" (*Von der Taufe, von der Wiedertaufe und von der Kindertaufe* [1525], SW 4:227–28; LCC 24:138–39).

[29] *Inst.* 1536, OS 1:140–42, cf. 144; *Institution*, 142–45, 147.
[30] Ibid., OS 1:138; *Institution*, 140.

the charge of departing from the ancient fathers of the church. The difficulty is that the fathers said many different things, and his opponents search for dung amid the gold: the good things that the fathers wrote they either fail to notice, or cover up, or misrepresent. And in his remarkable list of good patristic utterances (gold) is this: not the true body but the mystery of the body is in the Sacrament of the Supper. In the 1536 edition, Calvin comments: "Therefore, they [his Roman Catholic opponents] overstep the bounds when they make it [the] real and substantial [body]."[31] He changed this in the 1539 edition to read: "Therefore, they overstep the bounds when they imagine that [the body] is contained there, locally confined."[32] Why the change? Surely because in 1539 Calvin was living in Strasbourg and could not let an antipapal remark be taken as anti-Lutheran also. Perhaps to leave nothing to chance, in 1543 he altered his comment again (and, incidentally, attached it to a different patristic quotation): "Therefore they overstep the bounds who imagine that the substance of the bread and wine is transformed and ceases to exist when the Lord's words are repeated."[33] And in case anyone still misses the point, he adds in 1559: ". . . so as to be transubstantiated into the body and blood."[34]

In this way, the rejection of a real and substantial presence becomes, in the passage from one edition of the *Institutes* to the next, only a rejection of transubstantiation. But is this a change of mind, or a change of strategy? Is the door opened to a real, substantial presence, or is it simply that an unnecessary offense to fellow evangelicals is avoided? Unfortunately, the problem goes deeper: even *within* the very first edition of the *Institutes*, taken by itself, it is not difficult to discover reasons why Calvin's critics might think his views uncertain, ambiguous, perhaps devious. The blame was partly his. He seemed to stumble between the rival opinions of Luther and Zwingli rather than to harmonize them, wavering on both the Real Presence and sacramental causality.

[31] "Igitur modum praetereunt, cum faciunt reale et substantiale" (CO 1:18). The editors of CO attribute the assertion to the author of an unfinished homily on Matthew found in the works of Chrysostom (CO 1:18, n. 2). But when the same assertion is quoted in the 1539 edition, the footnote says: "Gelasius papa in concil. Rom" (CO 1:267, n. 8).

[32] ". . . quum localiter illic circumscriptum contineri fingunt" (CO 1:267).

[33] ". . . qui fingunt transmutari et desinere substantiam panis et vini" (CO 1:267). The quotation is now from Gelasius (see LCC 20:20, n. 23). Cf. n. 31 above.

[34] ". . . ut in corpus ac sanguinem transsubstantietur" (OS 3:19).

In the 1536 *Institutes*, Calvin does not question the belief that the body and blood of the Lord are "distributed" in the Sacrament.[35] This, of course, is the language of the Lutheran Augsburg Confession in its original, unaltered version (1530); it is, presumably, above Lutheran reproach.[36] And yet, in the main the "giving" of Christ's body suggests to Calvin, as it did to Zwingli, the surrender of the body to death at Calvary, not the offering of it to the communicant in the Supper. The Sacrament sends us to the cross; it is a remembrance, a declaration of Christ's death.[37] And while Calvin does write of our coming to possess entire the crucified Christ,[38] his emphasis is on sharing Christ's benefits: the promised benefits are extended to us in the Sacrament just as if Christ were present.[39] Just as if? Are we to conclude, then, that Christ is not, after all, present? Well, Calvin denies forthrightly enough that Christ's body and blood are exhibited naturally in the Sacrament, or that the true and natural body of Christ—its actual substance—is given there.[40] What we partake of is rather the symbol of the body (that is, bread).[41] Nevertheless, he thinks it appropriate to affirm that the body of Christ is exhibited and offered to us "truly and efficaciously,"[42] or that Christ exhibits himself as present "in power and virtue." For this, he says, is the bodily presence that the nature of a sacrament demands.[43] But what kind of bodily presence is that?

If Calvin thus proves himself shy of the language of bodily presence, there is no less equivocation in his remarks on our second problem: the instrumentality of the sacraments. In one place in the 1536 *Institutes* he mentions the Zwinglian objection that the very notion of a sacrament appears to transfer the glory and power of God to created things (*creaturae*). He answers: "We do not place any power

---

[35] OS 1:138; *Institution*, 140. Cf. OS 1:141; *Institution*, 144 (Christ distributed his body in the Last Supper).

[36] BELK, 64; BC, 34.

[37] OS 1:138, 145, 149; *Institution*, 141, 148, 153. The sacraments in general attest past redemptive events (OS 1:126, 130, 131, 138; *Institution*, 127, 131, 132, 140–41).

[38] OS 1:139; *Institution*, 142.

[39] OS 1:137; *Institution*, 140. Cf. OS 1:139, 142; *Institution*, 142, 145.

[40] OS 1:142; *Institution*, 145. He does say, however, that Christ's body "becomes one substance with us" (OS 1:137; *Institution*, 140), though not that this happens in the Lord's Supper.

[41] OS 1:149; *Institution*, 153. Cf. OS 1:152; *Institution*, 156.

[42] OS 1:140–142; *Institution*, 142, 145. These expressions are taken from his direct discussion of the Lord's Supper. On the second article of the Apostles' Creed he had already written: "Itaque quanquam in coelum sublatus corporis sui praesentiam e conspectu nostro sustulit, non tamen auxilio ac potentia desinit adesse suis fidelibus, manifestamque praesentiae suae virtutem ostendere" (OS 1:84; *Institution*, 76).

[43] OS 1:143; *Institution*, 146.

in the created things. All we say is that God makes use of such means and instruments (*mediis ac instrumentis*) as he himself foresees to be expedient, that everything may serve his glory since he himself is Lord and arbiter of all things."[44] And yet, just a few pages on, after asserting that the Lord represents spiritual things by physical, Calvin quickly adds: "Not that such spiritual gifts (*gratiae*) are tied to a sacrament, or enclosed in it, or that a sacrament is an implement or instrument (*organum ac instrumentum*) to the end that they may be conferred on us, but only because the Lord attests to us by this token his will to bestow these things upon us."[45] So, are the sacraments instruments, or not?

I would not wish to assert that the two statements just cited, though formally in contradiction with each other, are beyond reconciliation. But Calvin himself must have had second thoughts about the second one: he dropped from the 1539 *Institutes* the denial "that a sacrament is an implement or instrument."[46] Similarly, he carefully modified another sentence that read in 1536: "Sacraments are like heralds that announce and show the things given to us by God's bounty but do not bring them."[47] The negative phrase "do not bring them" becomes in 1539 "do not bestow any grace," which is then further modified in 1543 by the crucial addition of the two words *a se*: "They do not bestow any grace *of themselves*."[48] Perhaps it was always Calvin's intention to say what he says in the final, 1559 edition of the *Institutes*: "Whatever implements God employs, they detract nothing from his primary operation."[49] Or perhaps it took him a while to make up his mind. Meantime, the Lutherans are surely to be forgiven if they heard Calvin's trumpet give an uncertain sound. This brief look at the 1536 *Institutes* alone is enough to earn them our sympathy.

No serious discussion of Calvin's eucharistic theology can pass over the ambiguities his opponents and his interpreters have found in his language. Clear enough! But the difficulties should not be allowed to distract us from what was central in his teaching on the Lord's Supper. For it should also be clear enough from the very first edition

---

[44]   OS 1:121; *Institution*, 122.

[45]   OS 1:133; *Institution*, 134. What is said here of the sacraments in general has already been said of Baptism in particular: the water is not an instrument of regeneration or renewal; what is received in Baptism is not the cause of salvation, but only the knowledge and assurance of such gifts (OS 1:127; *Institution*, 128).

[46]   1536: ". . . aut quod sacramentum organum ac instrumentum sit, quo nobis conferantur" (OS 1:133; *Institution*, 134). 1539: ". . . quo eius virtute nobis conferantur" (CO 1:965).

[47]   OS 1:124; *Institution*, 124.

[48]   CO 1:950 (my emphasis).

[49]   *Inst.* 1559, 4.14.17 (2:1293).

of the *Institutes* that no discussion, if it wants to take Calvin on his own terms, can be wholly determined by the question of the Real Presence. From the first, Calvin shows his anxiety that all the wrangling over the Real Presence might push aside what is actually, for him, the main point. He deplores the frightful controversies over how Christ's body is present in the bread, and how the body is swallowed by us.[50] The question is why, or to what end, there is a Lord's Supper at all.[51] The answer, he believes, is disclosed in what the sign signifies: when we see the bread extended to us, our thoughts should be on the analogy of life-giving nourishment.[52] The Lord's Supper does not simply exhibit the body; it seals and confirms the promise by which Christ testifies that his flesh is food indeed (John 6:55)—food not for our bodies but for our souls, since the Sacrament is spiritual.[53] "Just as bread nourishes, sustains, and preserves the life of our body, so Christ's body is the food and protection of our spiritual life."[54] That is the heart of the matter. The Lord's Supper is a genuine feast (*convivium*), a holy banquet (*sacrosanctum epulum*), which recalls to our memories that Christ was made the bread on which we continually feed. It is this focal image of the banquet that made Calvin's doctrine (in his own estimate) simple, edifying, and irenic.[55]

Calvin, too, finds that he cannot avoid a "how" question: how Christ's body, which was once given up for us, becomes ours.[56] And, oddly enough, having set the analogy of the holy banquet at the center, he immediately turns to the nature not of spiritual nourishment, but of Christ's body.[57] It is arguable that in so doing he frustrates his own desire to shift attention from the controversy over the Real Presence to the meaning of the sacramental analogy.[58] But of course he has much

---

[50]   OS 1:139; *Institution*, 141–42.

[51]   Cf. *De la Cene*, OS 1:503; TT 2:164.

[52]   OS 1:138; *Institution*, 140.

[53]   OS 1:138-39; *Institution*, 140–42.

[54]   OS 1:138; *Institution*, 140.

[55]   OS 1:161; *Institution*, 167. Cf. OS 1:159 (*Institution*, 164), from which my epigraph for this chapter is taken. Although Calvin can locate the analogy in the bread, from his earliest thoughts on the Eucharist he found the analogy in the action rather than in the element as such: "Signa quae hic dantur, ceremoniae sunt" (OS 1:125; *Institution*, 126). In the *Breve et clarum doctrinae de coena Domini compendium*, we find it said expressly that the symbol in the Eucharist is not the bread or the wine but their distribution and reception (CO 9:686). But Calvin's authorship of the compendium is not certain.

[56]   OS 1:139; *Institution*, 142.

[57]   OS 1:140–45; *Institution*, 142–48.

[58]   Note that Calvin himself already in the 1536 *Institutes* uses the expression *realis corporis praesentia* but does not endorse it (OS 1:147; *Institution*, 150).

more to say about spiritual eating elsewhere, and in due time we shall look at what he says. For now, we have the right point of entry to his eucharistic theology: his own point of entry, not that of one or other of his critics. Calvin's appeal to the metaphor of spiritual food does not resolve the problems of the Real Presence and the instrumentality of created things, but it does put these problems in a distinct perspective. By entering his doctrine of the Lord's Supper at its center, we can see how it is linked with the rest of his theological system, which in 1536 was only beginning to take shape.

CALVIN'S SUMMARY OF PIETY

But do we not run into a difficulty if we try to approach Calvin in this way? Was the *Institutes* properly a systematic work? It may even be that I myself have cast doubts on his credibility as a systematician by uncovering changes and inconsistencies in his language. Perhaps that says no more than that Calvin was, after all, human. But the need to understand his thought as a frail human effort to come to terms with the particular problems of his own time is precisely what leads William Bouwsma to deny that Calvin should be considered a systematic theologian at all.[59] "The available intellectual and cultural resources of the period," Bouwsma writes, "made the production of what we usually understand by 'systematic thought' almost inconceivable, a circumstance that students of Calvin's thought have rarely kept in mind. There are no significant 'systematic' thinkers in the sixteenth century. . . . A systematic Calvin would be an anachronism."[60] Bouwsma does not say how systematic thought is "usually" understood, but it appears from his incidental remarks that he himself pictures the systematic theologian as a contemplative recluse striving to erect a complete, passionless, and totally self-consistent edifice of timeless abstractions. Bouwsma may be right when he says that studies of Calvin's thought continue to be shaped by the assumption that theological language is exempt from the confusion and incoher-

---

[59]   Bouwsma, "The Quest for the Historical Calvin" (1986): 47–57. The substance of this article became the introduction to Bouwsma's *John Calvin* (1988), where it is supplemented by chapter nine, titled "Knowing." In the conclusion to the book (p. 234) Bouwsma concedes that "the conception of Calvin as a tidy and systematic thinker… is not altogether wrong."

[60]   Ibid., 54.

ence that plague other regions of human discourse.[61] Some studies perhaps are, and insofar as their authors project such a notion of theology onto Calvin's own mind, they stand in need of Bouwsma's caution. But most studies of Calvin's theology that have appeared in our own century point in exactly the opposite direction: they puzzle over the obscurities and even contradictions in the *Institutes*.

At least since the work of Hermann Bauke (1922), the prevailing view has been that if a system is a logically self-consistent whole in which everything flows smoothly, with mathematical precision, from a single first principle, then Calvin was indeed no systematic theologian.[62] The older scholars who looked for the regulative first principle in the *Institutes* were unable to agree among themselves as to what it actually was. The quest for Calvin's fundamental principle, Bauke suggested, was the quest of a later generation for some defining characteristic of Reformed, as distinct from Lutheran, theology: it was a by-product of nineteenth-century confessional interests.[63] Like Calvin in *his* time, we may conclude, the historians who study him are trying to "come to terms with the utterly real and quite particular problems"[64] of *their* time. They look for things that previous generations did not look for, and they stop looking for much that once inspired the research of their predecessors. One reason why very few Calvin scholars nowadays look for a deductive system in his *Institutes* is that such a conception of theology has gone out of style; it survives, if at all, only in a few sheltered enclaves. Everywhere else the broken, fragmentary, time-bound character of theological statements has long been taken for granted. Such limitations are the price paid for historical existence, or, as the dialectical theologians liked to say, the price paid for trying to speak of the living God.[65] That Calvin himself did not manage to transcend the limits of finite human discourse may be taken as generally, if not universally, agreed. He did not aspire to a timeless system of doctrines in which everything could be deduced with mathematical precision from some unquestioned axiom.

There are more ways than one, however, to be systematic, if "systematic" means only, as the dictionary tells us, "arranged . . . according to a system, plan, or organized method."[66] We need to

---

[61]   Ibid., 47, 49, 54–55.
[62]   Bauke, *Die Probleme der Theologie Calvins* (1922), 30–31.
[63]   Ibid., 22–23.
[64]   Bouwsma's phrase ("Quest for the Historical Calvin," 47).
[65]   Cf. Wilhelm Niesel, *The Theology of Calvin* (1956), 17–20.
[66]   *Oxford English Dictionary*.

consider the question Bouwsma sets aside: whether there may not be a sense of the term "systematic theology" that would have seemed desirable to Calvin.[67] It is patently insufficient, once a cast-iron deductive system with a central dogma has been denied to Calvin, to say no more than simply that the basic elements of his theology lie side by side, dialectically juxtaposed.[68] That, too, was an interpretation of the *Institutes* that, however fruitful and illuminating, owed its currency to one of our own theological fashions. It is not even true to say, as Bauke said, that Calvin was "not a systematic theologian in the same sense and of the same kind as Schleiermacher."[69] He was a systematic theologian in exactly the same *sense* as Schleiermacher: he looked assiduously for the interconnections between doctrines, the way they "hang together" (their *Zusammenhang*).[70] What is true is that he was not a systematic theologian to the same *degree* as Schleiermacher, in whom, as Barth remarked, a system was achieved "in almost *suspiciously* brilliant fashion."[71] The somewhat looser organization of the *Institutes*, in comparison with Schleiermacher's *The Christian Faith*, is a consequence partly of its manner of production, but partly also of the Erasmian side of Calvin's thinking. With Erasmus, he shared in the sixteenth century's shift from a scholastic to a humanistic model for theology.[72] He was of one mind with the great humanist on the goal of the Christian philosophy. Nevertheless, in the final edition of his *Institutes* he left the topical method of Erasmus behind, and it is this that made Calvin not simply a systematic theologian but the preeminent systematician of the Protestant Reformation.

[67]   Bouwsma, "Quest for the Historical Calvin," 54.

[68]   Bauke, *Die Probleme der Theologie Calvins*, 32. The qualification in n. 84 is far too casual: "Dabei soll natürlich nicht bestritten werden, dass es einzelne Elemente und Elementengruppen gibt, die untereinander in besonderen, systematischen Verbindungen stehen. Das hat seine Wurzeln in der gemein-christlichen Ueberlieferung; hier für die Beschreibung des Charakteristischen der Dogmatik Calvins kommt es nicht in Betracht."

[69]   Ibid., 31. Bauke finds in Schleiermacher precisely a deductive system with an "absolutely unifying material principle," namely, the concept of religion as the feeling of absolute dependence, and he judges such a unifying principle to be Lutheranizing. But the more fundamental sense of system is given already in the title to Schleiermacher's work: *Der christliche Glaube nach den Grundsätzen der evangelischen Kirche im Zusammenhange dargestellt*, 7th ed., based on the 2d ed. of 1830–31, ed. Martin Redeker, 2 vols. (Berlin: Walter de Gruyter, 1960).

[70]   See B.A. Gerrish, "From Calvin to Schleiermacher: The Theme and the Shape of Christian Dogmatics" (1985).

[71]   Karl Barth, *The Theology of Schleiermacher: Lectures at Göttingen, Winter Semester of 1923/24*, ed. Dietrich Ritschl, trans. Geoffrey W. Bromiley (Grand Rapids, MI: Wm. B. Eerdmans Co., 1982), 190.

[72]   See B. A. Gerrish, *Grace and Reason: A Study in the Theology of Luther* (Oxford: Clarendon Press, 1962), chap. 10.

For Desiderius Erasmus (ca. 1469–1536), the aim of theological study was practical: to transform the heart and the mind. And not only the purpose but also the very sources of theology called, in his opinion, for a rhetorical rather than a dialectical method. True theology is a matter not of marshalling formal arguments more clever and subtle than those of one's opponents, but of grasping the poetics of scriptural discourse and letting it make a better person of you.[73] Calvin agreed. He did not object to the systematic theology of his day because it was systematic,[74] but because it was abstract, speculative, and unedifying. Hence his annoyance when Cardinal Jacopo Sadoleto (1477–1547) accused the evangelicals of seducing the people with thorny, subtle questions.

> What [Calvin says]? Have you forgotten what the times were like when our people first appeared, and what kind of doctrine it was that those who were preparing to teach the churches learned in the schools? You yourself know that it was mere sophistry—so contorted, tangled, twisted, and involved, that scholastic theology might well be described as a species of occult magic. The denser the darkness anyone spread around, the more he tormented himself and others with vexatious puzzles, the greater the prize he carried off for acumen and learning. And when those who had been turned out in that workshop wished to carry the fruit of their learning to the people, how skillfully, I ask you, did they edify the church? Not to run through every detail, was there then any discourse in Europe that showed the simplicity with which Paul wishes Christian people to be occupied their whole life long? . . .
>   Only a few allusions were sprinkled in from the word of God, to gain credit for such frivolities from the majesty of the word.[75]

Calvin's insistence on the edifying goal of a sound exegetical theology is fundamental to his thought.[76] To be sure, it would be a setback for our understanding of him if we then imagined an opposition in his mind between truth and usefulness, or between theological understanding and practical piety.[77] While he was not interested in useless truth, it would never have occurred to him that a doctrine could be useful if it was not first of all true. The business of theology

---

[73]   See Mary K. O'Brien Weintraub, "The Shape and Function of Dogma in the Theology of Erasmus" (Ph.D. diss., University of Chicago, 1987), 96–120.

[74]   As Bouwsma implies ("Quest for the Historical Calvin," 54).

[75]   *Responsio ad Sadoleti epistolam* (1539), OS 1:468; TT 1:40.

[76]   See, e.g., *Inst.* 1536, OS 1:29; *Institution*, 10–11. Calvin applied the rule of usefulness also to the work of exegesis itself, which the allegorizers, he believed, turned into an occasion for sport and speculation. See, e.g., Comm. Lev. 1.1 (CO 24:506); Comm. 2 Cor. 3:6 (CO 50:40-41); Comm. Gal. 4:22 (CO 50:236-37).

[77]   Bouwsma's remarks surely risk such a misunderstanding ("Quest for the Historical Calvin," 54–55).

is with knowledge— knowledge of God and of ourselves.[78] Nevertheless, there is no knowledge of God, in Calvin's view, where there is no
religion or piety.[79] The long subtitle of the first edition described the
Institutes not as a *summa theologiae* but as a *pietatis summa: Instruction
in the Christian Religion, Embracing an Almost Complete Summary of Piety
and Whatever it is Necessary to Know in the Doctrine of Salvation: A Work
Most Worthy of Being Read by All Who are Devoted to Piety, and Recently
Published* (1536). Even if not from Calvin's own hand, the subtitle was
entirely fitting in one respect: Calvin was determined to do theology
within the limits of piety alone.[80]

The antischolastic polemic of Calvin's letter to Sadoleto could
easily be matched many times over with similar protests in the
writings of Erasmus.[81] And yet, Calvin and Erasmus held different
views on the organization or arrangement that the new theology
required. When Erasmus entertained the need for a compendium of
theology, he envisioned it as the pursuit of individual topics.[82] Philipp
Melanchthon (1497–1560) achieved just such a compendium in his
famous *Loci Communes,* first published in 1521, and the second edition
of Calvin's own *Institutes* (1539) followed much the same procedure.
As Calvin expressly indicated in a preface to the French version (1541),
his purpose was simply to treat the principal matters comprised in the
Christian philosophy.[83] In the 1559 edition, however, the topical
method is left behind, and Calvin has come to think of order not as
mere sequence but as logical or organic connection.

[78]   *Inst.* 1559, 1.1.1 (1:35).
[79]   Ibid., 1.2.1 (1:39).
[80]   See my essay "Theology within the Limits of Piety Alone: Schleiermacher and
Calvin's Doctrine of God" (1981), reprinted in *The Old Protestantism and the New* (1982),
chap. 12.
[81]   Most familiar perhaps are his mischievous remarks on theologians in *Moriae
encomium, id est stultitiae laus* (1511). See the critical edition by Clarence H. Miller in the
Amsterdam edition: *Opera omnia Desiderii Erasmi Roterodami,* 4, 3 (Amsterdam: North-
Holland Publishing Co., 1979), 144–58. With his translation of the *Encomium* Miller
included the letter to Martin Dorp (1514) in which Erasmus offered his own comments
on the work: Erasmus, *The Praise of Folly,* trans. and ed. Clarence H. Miller (New Haven:
Yale University Press, 1979); see pp. 87–98, 153–55. Erasmus's constructive proposals
for a better theology in his *Ratio seu methodus compendio perveniendi ad veram theologiam*
(1519) are most conveniently accessible in Desiderius Erasmus Roterodamus, *Ausgewählte
Werke,* ed. Hajo Holborn in collaboration with Annemarie Holborn (1933; reprint ed.,
Munich: C. H. Beck, 1964), 175–305.
[82]   See Weintraub, "Dogma in the Theology of Erasmus," 121–30.
[83]   CO 31:xxiii. This is translated in LCC 20:6–8 as a preface to the French edition
of 1560 (rather than 1541), but see CO 31:xxii and Jean Calvin, *Institution de la Religion
Chrestienne,* critical ed., ed. Jean-Daniel Benoit, 5 vols., Bibliothèque des Textes
Philosophiques (Paris: J. Vrin, 1957–63), 1:25–26.

As befits the author of a *pietatis summa*, Calvin now begins with introductory chapters on the nature of piety. He then proceeds to unroll the magnificent tapestry of the twofold knowledge of God—as creator and redeemer. Notoriously, there are differences of scholarly opinion about this new structural principle that Calvin introduces—with deliberate emphasis—into the final edition of his *Institutes*. In particular, how inclusive is the theme of God the Redeemer? Does it embrace the whole work after book one, or only book two? For my present ends, however, it is enough to establish that Calvin's strong sense of logical connection, now made explicit, invites the reader to anticipate thematic links between one doctrine and another and to grasp the part always in relation to the whole, not dissecting the work into relatively self-contained topics or *loci communes*. [84]

To return, then, to the Eucharist in Calvin's theology, our task is to see how this "spiritual feast" fits into his "summary of piety," or "sum of godliness," whether or not we can reconcile every inconsistency in his statements on the Real Presence and sacramental signs. It was his intention, from the very first, to focus our thoughts on the analogy (the *analogia* or *similitudo*) of life-giving food. From this focal point he opens up the theme of grace and gratitude that brings his teaching on the Lord's Supper into harmony with other parts of the whole. In itself, the meal is a gift of God, but—like every gift—it is also an invitation to give thanks. [85] He writes:

> We call it either "the Lord's Supper" or "the Eucharist" because in it we both are spiritually fed by the liberality of the Lord and also give him thanks for his kindness . . . . In this sacrament . . . the Lord recalls the great bounty of his goodness to our memory and stirs us up to acknowledge it; and at the same time he admonishes us not to be ungrateful for such lavish liberality, but rather to proclaim it with fitting praises and to celebrate it by giving thanks . . . . We see that this sacred bread of the Lord's Supper is spiritual food, sweet and delicious to those to whom it shows that Christ is their life. . . . All the delights of the gospel are laid

[84]   For further consideration of the shape of Calvin's system, see the essays referred to in nn. 70 and 80 above. Edward A. Dowey, Jr. returns to a central theme of his earlier study (1952)—the knowledge of God the Creator and the knowledge of God the Redeemer—in "The Structure of Calvin's Theological Thought as Influenced by the Two- Fold Knowledge of God" (1984). The view that Calvin intended only the second book to contain his discussion of God the Redeemer was put forward by T.H.L. Parker (1952). Cf. Gerrish, *The Old Protestantism*, 199.

[85]   *Inst.* 1536, OS 1:155 (*Institution*, 160): "Siquidem coena ipsa donum Dei est, quod cum gratiarum actione accipiendum erat." Cf. OS 1:126 (*Institution*, 127), where Calvin uses the expression *coena eucharistiae*.

before us. Surely the Devil could have found no shorter way to destroy people than by so deluding them that they could not taste or savor this nourishment with which their good (*optimus*) Heavenly Father wanted to feed them.[86]

These eloquent sentences are quoted from the first edition of the *Institutes*. But Calvin never wavered, right up to the final edition, in setting first the image of the spiritual banquet (*spirituale epulum*) that the best of fathers spreads before his children.

What becomes clearer in the final edition of Calvin's *Institutes* is that the father's liberality and his children's answering gratitude, or lack of it, is not only the theme of the Lord's Supper but a fundamental theme, perhaps the most fundamental theme, of an entire system of theology. It conveys, as nothing else can, the heart of Calvin's perception of God, humanity, and the harmony between them that was lost by Adam and restored by Christ. The cardinal role of grace and gratitude is not surprising, since piety or godliness, as Calvin understands it, *is* grateful acknowledgement of the father's gifts. Piety and its renewal as faith in Christ—this is the subject of Calvin's *pietatis summa*. The holy banquet is simply the liturgical enactment of the theme of grace and gratitude that lies at the heart of Calvin's entire theology, whether one chooses to call it a system or not. It is, in short, a "eucharistic" theology. Or, at least, that is what the remaining chapters will have to show.

---

[86]   Ibid., OS 1:136, 145, 146, 148 (cf. 161); *Institution*, 139, 148, 149, 152 (cf. 167).

TWO

THE FOUNTAIN OF GOOD AND
THE SHAME OF ADAM

> *Only let my readers keep this firmly in mind: The first step to*
> *piety is to recognize that God is a father to us—to watch over*
> *us, to guide and cherish us, until he gathers us into the eternal*
> *inheritance of his kingdom.*

If, as Calvin says, the Lord's Supper is a holy banquet that presents
Christ to us as the bread of life, then the right approach to the Eucharist
must lead through reflection on the person and work of Christ. This,
at least, is what Bullinger and Calvin decided. The two reformers did
not fall out for very long over the meaning of the Supper. After a sharp
exchange of criticisms, they reached agreement in the Zurich Consensus (1549). The second article declares that, because the sacraments are
"appendages" of the gospel, only one who begins with Christ can
fittingly and usefully discuss their nature, power, function, and
benefit. And this means not just mentioning Christ's name incidentally, but grasping the purpose for which he was given to us by the
father and the good things he has brought us.[1] But, obviously, the
saving work of the mediator presupposes a great deal about God and
humanity that, in the final edition of the *Institutes*, Calvin deals with
first, and this is where we, too, need to begin, tracing the story back to
the Garden of Eden. In Calvin's words: "We are occupied, for now,
with the knowledge that stops at the creation of the world and does not
ascend to Christ the mediator."[2] And our question is this: What kind
of a God is it that fashioned the world, and how did the human species

[1]   *Consensus Tigurinus* (published 1551), OS 2:247: TT 2:212–13.
[2]   *Inst.* 1559, 1.10.1 (1:97).

find its place in God's creation? From here we can move on to faith in
the mediator (in chapter three) and the purpose of the sacraments (in
chapters four, five, and six), showing how the pieces all fit together in
a single "eucharistic" scheme.

THE FATHER AND FOUNTAIN OF GOOD

Everyone knows the popular image of Calvin's God as the absolute
monarch whose autocratic will is the inflexible cause of all that
happens. Remote, terrible, and inexorable, there seems to be little
better to say of this God than was said by historian Preserved Smith:
"The God of Calvin may have been a tyrant, but he was not corruptible
by bribes."[3] Calvin's tyrannical God is by no means an image peculiar
to non-theological literature, or it might be dismissed as an instance of
the misinformation that lies beyond the boundaries of any and every
discipline. Neither is it wholly the creation of confessional or party
polemics. The Lutherans in Germany, the high churchmen and the
Latitudinarians in England, certainly had their reasons for not being
generous to the Calvinist creed. W. B. Selbie, on the other hand, as an
English Congregationalist and onetime principal of Mansfield College, Oxford, stood formally within the Calvinist tradition, and his
remarks on the Calvinistic picture of God may be taken to exemplify
a common internal judgment. For his book on the fatherhood of God,
Selbie found no help at all in Calvin or his professed disciples. "The
whole Calvinistic system," he explains, "is built on the idea of God's
greatness and remoteness from man. He is an absolute sovereign, and
His arbitrary will governs all things." The most essential attributes of
this God are holiness and righteousness. "Grace," Selbie concedes, "is
also predicated of Him, but it is the graciousness of a sovereign rather
than the love of a Father." Like Preserved Smith, Selbie can manage
only a backhanded compliment to Calvinism: "It is a grim creed which
made strong men." He adds (writing in 1936): "It has its counterpart
to-day in the theology of Karl Barth."[4]

From the theological discussions, whether externally polemical or
internally self- critical, the image of Calvin's divine despot has passed

[3]   Preserved Smith, *The Age of the Reformation* (New York: Henry Holt & Co., 1920), 746.
[4]   W. B. Selbie, *The Fatherhood of God* (London: Duckworth, 1936), 75–76. It is
significant that Selbie goes on to quote John McLeod Campbell (1800–72), whose protest
is commonly taken to be anti-Calvinistic. See my *Tradition and the Modern World* (1978),
89–94.

into the general literature, where it is judged not only erroneous but psychologically harmful. Erich Fromm, for example, ascribed to Calvin's God all the features of a tyrant without any quality of love or even justice.[5] He believed he could take Calvin to represent an authoritarian, as distinct from humanistic, religion, in which people submit themselves in obedience to a transcendent power not because of its moral qualities but simply because it has control over them. "God" in authoritarian religion is a symbol of power and force. Calvin's religious experience is accordingly a matter of despising everything in oneself, since in comparison with God humans are utterly powerless.[6] Those who trouble to check Fromm's rare citations from the *Institutes* may find their trust in his confident pronouncements greatly weakened. He quotes disapprovingly a passage in which Calvin rejects the teaching of the Schoolmen that love is prior to faith and hope, but he leaves out Calvin's reason: because it is faith that engenders love.[7] Calvin had no intention of belittling love, as Fromm's readers might suppose. On the contrary, he had just asked: "How shall the mind rise up to taste the divine goodness [that is, by faith] and not at once be wholly set on fire with answering love for God?" (Fromm does not quote that sentence.) The priority of faith over love in Calvin's thinking is an expression not only of dogmatic insight but of psychological insight, too—a point to which I shall return later. But Fromm's unfortunate misreading of the text leaves him in good company: he says no more than most readers will expect to hear. It would come as a surprise to them to learn that scholars who have devoted a lifetime to Calvin research have arrived at exactly the opposite reading of his doctrine of God.

In an essay first published in 1909, Benjamin Warfield concluded that Calvin's doctrine of God is "preeminent among the doctrines of God given expression in the Reformation age in the commanding place it gives to the Divine Fatherhood."[8] One year later, Émile Doumergue showed that in Calvin's theology "father almighty" is not simply a conventional trinitarian phrase taken from the Creed, but expresses the two principal attributes of his God: fatherhood and

---

⁵   Erich Fromm, *Escape from Freedom* (New York: Rinehart, 1941), 87–88.
⁶   Erich Fromm, *Psychoanalysis and Religion* (New Haven: Yale University Press 1950), 34–36. Calvin's religion, as will become clear, was neither authoritarian nor humanistic in Fromm's sense. The alternative, humanistic type of religion makes God a "symbol of man's own powers."
⁷   *Inst.* 1559, 3.2.41 (1:589); quoted in *Escape from Freedom*, 88.
⁸   Benjamin B. Warfield, "Calvin's Doctrine of God" (1909a): 425.

power. Doumergue begins with the Divine Fatherhood. He remarks that although it is so often declared to have been forgotten or denied by him, Calvin in fact insisted on God's *paternité* with a quite distinctive energy.[9]

The truth seems to be that to make arbitrariness the heart of Calvin's doctrine of God is itself a remarkable exercise of arbitrariness, requiring, as it does, a willful selection, arrangement, and editing of the sources. Such plausibility as the results appear to have is borrowed partly from our image of later Calvinism and partly from the attempt of modern scholarship to link Calvin's theology with the voluntaristic strand in later medieval thought. There is no need to deny the real lines of continuity between Calvin and Calvinism, or to reject out of hand the possibility that his language about God may very well have been shaped by Scotist and Nominalist patterns of thinking. But to claim that the notion of arbitrary, despotic will is the key to his doctrine of God does scant justice either to Calvin's own explicit statements about where the primacy lies or to the implications of his careful systematic order. Even when a serious attempt is made to document the divine tyrant from Calvin's *Institutes*, the assumption is usually made that one need look no further than his discussions of providence in book one (chapters 16—18) and predestination in book three (chapters 21—23). And this can only be judged a failure to take him seriously as a systematic thinker.[10]

What is primary in Calvin's notion of God appears already, as we could reasonably expect, in the very first paragraph of the 1559 *Institutes*. The precious gifts with which we are endowed, he asserts, are by no means from ourselves: "By these good things (*bonis*), shed upon us drop by drop from heaven, we are led, as if by rivulets, to the fountain (*ad fontem*)."[11] If, instead, we start not from our wealth but from our poverty, it is even clearer what an infinity of good things resides in God, for our very need itself turns our eyes upward to seek from there what we lack. Changing the metaphor in the next paragraph, Calvin then reverses the direction of our thoughts. Such is the perfection of God's justice, wisdom, and virtue that, when we raise our eyes to God, we are dazzled as if by the intense light of the sun; turning

9   É[mile] Doumergue, *La Pensée religieuse de Calvin* (1910), 89. See further Garrett A. Wilterdink, "Irresistible Grace and the Fatherhood of God in Calvin's Theology" (Ph.D. diss., University of Chicago, 1974), published as *Tyrant or Father? A Study of Calvin's Doctrine of God* (1985).
10   See further Gerrish, *The Old Protestantism and the New* (1982), 199–203.
11   *Inst.* 1559, 1.1.1 (1:36).

our eyes earthward again, we find that what had once seemed admirable in ourselves now looks dull and tarnished, a mere show.[12] Thus knowledge of God and knowledge of ourselves are mutually connected. If we begin with ourselves, our minds are carried up to the fountain; but until we have lowered our eyes from the sun to ourselves, we can scarcely be said to know ourselves at all.

In the first chapter of the *Institutes*, Calvin has given us not metaphysical attributes but favored images of God, and he moves on in chapter two to make quite sure we have realized what sort of a knowledge of God he is talking about. In a word, he is discoursing on *pietas*, "piety" or "godliness." For, properly speaking, we cannot say that God is known where there is no piety or religion. In a *pietatis summa*, "God" and "piety" are correlative concepts: the proper definition of "God" will be, quite simply, the referent of a rightly defined "piety."[13] Moreover, if the sole intention in talking of God is to evoke a right attitude toward God, then the appropriate language will be, to put it in Schleiermacher's terms, rhetorical rather than dialectical.[14] Hence, when Calvin comes to the biblical attributes of God (in chapter ten), he asserts that in some especially useful passages of Scripture the true countenance of God is so displayed that it can be visualized through images (εἰκονικῶς *visenda*). Now Schleiermacher thought that the dogmatic task was to regulate the content of sermons by moving, if only provisionally, beyond the metaphorical language of Scripture. For Calvin, by contrast, the dogmatic task was more immediately in the service of piety and preaching. The knowledge of God with which he was concerned is a direct invitation to fear and trust God; it teaches us to worship God and to depend wholly on the divine goodness. This is its use, aim, or function (its *scopus*),[15] and its language is accordingly metaphorical.

Calvin had various ways of asserting that his concern was with a quite specific kind of knowledge of God. The question is not what God is, but what God is like, or what God is like to us, so that recognition of God will consist in living awareness (*vivo sensu*) rather than idle,

---

[12]   Ibid., 1.1.2 (1:38).
[13]   Ibid., 1.2.1 (1:39–41).
[14]   Friedrich Schleiermacher, *Der christliche Glaube nach den Grundsätzen der evangelischen Kirche im Zusammenhange dargestellt*, 7th ed., based on the 2d ed. of 1830–31, ed. Martin Redeker, 2 vols. (Berlin: Walter de Gruyter, 1960), § 16 (1:107–12); Eng. trans., *The Christian Faith*, ed. H. R. Mackintosh and J. S. Stewart (1928; reprint ed., Philadelphia: Fortress Press, 1976), 78–83.
[15]   *Inst.* 1559, 1.10.2 (1:97-98).

absent-minded speculation.[16] But with the cardinal point in mind—
that he is interested only in *pietas*—let me venture to quote at length the
passage which, it seems to me, by its very location at the beginning of
the *Institutes*, must be taken as regulative for everything that follows.

> It is not enough simply to hold that God is one who should be wor-
> shipped and adored by all, unless we are persuaded also that he is the
> fountain of all good, so that we should seek nothing anywhere else but
> in him. I take this to mean not only that he sustains this world, as he once
> established it, by his boundless power, governs it by his wisdom,
> preserves it by his goodness, and in particular rules the human race by
> his justice and judgment, supports it in his mercy, looks after it with his
> protection; but also that not one drop of wisdom and light, or justice, or
> power, or uprightness, or genuine truth will be found that does not flow
> from him, and of which he is not the cause.[17]

There, surely, you have at the outset Calvin's fundamental definition
of God (or, if you prefer, his fundamental image of God): the deity is
fons omnium bonorum, the spring or fountain of all good. And Calvin
immediately goes on, in this selfsame passage, to give the correlative
definition of piety. He continues:

> And so we should learn to look for, and to ask for, all these things from
> him, and when we receive them to ascribe them thankfully to him. For
> it is this sense of the divine perfections (*hic virtutum Dei sensus*) that is
> our proper teacher of the piety from which religion is born. By "piety"
> I mean the reverence joined with love for God that the knowledge of his
> benefits induces. For until people sense (*sentiant*) that they owe every-
> thing to God, that they are cherished by his fatherly care, that he is the
> author of their every good, so that they should ask for nothing apart
> from him, they will never bow to him in willing reverence. No, unless
> they fix their happiness firmly in him, they will never devote them-
> selves wholly, truly, and sincerely to him.[18]

The pivotal description of God as source or fountain of good reappears
later in chapter two of book one[19] and countless times elsewhere in
Calvin's writings,[20] and it clearly determines his entire conception of

---

[16]   Ibid., 1.2.2 (1:41), 10.2 (1:97).

[17]   Ibid., 1.2.1 (1:41).

[18]   Ibid., 1.2.1 (1:41). On the historical background of the word *pietas* and its place
in Calvin's "spirituality," see Lucien Joseph Richard, *The Spirituality of John Calvin*
(1974). As John Burkhart points out in a personal communication (20 December 1991),
pietas —both etymologically and in Calvin's actual usage — is "inherently relational,
and most appropriately instanced as filial and familial."

[19]   God is *bonorum omnium fons et origo* or *bonorum omnium author* (ibid., 1.2.2 [1:42]).

[20]   Often the description is expressly invoked as conveying the sum and substance
of the proper attitude to the Deity. "La saincteté du nom de Dieu est une maiesté tant
sacrée que cela doit nous esmouvoir tous à luy faire hommage, et à luy porter telle

what genuine religion is. Conversely, we may say that the only God that has a place in Calvin's theology is the God who corresponds to the attitude of piety, from which come the outward activities of religion. For, as Calvin insists, you cannot perceive God clearly unless you recognize him as the source and origin of every good, and it is from this recognition that the desire to cleave to God and confidence in God are born—or would be if the human mind were not seduced by its own perversity.[21]

It will have been noticed that in my extended quotation from Calvin the metaphor of the fountain drops out, and another takes its place: Calvin speaks not only of the divine fountain but also of God's fatherly care (*paterna cura*). There is of course no conflict between these two images, the "fountain" and the "father." They say the same thing, one by a metaphor taken from nature, the other by a metaphor from personal relationships. Hence, having connected piety with the persuasion that God is fountain of good, Calvin can equally well assert later on that the first step to piety is to recognize God as father,[22] and that none will devote themselves freely to God's service unless they taste his fatherly care and are coaxed to love and worship him in return.[23] As the *Institutes* unfolds, it is in fact the familial rather than the natural imagery that dominates — in part, no doubt, because it is more readily adapted to Calvin's other themes. At every critical turn in his progress through the principal matters contained in the Christian philosophy, he invokes the child-father relationship with an acuteness that fully justifies Warfield's verdict: in the Reformation era Calvin was preeminently the theologian of divine fatherhood.

---

reverance que nous ne pensions de luy et n'en parlions point sinon cognoissant qu'il est la source de tout bien" (Serm. Luke 1.49, CO 46:123). "Nunc ad summum gradum gloriandi conscendit. Nam dum gloriamur Deum esse nostrum, quidquid fingi vel optari potest bonorum, consequitur et ex hoc fonte manat. Non enim supremum tantum bonorum omnium est Deus, sed summam quoque ac singulas partes in se continet: factus est autem noster per Christum. Ergo huc fidei beneficio pervenimus, ut nobis ad felicitatem nihil desit" (Comm. Rom. 5.11, CO 49:94). Other passages are cited elsewhere in this volume; there is no need to repeat them here.

[21]   *Inst.* 1559, 1.2.2 (1:42).

[22]   Ibid., 2.6.4 (1:347), the source of my epigraph for this chapter.

[23]   Ibid.,1.5.3 (1:55). To underscore the fact that the word "father," in Calvin's usage, is generally a metaphorical description of God and not a merely trinitarian name, I have not capitalized it except where the inner-trinitarian relationship is clearly intended. Even in speaking of the relation of the incarnate Christ to the first person of the Trinity, Calvin's thought is often better expressed by the lower-case "father" and "son," since it is not an eternal begetting that he has in mind but paternal love and answering filial obedience.

The paternal image of God brought Calvin's language into line with the language of the Bible. But one cannot fail to notice that it had a quite personal appeal to him that goes beyond scriptural warrant alone. Its primary connotation in his mind was not power or authority but devoted, affectionate care, which the natural image of the fountain could not convey. Indeed, Calvin writes expressly: "He names himself our father, and that is how he wants to be called by us. He takes away all our mistrust by the utter winsomeness of this name, since a more loving disposition (*amoris affectus*) could not be found anywhere else than in a father."[24] I admit that this is the sentiment of one who has been redeemed: I take it from Calvin's exposition of the Lord's Prayer in book three. Further, it is linguistically possible to translate, as the standard English version does: "... since no greater feeling of love can be found elsewhere than in *the* Father."[25] But that would not explain *why* God calls himself "father," which is the entire aim of the passage. Calvin's point, whether one likes it or not, is general, and that is why I make use of it here even before turning directly to the story of redemption. He must really have thought it a universal truth that you could not find a greater love than father love. [26]

It does not follow that "father" is the only legitimate image of deity. The pious mind acknowledges God also as lord and as a just judge armed with severity to avenge wrongdoing.[27] But that, properly speaking, is not what makes it a pious mind. Piety arises strictly out of the knowledge of God's benefits, and for itself the pious mind needs no threats of punishment: even if there were no hell, it would still shudder merely to offend him. Calvin does not, I think, mean to say that "*because* it loves and reveres God as Father, [the pious mind] worships and adores him as Lord." (This is how the standard translation renders him in English.)[28] The phrases are in apposition: because the pious mind loves and reveres God as father, worships and adores him as lord, therefore it shudders to offend him. The pious mind, in other words, never forgets that the father is lord, but it is a *pious* mind

[24]   Ibid., 3.20.36 (2:899). Doumergue points out (see n. 9 above) that for Calvin God is the one to whom the name "father" properly belongs: "Tandis qu' en général on appelle Dieu *Père* par métaphore, c'est l'homme qui est *père* par métaphore, et c'est Dieu qui l'est en réalité."

[25]   LCC 2:899, my emphasis.

[26]   In the OS text of the parallel passage in the 1536 *Institutio* (1:105), the initial *p* of *patre* is lower case; in the text of the 1559 edition (4:346) it is capitalized (but not in CO 2:662!).

[27]   *Inst.* 1559, 1.2.2 (1:43); cf. 3.2.26 (1:572). See further p. 67, n. 71 below.

[28]   My emphasis (see LCC 20:43).

only because it has tasted the father's benefits. There is, as we shall see, an exact parallel in this respect between piety and faith; for although faith believes every word of God, it rests solely on the word of grace or mercy, the promise of God's fatherly goodwill.[29]

If Calvin is as good a systematic theologian as I believe, it should be possible to demonstrate that God's goodness and paternal care decisively shape the knowledge of God the Creator that constitutes the overall theme of book one. I cannot hope to do that in detail here. Elsewhere, I have tried to show how the God of faith and piety is related to the theme of God's hiddenness in Calvin's doctrine of providence, which completes his doctrine of creation.[30] Although providence is about God's care for the whole human race, and especially for the church, neither God's fatherly kindness nor the strictness of his judgments is always apparent; sometimes, the causes of events are concealed. Or, to put it more correctly: since the will of God is the cause of every event, the justice of God is often concealed, and the thought insinuates itself that human affairs are whirled around under the blind impulse of fortune.[31] Calvin could portray the terror of this thought with astonishing effectiveness. His purpose, however, was not to unravel his previous reflections on God's fatherly care but to commend them. He does speak of God's hidden, inscrutable will,[32] but the function of his remarkable utterances on the terrifying abyss in God can only be, in a summary of piety, to drive the pious mind all the more eagerly to the fatherly goodwill of God disclosed in Scripture.[33] To focus on the hidden will would be totally wrongheaded. It is with the revealed will of the heavenly father that piety and therefore theology are concerned. Hence Calvin winds up the discussion in

---

[29]   *Inst.* 1559, 3.2.28-30 (1:573–76). It is clear from 1.2.2 that the image of God as judge is correlated with the activities—and the destiny—of the wicked. For the "pious," God is father and lord, and to them, as we will note later, God's punishment is only paternal discipline. The close connection between *fides*, *pietas*, and *religio* is clear from the fact that Calvin actually changes at the end of 1.2.2 from *pietas* to *fides*: "En quid sit pura germanaque religio, nempe fides cum serio Dei timore coniuncta" (1:43).

[30]   "'To the Unknown God': Luther and Calvin on the Hiddenness of God" (1973), reprinted in *The Old Protestantism*, chap 8; cf. chap. 12, 203.

[31]   Inst. 1559, 1.17.1 (1:210–11).

[32]   On the other hand, he expressly rejects the medieval notion of God's *absolute* will, which is sometimes said to account for the despotic Calvinist God: ibid., 1.17.2 (1:214), 3.23.2 (2:950).

[33]   See, e.g., *Inst.* 1559, 1.17.11 (1:224–25). In the article referred to above (n. 30) I tried to convey something of the psychological power of Calvin's utterances on "dread" (*anxietas, formido*) and to show what they meant for his concept of faith. William J. Bouwsma's recent work (*John Calvin: A Sixteenth-Century Portrait*, 1988) takes them as important clues to Calvin's own psyche in the context of his times.

these words: "So the incalculable happiness of the *pious* mind becomes obvious. . . . In short, not to delay any longer over this point, you will easily perceive, if you pay attention, that ignorance of providence is the ultimate misery; in knowledge of providence lies the highest blessedness."[34]

Taking Calvin's advice, and not letting ourselves be diverted any longer, we can fairly sum up the main line of his argument in three thoughts. First, the creation was an act of God's pure goodness.

> If we ask the reason why he was once induced to create all these things, and now is moved to preserve them, we shall find it was because of his goodness alone. But if this is the only reason, it should be more than enough to draw us gently to his love, for there is no creature (as the prophet tells us) on which his compassion (*misericordia*) has not been poured out.[35]

Second, as this passage already hints, by his providence the Maker tends the world with the same loving care that first brought it into being. The identification of the cause of all events with the heavenly father of *pietas* appears constantly throughout Calvin's reflections on providence;[36] the security of the godly rests upon it.

> When once the light of divine providence has shone on devout people (*homini pio*), they are relieved and released not only from the extreme anxiety and dread that crushed them before, but from every care. As they justly shudder at fortune, so they dare commit themselves fearlessly to God. Their comfort, I say, is understanding that the heavenly father so holds everything in his power, so rules by his authority and command, so governs by his wisdom, that nothing falls out unless by his design. Since they have been received into God's keeping, entrusted to the care of the angels, no harm from water, or fire, or iron can touch them, except insofar as it has pleased God the governor (*Deo moderatori*) to make room for these things.[37]

Third, the human race was placed in the world to be the privileged recipients of the father's special care. Though God's compassion is

---

[34]   Ibid., 1.17.10 (1:223; my emphasis), 17.11 (225).
[35]   Ibid., 1.5.6 (1:59). The allusion is to Psalm 145:9: "The Lord is good to all, and his compassion is over all that he has made" (RSV). Cf. ibid., 1.5.9 (1:62).
[36]   On the hand of fatherly kindness in the governance of the world see, e.g., *Inst.* 1559, 1.5.7–8 (60), 16.1 (198), 16.5 (204), 16.7 (206), 17.1 (210–11), 17.6 (219). God's fatherly providence extends not only to all humankind but to every living creature (Comm. Ps. 136.25 [CO 32:367]).
[37]   *Inst.* 1559, 1.17.11 (1:224). Though some adjustments may be needed to avoid pejorative connotations, our modern ears can probably hear "piety" and "pious mind" without too much difficulty, and I have tried to suggest the Latin original consistently even though the English language would sometimes prefer "devout" or "godly." But "pious people," I suspect, is too much, and I have avoided unnecessary use of the sex-specific word "man" (which in Calvin's Latin would of course be *vir*, not *homo*).

over all his works, humanity is unique as a cosmos in miniature, an exceptional specimen of God's power, goodness, and wisdom, and a clear mirror of God's works. "By adorning us with such excellence, he proves he is our father."[38]

> We should note God's fatherly love to humanity in the very order of creation (*in ipso . . . ordine rerum*). He did not create Adam until he had enriched the world with full abundance of good things. . . . He shows his wonderful goodness to us by assuming the burden (*curam*) of a prudent and conscientious head of the family (*patrisfamilias*).[39]

THE GOD OF THE PHILOSOPHERS

Calvin's vision of cosmic goodness and benevolence, though often expressed in a distinctive style, was not in itself greatly original.[40] He drew from a common store of religious ideas and worked them into a whole that bore his characteristic stamp. The image of God as fountain of good was equally well-liked by Luther and Zwingli. In his exposition of the First Commandment in the *Large Catechism* (1529) Luther wrote: "It is God alone (as has been said often enough) from whom we receive all that is good . . . . He is an eternal fountain overflowing with sheer goodness; from him pours forth all that is good and is called good."[41] Calvin's reading of the First Commandment in the 1536 *Institutes* is so close to Luther's that direct influence, through the Latin translation of the *Large Catechism*, seems likely.[42]

[38]   Ibid., 1.5.3 (1:55).

[39]   Ibid., 1.14.2 (1:161–62); cf. 14.20, 22 (180, 182). Calvin's perception of nature has been redeemed from the vexed epistemological problem of a *theologia naturalis* and discussed in its full scope by Susan E. Schreiner, *The Theater of His Glory* (1991).

[40]   "Vision" is the right word, not least because of the strongly aesthetic language Calvin employs. The divine wisdom is exhibited in the excellence of the divine art (*Inst.* 1559, 1.5.2 [1:53]). The world is a theater (1.5.8, 6.2, 14.20 [1:61, 72, 179]; 2.6.1 [1:341]), or a place of beauty and harmony (1.5.11, 14.2 [1:63, 162]). God's perfections are depicted in his works, and especially in the whole, as in paintings (1.5.10 [1:63]). See further Léon Wencelius, *L'Esthétique de Calvin* (1937), 36–49.

[41]   *Der grosse Katechismus*, BELK, 565–66; BC, 368. "Tribuere autem Deo gloriam est credere ei, est reputare eum esse veracem, sapientem, iustum, misericordem, omnipotentem, in summa: agnoscere eum authorem et largitorem omnis boni" (Comm. Gal. 3.6 [1535], WA 40¹. 360.21; LW 26:227). "Quid possumus tribuere ulli maius quam veritatem et iustitiam et absolutam prorsus bonitatem?" (*De libertate christiana* [1520], WA 7.53.38; LW 31:350).

[42]   OS 1:42; *Institution*, 26. A Latin translation of the *Large Catechism* appeared already in 1529. Calvin's formula *timeri et amari* also echoes the familiar language of Luther's *Small Catechism*, published the same year (*Der kleine Katechismus*, BELK, 508–9; BC, 342–44).

Zwingli, too, in his *Commentary on True and False Religion* (1525), finds in God "the fountain and spring of all good" (*omnium bonorum fons et scaturigo*). God, the source and spring of being, must also be good because we are told that everything made by God was good. The highest good is by nature kind and bountiful, but not as we are bountiful who look for something in return. God simply loves to impart himself (*distrahi amat*) out of his abundant goodness. Piety or religion, then, is clinging to God as the only good, as a child clings to a parent; it arises when one contrasts one's own poverty with the abundance of the Creator-father.[43] Similarly, in his *Sermon on Providence* (1530) Zwingli identifies the supreme Deity with the highest good, not because he is better than other goods, as gold is better than silver, but because he is the only thing good by nature. Everything else is good by participation, or rather by "supplication" (*precario*); its goodness is borrowed. The divine goodness is manifested even in the Fall, not in the works of creation and redemption alone. If God knew Adam and Eve would fall, does his goodness come under suspicion because he did not prevent it? By no means. God made humans able to fall because goodness cannot be truly known where there is no evil with which to compare it. Rightly understood, therefore— that is, in relation to the good it was to serve—even the Fall must be subsumed under the goodness of God.[44]

In their emphasis on the goodness of God, the fountain of good, the three reformers stood on common ground. What becomes clear in Zwingli is that it was not exclusively biblical ground. The goodness of the Lord is, of course, an Old Testament theme, especially in the Psalter, and Zwingli managed to press other biblical affirmations into service. He inferred the goodness of the Creator from the goodness of creation (Gen. 1:31), and he liked Jesus' assertion that there is none good but God (Matt. 19:17). But he recognized that cosmic good was also a favorite philosophical theme. For, first, he remarks that "the philosophers" knew the identity of the good with the true; and, second, he quotes Seneca's reference to the goodness of the Platonic Artificer-God. [45]

The question needs much closer attention, but is it not almost certain that Zwingli here makes explicit one of the philosophical

---

[43]   *De vera et falsa religione commentarius* (1525), SW 3:645, 650–51, 668; LWZ 3:64, 70–71, 91. Jackson and Heller translate *distrahi amat* as "loves to impart itself."
[44]   *Sermonis de providentia dei anamnema* (1530), SW 6, 3:70–75, 140–50; LWZ 2:130–32, 174–80.
[45]   Ibid., SW 6, 3:71–72, 107; LWZ 2:131, 151–52.

sources from which the reformers drew their language about God? Zwingli was more eager than Luther, or even Calvin, to voice philosophical debts. At one point in his great treatise on providence, he admits that he has been dealing with his theme—God as the fountain of all being—a bit philosophically (*paulo* φιλοσοφικοτέρως), and he notes that there are certain people who are not ashamed to make truth odious by attributing it to the philosophers. Who are these "certain people"? Perhaps Zwingli had Luther in mind. In any case, he states his own principle that truth, whoever brings it to light, is from the Holy Spirit.[46] This is his warrant for saying later on: "I am happy, therefore, to introduce here what Seneca says about Plato's view, chiefly because everything I have said so far in this book, and everything I am going to say, is derived from a single source (*fonte*): the nature and character of the supreme deity. Plato also tasted this fountain (*fontem*) and Seneca drank from it."[47] Although Calvin was inclined to be more cautious (he did not want the *mistakes* of the philosophers to be overlooked), he, too, insisted that all truth comes from God, whose Spirit is the one fountain of truth; it would therefore be mere superstition not to risk borrowing from non-Christian writers.[48] Calvin did not doubt that it was God who sowed by the hand of the philosophers the excellent thoughts that are to be found in their writings.[49] And we know from recent scholarship that Calvin not only wrote his first book on a treatise by Seneca but was still studying and annotating his classical authors in the turbulent 1540s, when one might have expected him to be too busy reforming the Genevans.[50]

Plato, according to Calvin, was "the most religious of all the philosophers and the most sensible (*inter omnes religiosissimus et maxime sobrius*)."[51] Although the compliment appears in the midst of a criticism, it unquestionably expresses a special regard for Plato, which reappears many times in Calvin's writings.[52] He knew well the discourse on the Good in Plato's *Republic*; from it he borrowed and

---

[46]   Ibid., SW 6, 3:94; LWZ 2:144.
[47]   Ibid., SW 6, 3:106–7; LWZ 2:151.
[48]   Comm. Tit. 1.12, CO 52:414–15.
[49]   Comm. John 4.36, CO 47:96. But the seed was *adulteratum . . . ab ima radice.*
[50]   See Alexandre Ganoczy and Stefan Scheld, *Herrschaft—Tugend—Vorsehung* (1982).
[51]   *Inst.* 1559, 1.5.11 (1:64).
[52]   Calvin's relation to the Platonic tradition has been explored in a number of interesting studies: Roy W. Battenhouse (1948), Jean Boisset (1959), Gerd Babelotzky (1977), Charles Partee (1977). But they focus on other themes than the one that interests me here.

adapted the allegory of the cave to describe faith's indirect illumination by the "radiance" of God.[53] The Platonic idea of the Good is not defined in the *Republic*, but symbolized. In itself, it remains ineffable; one can only point to it through such images as the radiance of the sun, which is the source of both light and life. Just as the sun not only makes visible the objects we see but also brings them into existence and nurtures them, it is the Good that makes it possible to know the things we know and that gives them their very existence.[54] The last thing to be "seen" in the world of knowledge is the idea of the Good, which is the cause (*αἰτία*) of all that is right and beautiful; without perceiving this idea, no one can act wisely either in private or in public life.[55]

It would, of course, be unjustifiable simply to identify Plato's idea of the Good as the immediate source of Calvin's *fons bonorum*. The point, rather, is that the idea of the Good entered into the common fund of Christian ideas, from which Calvin drew. And so did Plato's explanation, in the *Timaeus*, of the reason why the Artificer made the world: because he was good, and, being totally ungrudging (devoid of *φθόνος*), he desired everything to be like himself as much as possible. "This principle, then, we shall be wholly right in accepting from men of wisdom as being above all the supreme originating principle (*ἀρχὴν*) of Becoming and the Cosmos. For God desired that, so far as possible, all things should be good and nothing evil."[56] In Christian thinking the good Artificer and his model, the idea of the Good, coalesced in the notion of the one supremely good God.[57] It is always difficult, often impossible, to trace the lines of influence with any kind of assurance. But when Calvin writes: "If we ask the reason (*causa*) why [God] was once induced to create all these things, and now is moved to preserve them, we shall find it was because of his goodness alone," it is impossible not to hear at least an indirect echo of Plato's *Timaeus*.[58] As Seneca writes in the passage quoted by Zwingli: "The Maker is God . . . . Do you ask what God's intention may be?

---

[53]   *Inst.* 1559, 3.2.19 (1:565). Cf. *Republic*, Books VI–VII, 505A–518B. The allegory of the cave is in Book VII, 514A–517A.

[54]   *Republic*, 509B.

[55]   Ibid., 517B–C.

[56]   *Timaeus*, 29D–30A, trans. R. G. Bury (LCL, *Plato*, 9:55). Plato's use of the word *φθόνος* is in striking contrast to the famous verdict of Herodotus: *τὸ θεῖον πᾶν ἐὸν φθονερόν* (the attitude of the gods is wholly one of envy: *Hist.*, I, 32).

[57]   That this was by no means Plato's own intention is commonly agreed. See, e.g., A. E. Taylor, *Plato: The Man and His Work*, 6th ed. (London: Methuen, 1949), 288–89, 441–44.

[58]   *Inst.* 1559, 1.5.6 (1:59).

Goodness. So, at least, Plato says: 'What was the reason (*causa*) why God made the world? He is good; what he made is good; no good person is ever grudging with anything good.'"[59]

The divine goodness became an especially prominent theme in Christian mysticism, of which Calvin was in some respects deeply suspicious. For the immensely influential Pseudo-Dionysius (fifth century), God was precisely the universal cause and fountain of goodness.[60] Nearer to Calvin's own day, the *Theologia Germanica*, discovered and published by Martin Luther in 1516, taught that eternal bliss lies in one thing only: the good. Not this good, or that good, but the good above good: that is, the God who is the goodness in every good thing.[61] The "Teutonic Knight," nameless author of the book, sees the absolute goodness of God attested in the life of Jesus, who called even Judas, his betrayer, "friend." It is as though God in human nature were saying: "I am pure, single Goodness, and therefore I cannot will, or desire, or hope, or do, or give anything but goodness. If I am to reward you for your evil and wickedness, I must do it with goodness, for I am and have nothing else."[62] One would expect Calvin's mind to resonate with these testimonies to the fountain of good. It is true that other strands in Christian mysticism made him mistrustful. He thought *The Celestial Hierarchy* of "that Dionysius, whoever he was," in part subtle and acute, but on closer inspection mostly idle chatter, which might divert the ear but would hardly strengthen consciences.[63] And he wrote a letter to the French Protestants in Frankfurt, where the *Theologia Germanica* was supposedly written, warning them that though the book contained no obvious errors, anyone who looked more closely would discover in it a hidden venom fit to poison the church. He begged them to flee like the plague

[59]   See Seneca, *Ad Lucilium epistolae morales*, no. lxv. Zwingli cites the letter as the sixty-sixth (which is how it was numbered in older editions) and gives a wording that differs slightly from modern texts. I have translated the quotation as he gives it (SW 6, 3:107).
[60]   *De divinis nominibus*, IV, ii (MPG 3:696). The whole of the profoundly Platonic chapter four and the beginning of chapter five (secs. i–iv) are a hymn of praise to the Good, the source and end of all things. My attention was drawn to these passages by my colleague Bernard McGinn.
[61]   *Theologia Germanica*, ed. Joseph Bernhart, trans. Susanna Winkworth (New York: Pantheon Books, 1949), 128, 177; from chaps. 9 and 36. The old, nineteenth-century translation of Susanna Winkworth (1820–84) was revised for this edition to conform with the German edition of Joseph Bernhart, *Der Frankfurter: Eine deutsche Theologie* (Leipzig: Im Insel-Verlag, 1920).
[62]   Ibid., 172–73 (chap. 33). I have adapted the Winkworth translation by changing "thee" to "you."
[63]   *Inst.* 1559, 1.14.4 (1:164–65).

those who tried to infect them with such excrement (*de telles ordures*).[64] And yet, it must surely be said, to borrow Zwingli's image, that whatever else they may have learned, Pseudo-Dionysius, the anonymous Teutonic Knight, Zwingli, and Calvin himself all drank of the same Platonic stream.

Calvin also adopts the more Aristotelian notion of the *summum bonum*, notably in the third question of his *Geneva Catechism* (1545): "What is the highest human good?" In this context the good is the goal of human activity, virtually synonymous with the chief end (*finis*) of human life, which is to know the God who made humans to glorify him.[65] Calvin in fact begins with the question of the chief human *end:* "What is the chief end of human life?" (Question 1). When he adds that the highest human *good* is the very same thing—to know and to glorify God—his point is simply that human happiness consists in fulfillment of the end for which humans were created. Take away the activity of knowing and glorifying the Maker, and our condition is less happy than that of any of the beasts. Hence in Question 5 (which is not really a question at all) the teacher says: "So, then, we see clearly enough that the greatest unhappiness that can befall someone is not to live to God." And the pupil's response is: "*Sic res habet* (that's the way it is)."[66]

The thought that the good of anything lies in the performance of its function or end was in particular Aristotle's (384—322 B.C.E.), for whom the highest human good was the exercise of the noblest human capacity: intellectual contemplation.[67] In the Christian Aristotelianism of Thomas Aquinas (ca. 1225-1274) the highest good, "beatitude," is defined as vision of the divine essence, the activity in which the human intellect is perfected.[68] Calvin's understanding of the end of knowing and glorifying God is paradoxical insofar as it calls for a corresponding human abnegation. If the exaltation of God requires the humbling of ourselves, how can God's glory be our highest good? As Calvin explains it in his Catechism and many times elsewhere: although we ought to look to God's glory alone and to have no regard for our own advantage, God's infinite goodness has so arranged things that what

---

[64]   Calvin to the French Congregation at Frankfurt, 23 February 1559, CO 17:441–42.

[65]   *Catechismus ecclesiae Genevensis* (1545), OS 2:75; TT 2:37.

[66]   Ibid., OS 2:75; TT 2:37–38.

[67]   Aristotle, *Nichomachean Ethics*, I, 1094A–B, 1098A; X, 1177A–1179A.

[68]   Thomas, ST IaIIae, Q. 3, a. 8. See also ibid., I, Q. 12, a. 1; IaIIae, Q. 3, a. 1, ad 2. Augustine identified the highest good with the vision of God (*De trinitate*, I. xii, 31; cf. VIII. iii, 4–5).

makes for God's glory is also good for us.[69] An unrealistic resolution of the paradox, it may be. At any rate, Calvin can admit that to prefer God's glory to life itself is impossible for us without the hope of a better life to come.[70] His thoughts on the goal of human activity come closer to the Aristotelian-Thomistic notion of an appetitive drive than first appears. [71]

The more Platonic image of God as source of good, on the other hand, while it by no means excludes a reciprocal yearning for God, reverses the direction of thought: in this image, the primary movement is from creator to creature. And it is interesting that Calvin's Catechism passes over from "highest good" to "author of good" as soon as it asks for details on how we should give God the honor that is his due. Question 7 asks: "But what is the rule for duly honoring him (rite honorandi ratio)?" The answer is this: "To place all our confidence in him, to be eager to revere him all our life by yielding to his will, to call upon him when burdened by any need, seeking in him our safety and every good we can desire, and, finally, to acknowledge him with both heart and mouth as the only author of all good things (bonorum omnium solum authorem)."[72]

The cardinal importance of the image of the fountain of good in Calvin's doctrine of God has not, as far as I know, received the attention it deserves. Consequently, its place in the wider philosophical and theological tradition needs further exploration. Unfortunately, it is often assumed that to have a philosophical thought is un-Protestant, and that a good Reformation scholar should rise to the defense of the Protestant reformers if some possible influence from philosophy is suggested.[73] I doubt if Zwingli and Calvin, at least, would have been anxious to have their honor maintained by this defense. (I am not so sure about Luther.) At any rate, it tends to cut off exploration of some interesting parallels, and it may leave untested

---

[69]   Catechismus, OS 2:119; TT 2:75.
[70]   Comm. Dan. 3.16–18, CO 40:633–34.
[71]   "Ratio enim boni in hoc consistit, quod aliquid sit appetibile, unde Philosophus dicit quod bonum est quod omnia appetunt" (Thomas, ST I, Q. 5, a. 1; cf. Aristotle, Nic. Eth., I, 1094A). For all his emphasis on the benefits lavished upon Adam by the Creator, Calvin's perspective is not strictly anthropocentric precisely because the end of humanity is the glory of God; what he wishes to convey is the special place of humanity in a theocentric universe. Even if God has so ordered things that salvation lies in glorifying God, preoccupation with being saved is bad theology and bad religion (Responsio ad Sadoleti epistolam [1539], OS 1:463–64; TT 1:33–34).
[72]   Catechismus, OS 2:75; TT 2:38.
[73]   This defensiveness is no doubt a remote by-product of the debate over "natural theology" in the 1930s. See, e.g., Wilhelm Niesel, The Theology of Calvin (1956), 39–53.

the assumption that Christian beliefs are more distinctive than they really are. This certainly applies to Calvin's other favorite image, God as father, which belonged very closely in his mind with the image of the fountain. For the heavenly father is not only supremely good but goodness itself (*ipsa etiam bonitas*).[74]

The fatherhood of God is sometimes taken to be a distinctively, if not uniquely, Christian theme grounded in the message of Jesus. The New Testament scholar, of course, must take due note of the fact that Jesus is reported speaking of God as father much more frequently in Matthew than in Mark or Luke, and this invites the question whether a partiality for the name "father" should, after all, be credited to Matthew as much as to Jesus.[75] Be that as it may, the divine fatherhood is certainly a prominent theme in the New Testament. This, however, does not make it a uniquely Christian theme. It was common, for instance, not only in Judaism but also in the later Stoics, including Seneca (ca. 4 B.C.E.—65 C.E.), in whom Calvin had a special interest.

Calvin himself conceals the affinity between his notion of God and Seneca's by indignantly repudiating any resemblance between providence and the Stoic dogma of fate. The difference, he claims, is that whereas the Stoics invent an immanent causal necessity in nature, he himself, in his doctrine of providence, affirms a God who makes decisions (*Deum arbitrum*) and now carries out by his power what he decreed in his wisdom in eternity.[76] But Seneca, at least, as Calvin must have known, had no hesitation in using personal language of the ultimate reason in things, and he sometimes distinguished God as first cause from the causes that depend on God. This is why it is futile, in Seneca's opinion, to say that we are indebted not to God but to nature. The universe is sustained by God's benefit (*beneficio*). There is no nature without God, and no God without nature; the two differ only in function (*officio*). Perhaps this is still not transparently clear, but Seneca goes on: "Not to be drawn aside into further controversy, God bestows upon us very many and very great benefits, with no thought of any return, since he has no need of having anything bestowed, nor are we capable of bestowing anything on him."[77]

---

[74]   *Catechismus*, OS 2:120; TT 2:75.
[75]   According to McGiffert the figures are: forty-four times in Matthew, fifteen or sixteen in Luke, and only four times in Mark. Arthur Cushman McGiffert, *The God of the Early Christians* (New York: Charles Scribner's Sons, 1924), p. 14.
[76]   *Inst.* 1559, 1.16.8 (1:207).
[77]   Seneca, *De beneficiis*, IV.vii. 1–ix.1, trans. John W. Basore (LCL, *Seneca: Moral Essays*, 3:216–21).

Seneca's gods (he uses the singular or the plural indifferently) are by no means trapped in the forces of nature. Rather, like Calvin's providence, they do not change their minds once they have decided; and, like Calvin's Creator, they designed the world with particular love for humanity, giving us this most beautiful home and making us rulers of the earth. Gratitude would be the right human response.[78] And yet the gods continue to bestow their benefits even on the thankless; for the sun rises also on the wicked, and the sea lies open even to pirates.[79] For Seneca, as for Calvin, "father" is the natural image to describe a beneficent maker: he finds a bond of affinity between God and humans, who are God's pupils, imitators, and true offspring. But Seneca's God is tough in bringing up his children, as strict fathers are; he does not wish to spoil a good person.[80]

There are certainly differences between Calvin's and Seneca's perceptions of God. The crucial difference I leave for later: Calvin's persuasion that we cannot have a firm confidence in the paternal beneficence of God unless access to God is opened by Jesus Christ. But, in addition to this crucial point, Calvin worried also that the Stoics in general did not sufficiently distinguish God from nature,[81] and that by their doctrine of "apathy" (ἀπάθεια) they left no room for sadness or tears at the human condition. "We have nothing to do with this iron philosophy, which our lord and master condemned not only by word, but also by his example. For he sighed and wept over the evils that befell both himself and others."[82] There is, besides, one other point at which Calvin took a different path from Seneca. They both applied the image of father to God, but Calvin did not, like Seneca, take this to exclude the motherhood of God.

Fathers and mothers, in Seneca's view, do not show their affection in the same way. A father insists that the children must be called early to get on with their assignments, and he will not let them do nothing even on holidays; he draws sweat out of them, sometimes tears. But a mother caresses her children on her lap, wants to keep them out of the sun, wants them never to be unhappy, or to cry, or to have to work. "Toward good men," Seneca concludes, "God has a father's mind and

---

[78]   Ibid., VI.xxiii.1–8, 406–13; II.xxix.3–6, 108–111.

[79]   Ibid., IV.xxvi.1, 256–57. Seneca accepts this sentiment for the interesting reason that it simply is not possible to separate the bad from the good (IV.xxviii.1, 260–61).

[80]   De providentia, I.i.5–6.

[81]   Inst. 1559, 1.5.5 (1:58). See LCC, n. 22 ad loc.: "These sentences reflect statements of Lactantius, who credits Seneca with being the best of the Stoics, since he 'saw nature to be nothing else than God.'"

[82]   Inst., 1559, 3.8.9 (1:709).

loves them with a manly love."[83] Calvin, on the other hand, thought that God's love was as much like a mother's as like a father's, and better than both. On Isaiah 42:14 ("I [the Lord] will cry out like a woman in labor") Calvin comments:

> By this comparison he expresses an amazing warmth of love and the most tender affection. For he compares himself to a mother whose love for her baby, though she gave birth to it in intense pain, has no parallel (*unice amat*). This may not seem to fit God, but only by such figures of speech can his passionate love for us be expressed.

Like all analogies, this one is only partially adequate. Divine love, Calvin points out, is actually *more* perfect than human love, and if, in respect of love, God is like a mother, in power God is more like a lion or a giant. Still, where God's love is concerned, fatherhood is not the only comparison: motherhood is also suitable.[84]

In one of his sermons on Job, Calvin declared that God's word is meant to tame us, but, thinking perhaps that to liken his flock to savage beasts went too far, he added: "True, our Lord for his part becomes more familiar with us than anything else. He is like a nurse, like a mother. He does not compare himself just with fathers, who are kind and good-natured to their children. He says he is more than a mother, or a nurse. He uses such familiarity so that we shall not be like savage beasts any more."[85] No doubt, Calvin was thinking of Isaiah 49:15: "Can a woman forget her sucking child?" His commentary on this text says:

> By an apt comparison he [God] shows how strong is the concern he bears for his own. He compares himself to a mother, whose love for her baby is so engrossed and anxious as to leave a father's love a long way behind. Thus he was not content with using the example of a father, which he frequently employs elsewhere. To express his burning affection, he preferred to compare himself to a mother, and he does not call them just "children" but his "baby" (*foetum*), since affection for a baby is normally stronger. The affection a mother feels for her baby is amazing. She fondles it in her lap, feeds it at her breast, and watches so anxiously over it that she passes sleepless nights, continually wearing herself out and forgetting about herself.[86]

But the text says that a mother *may* forget her baby, and Calvin reverts to his usual point: the affection of God toward us is far stronger and

---

[83]   *De providentia*, II.ii.5–6.
[84]   Comm. Is. 42.14, CO 37:69–70.
[85]   Serm. Job 22.18–22, CO 34:316.
[86]   Comm. Is. 49.15, CO 37:204.

warmer even than any mother's love. We are to bear Christ's words in mind: "If you then, who are evil, know how to give good gifts to your children, *how much more* will your Father who is in heaven give good things to those who ask him!"[87] And so, the gospel text itself brings him back to God's father-love: "Men and women (*homines*)," he says, "though perverse and lovers of themselves, take care of their children. What of God, who is goodness itself? Will he be able to cast aside his fatherly affection? By no means."[88]

MIRRORS OF GOD'S GOODNESS

Not the divine despot but the Parent-God, who is goodness itself, was the object of Calvin's piety and therefore the main theme of his doctrine of God. His dominant image of the Deity was by no means innovative; it placed him in the religious-philosophical tradition inherited by the church from antiquity. But as a biblical theologian, he thought it necessary in part to correct the pagan thinkers; and in part, sometimes unconsciously perhaps, he went beyond his favorite classical authors—as, for instance, in his affirmation of the motherhood of God. It may even be that his recognition of mother-love as an image of divine goodness left him in conflict with his own other self, since one side of him clearly perceived father-love as unsurpassable. Or perhaps, if we could ask him, he might say that the two types of parental love are not identical, and each is unsurpassable in its own kind. But that, I admit, is speculation and can safely be set aside. It is time to change the perspective and to ask: what kind of human race corresponds to God the bountiful parent? The answer is obvious enough: grateful sons and daughters. But we have to make a distinction. There is a twofold knowledge of humanity, before and after the Fall.[89] The heart of the matter can then be summed up if we say that the existence of humanity in God's design is defined by thankfulness, the correlate of God's goodness, and the existence of humanity in sin is defined by thanklessness, the antithesis of God's goodness. [90]

---

[87]   Matt. 7:11, my emphasis.

[88]   Comm. Is. 49.15, CO 37:204–5. Jane Dempsey Douglass compares Luther and Calvin on Is. 42.13–14, 46.3, and 49.15 in "Calvin's Use of Metaphorical Language for God: God as Enemy and God as Mother" (1986): 133–36.

[89]   *Inst.* 1559, 1.15.1 (1:183). Cf. ibid., 1.2.1 (1:39–40), 6.1 (70–71); 2.6.1 (1:341).

[90]   For a more detailed treatment see my essay "The Mirror of God's Goodness: Man in the Theology of Calvin" (1981), reprinted as "The Mirror of God's Goodness: A Key Metaphor in Calvin's View of Man" in *The Old Protestantism*, chap. 9, in which I tried

In God's design the world is the theater of God's glory, and humans are placed in it as privileged spectators of his works.[91] Whether they look within, at their own special gifts, or without, at the evidences of a divine hand in nature, their thoughts are drawn irresistibly to the Maker. Since they have inside them a workshop adorned with countless works of God, a store packed with incalculable riches, they should break out in praise. Whether they want to or not, they cannot help knowing that all their various gifts are tokens of divinity (*divinitatis signa*).[92] As the apostle Paul said at Athens (Acts 17:27), God is not far from each one of us: everyone feels within the heavenly grace that imparts life, and to apprehend God there is no need to go outside ourselves.[93] If, however, we do carry our thoughts further to the world of nature outside us, in no corner of the universe will we fail to discover at least some sparks of God's glory flashing out.[94] It is, of course, true that the earth's abundance belongs to all the many species of living creatures. But everything was made chiefly for humankind, that they might recognize God as father.[95] Nothing could be more absurd than for humans not to know their author, since they were given the special gift of understanding mainly for this use.[96] The end of their life is to be heralds of the glory of God.[97]

Calvin can make the same point by appealing to the traditional notion of the image of God in humanity: he states expressly that the image embraces the knowledge of the One who is the highest good.[98] Now there would be no image of God in humanity unless the human species were uniquely endowed with souls. But the soul is not itself all that Calvin means by the divine "image." To have God's image includes an activity; it is a mode of personal existence rather than simply human nature as such, a relationship rather than simply a

---

to show how God as *fons bonorum* and humanity as constituted by the act of thankfulness are correlative ideas in Calvin's theology. The essay was an expansion of part of an earlier study, "John Calvin," in Gerrish, ed., *Reformers in Profile* (Philadelphia: Fortress Press, 1967), 142–64; see pp. 152–56.

[91]   Comm. Gen., argument (CO 23:10–11); Comm. Acts 17.26 (CO 48:414). Like so much else in Calvin, the image of *homo spectator* is found in the ancient Stoics along with the conviction that the gods furnished the world for humanity. See in particular Cicero, *De natura deorum*, II.lvi.140, lxi.153–154.

[92]   *Inst.* 1559, 1.5.4 (1:55).

[93]   Ibid., 1.5.3 (1:54–55).

[94]   Ibid., 1.5.1 (1.52). See further Calvin's preface to the New Testament, published in the French Bible of his cousin Olivétan (1535): CO 9:793; LCC 23:59–60.

[95]   Comm. Ps. 115.17–18, CO 32:192.

[96]   Comm. Acts 17.27, CO 48:415.

[97]   Comm. Ps. 115.17, CO 32:192.

[98]   Comm. Gen. 2.9, CO 23:39.

natural endowment. Often, though not always, Calvin has in mind a reflection in a mirror: the soul with its faculties is then the mirror, and the image is the reflection. "A full definition of the image is not given," Calvin writes, "until we clearly grasp the faculties in which humans excel and which require us to think of them as mirrors of God's glory."[99] "Humans were created in the image of God: the creator himself wanted his glory to be beheld in them as in a mirror."[100] But if, as Calvin holds, every creature without exception is a mirror in which we are to contemplate the immense riches of God's wisdom, justice, goodness, and power, and if the image of God in humanity is intended to set humans apart from the rest of the earthly creation,[101] then the question must surely be asked: in what special way are humans mirrors of deity—or how do they uniquely reflect the glory of God?

The answer is that while the whole created order reflects God's glory, humanity is distinguished from the mute creation by its ability to reflect God's glory in a conscious response of thankfulness. Even the brute beasts owe their existence to God, but they do not know it.[102] Human beings, by contrast, are endowed with understanding, or a soul, by which they can consciously acknowledge the fountain of good and in this sense image or reflect God's goodness.[103] In Calvin's view, it is this that makes humans the apex of creation: the whole created order has its meaning and purpose in the praise that they alone, of all God's earthly creatures, can return to him, and his design in making the entire order of nature would be subverted if at any time there were no people to call upon him.[104] Torrance suggests, by way of summing

---

[99]   *Inst.* 1559, 1.15.4 (1:189).

[100]   Ibid., 2.12.6 (1:471). See also Comm. Ps. 8.1 (CO 31:88), Serm. Job. 14.1–4 (CO 33:660). Sometimes, however, the *imago* suggests to him an engraving rather than a reflection (e.g., *Inst.* 1559, 1.15.3 [1:188], 2.12.6 [1:471]). Torrance, to whom we are all greatly indebted on this theme in Calvin, argues that Calvin never dissociates the metaphor of an engraved image from the idea of the mirror (*Calvin's Doctrine of Man* [1949], 36). Mary Potter Engel states more cautiously, in her carefully balanced treatment of the image of God in Calvin's theology (*John Calvin's Perspectival Anthropology*, 1988), that "the mirror metaphor is only one among many and not the controlling metaphor" (p. 68, n. 55).

[101]   *Inst.* 1559, 1.14.21 (1:180), 15.3 (186, 188); 2.12.6 (1:471).

[102]   Comm. Heb. 11.3, CO 55:144–46.

[103]   *Inst.* 1559, 1.15.3 (1:188): the soul is the "seat" (*sedes*) of the image. Calvin's thought that even the upright posture of the human body is at least a token of humanity's proper element was apparently borrowed from Cicero, *De natura deorum*, II.lvi.140.

[104]   Comm. Ps. 115.17–18, CO 32:192; cf. Comm. Ps. 105 44–45, CO 32:114–15.

up Calvin's doctrine of humanity in the 1536 *Institutes*, that "Calvin practically equates the *imago* with the *actio* of gratitude."[105]

To have the image of God is, in fact, to possess what we have already identified as a "pious mind," for it is piety that thankfully receives every good from God the fountain of good. There is a perfect fit between Calvin's constitutive notion of deity and his constitutive notion of humanity. Hence his full definition of the image of God reads like this: "Accordingly, this expression [*imago Dei*] signifies the integrity with which Adam was endowed when he possessed the power of right understanding, kept his affections subordinate to reason and all his senses regulated in due order, *and when he properly ascribed his excellence to the extraordinary gifts of his maker.*"[106] Without the recognition that their talents and distinctive constitution are divine gifts, humans are not—in the full sense—images of God. For in saying they were created in God's image, Scripture informs us that their blessedness lay not in good things of their own, but in their participation in God.[107]

Not only the gifts within but the gifts without, too, have the one purpose of evoking gratitude, and it becomes clear in the second book of the 1559 *Institutes* that the gifts without include, besides the fruits of nature, the entire achievement of civilization and the very structure of society. Humans are by nature social animals, and some "seed of political order" has been sown throughout their race; with it goes a grasp of the principles of laws. The ordering of social life is, to be sure, the work of human reason, and so also are the arts and sciences, philosophy, and civic virtue. But, like reason itself, they are nonetheless gifts of God that should move us to gratitude; and God proves that they are gifts of grace by distributing them unequally, giving more to some than to others.[108]

> If we regard God's Spirit as the sole fountain of truth [Calvin says], we will neither refuse the truth itself nor disdain it wherever it appears, unless we want to insult God's Spirit. For the Spirit's gifts cannot be held in light esteem without despising and reproaching the Spirit itself. . . . Shall we consider anything to be excellent or worthy of praise and not recognize that it comes from God? We should be ashamed of such ingratitude, into which not even the pagan poets fell: they acknowl-

---

[105]   Torrance, *Calvin's Doctrine of Man*, 71, n. 6. But once again I refer the reader to Mary Potter Engel (n. 100 above) for a more cautious interpretation.

[106]   *Inst.* 1559, 1.15.3 (1:188), emphasis mine.

[107]   ". . . quo scilicet insinuat, non propriis bonis sed Dei participatione [hominem] fuisse beatum" (ibid., 2.2.1 [1:256]).

[108]   Ibid., 2.2.13–17 (1:271–77), 3.4 (293).

edged that philosophy, laws, and all the noble arts were inventions of the gods.[109]

Finally, even the good deeds of one person to another are occasions of gratitude to God, since many of God's benefits reach us only through the network of social relations. In the Garden of Eden, according to Genesis, Adam and Eve had only each other for mutual society; perhaps that is the reason why, in book one of the 1559 *Institutes*, Calvin speaks chiefly of God's bounty in the world of nature—the setting in which the first humans were placed by the creation. For us, however, God's blessings do not all come solely or directly from nature, or from our own natural gifts; some reach us through the hands of other persons. The section on prayer in the *Geneva Catechism* begins—a little surprisingly—from exactly this point. We are to invoke God alone in every need, and yet this does not exclude our requesting the help of others. For it is God who has conferred on them their ability to help and has appointed them "ministers" of his beneficence. Whatever benefit we receive from others we should regard as coming from God, who alone bestows every benefit through their "ministry." Then comes the interesting question (Q. 237): "But should we not be grateful to other people when they perform some service for us?" Answer: "Of course we should, precisely because God honors them by channelling through their hands the good things that flow to us from the inexhaustible fountain of his generosity. In this way he puts us in their debt, and he wants us to acknowledge it. Anyone, therefore, who does not show gratitude to other people betrays ingratitude to God as well."[110] The Catechism is addressed to the redeemed. Nonetheless, what Calvin speaks of here is the web of natural human relationships, and it belongs to the order of creation.

Calvin sums up his vision of this created order, which includes the continuing providential care of God,[111] in these words: "Finally—to conclude once and for all— whenever we name God 'creator of heaven and earth,' we should recall at the same time that the management of

---

[109]   Ibid., 2.2.15 (1:273–74). Cf. Cicero, *Tusculanae disputationes*, I.xxvi.64. I owe this reference to the editorial note in the LCC translation.

[110]   *Catechismus*, OS 2:113–14; TT 2:70–71. In his *Large Catechism* Luther, too, refers to the human means by which many of God's blessings reach us, but he does not, like Calvin, urge us to be grateful to the "channels" as well as to the fountain. "Denn die Kreaturn sind nur die Hand, Rohre und Mittel, dadurch Gott alles gibt . . . " (BELK, 566; BC, 368).

[111]   *Inst.* 1559, 1.16.1 (1:197): ". . . nisi ad providentiam eius usque transimus, nondum rite capimus quod hoc valeat, Deum esse creatorem."

everything he has made is in his hands and power, that we are in truth his children, whom he has received into his faithful care (*in suam fidem custodiamque*) to feed and bring up."[112] This, however, although it sums up the meaning of our creation, is not the end of the story: Calvin must turn from God's design to Adam's shame.

In what did Adam's sin consist? It would be childish to suppose that in eating the forbidden fruit Adam merely yielded to gluttony. The prohibition was a test, an opportunity for him to prove he was content with his lot. But he was not content. Augustine, therefore, was not far from the truth when he said that pride was the beginning of all evils. Calvin, however, thinks he can carry the anatomy of human sin still further back and discover the root of Adam's pride in his disobedience and infidelity, which is contempt for the word of God. And once Adam had cast off reverence for God, he threw himself wherever his desire carried him. It was infidelity that generated pride, and with pride went ungratefulness: by seeking more than was granted him, Adam shamefully spurned the great bounty of God that had been lavished upon him.[113] Subverting the order of creation, he dragged all humanity into his shame.[114] The special race created to reflect the bounty of God in thankful acknowledgment thus fell into the thankless pride that spurns God's bounty. In this sense, the divine image was lost: the reflection is no longer there.[115] We now sit like blind spectators in the theater of God's glory.[116] We enjoy the gifts but ignore the giver, or ascribe his bounty to fortune or to nature itself.[117] It is true that the sense of deity can never be wholly erased in us, but it does not grow into genuine piety; rather the tokens of divinity are suppressed, and in the place of the true God we set up idols of our own fancy.[118]

---

[112]   Ibid., 1.14.22 (1:182).

[113]   Ibid., 2.1.4 (1:245).

[114]   Ibid., 2.1.5 (1:246). Luther, too, traced the "Fall" (in his own day as well as in Adam's) to its root in questioning the word of God: the temptation of Eve is the pattern of all temptations (*In primum librum Mose enarrationes* [1535–45], WA 42.119.2; LW 1:158).

[115]   The ambiguity in Calvin's statements about the effects of sin on the *imago dei*— was the image lost, or only damaged?—arise in part out of the two-sidedness of his conception of the image itself, which is both an endowment and its proper use. See Gerrish, *The Old Protestantism*, 154–55. Mary Potter Engel sorts out many of Calvin's divergent statements by her "perspectival" approach (*John Calvin's Perspectival Anthropology*, 54–61).

[116]   *Inst.* 1559, 1.5.8 (1:61).

[117]   Ibid., 1.4.1–2, 5.4–6, 5.11, 5.15 (1:47–49, 55–59, 69). Cf. Comm. Acts 17.26, CO 48:414.

[118]   *Inst.* 1559, 1.3.3, 4.1, 11.1, 11.8 (1:45–46, 47–48, 100, 108).

Calvin's denunciations of human depravity are sometimes exces-
sive when judged by modern sensibilities. He tells us, for example,
that the human heart is so thoroughly smeared with the poison of sin
that it can give off only a foul stench.[119] We may be tempted to rise in
defense of our species. But Calvin urges us to admit that what is
needed is not a defense attorney, but a physician.[120] And his point is
not that human nature is wholly villainous, but that it is diseased or
infected even at its noblest and best.[121] Hence in his chapters on sin he
is eloquent about the intellectual and moral achievements of fallen
humanity, which we cannot deny without offense to the fountain from
which every truth and every virtue comes.[122] But the fatal flaw of even
the great heroes of antiquity was precisely that they did not refer their
excellence to the goodness of the Maker. Their ambition always drove
them on; and where there is no zeal to glorify God, the chief part of
uprightness is missing.[123] Calvin's disgust at human ingratitude,[124] not
disgust with humanity, lies behind his rhetoric of sin and depravity.
He assures his readers that he does not want the nobility of our race,
which distinguishes us from brute beasts, to remain buried: the point
of contrasting our original and our fallen conditions is to kindle a new
zeal to seek God, in whom each of us may recover the good things we
have lost.[125]

The problem is, however, that sinful humanity has ceased to turn
to God as the source of good, or to think of God as the father who gives
good things to his children. In the natural order of things, the very
fabric of the world should have been the school of piety from which we
would pass to the blessedness we were created for. But since the Fall
it is God's curse that meets us wherever we turn our eyes, and we
cannot any longer infer from viewing the world that God is our father,
even though God still wants his paternal favor to be visible to us. Our
conscience shows us in our sin every reason for God to disown us and

---

[119]   Ibid., 2.5.19 (1:340).
[120]   Ibid., 2.5.18 (1:339).
[121]   Comm. John 3.6, CO 47:57: the gifts of creation remain, but the contagion of sin
spreads to every part "atque vinum vasis sui foetore prorsus infectum ac imbutum boni
saporis gratiam perdit, imo gustu et amarum et noxium est." Note that in this passage
Calvin affirms (among the gifts of creation) the emergence of *aliqua Dei notitia.*
[122]   *Inst.* 1559, 2.2.15, 3.3–4 (1:273–74, 292–93).
[123]   "Praecipua pars rectitudinis deficit ubi nullum est illustrandae Dei gloriae
studium " (ibid., 2.3.4 [1:294]; cf. 3.14.3 [1:770]).
[124]   "Haec sane turpis est hominum ingratitudo, quum vita communi fruantur
omnes, non reputare quorsum Deus illis vivere dederit" (Comm. Acts 17.26, CO 48:414).
[125]   *Inst.* 1559, 2.1.1, 1.3, 2.10 (1:242, 244, 267).

not to consider us his children.[126] Thus is born that servile religion of
fear that many take to be Calvinism, but that Calvin held to be the
complete negation of genuine religion, which springs from piety
alone—that is, from confidence in God the heavenly father and
fountain of good. The poet Statius (ca. 40—ca. 96) said that it was fear
that first made the gods. But his saying fits only that servile religion
which is in fact *impietas* ("impiety" or "irreligion"), an empty, decep-
tive shadow of religion, and not the thing itself.[127]

In sum, the meaning of creation for Calvin is that the father and
fountain of good has spread a table of good things before his children.
Not everyone receives the same liberality as the psalmist who wrote:
"You prepare a table before me . . . . My cup overflows." But there
is no one who is not bound to thankfulness for benefits received from
the kind and generous father; the more abundantly the benefits are
bestowed, the greater should be the gratitude.[128] It is through his
fatherly kindness and mercy that the Creator of heaven and earth
deals with his children, simply and solely because of his goodness.[129]
Before ever he fashioned the human race, he wanted to commend his
fatherly concern by making everything ready. "What ingratitude
would it then be to doubt whether this best of fathers has us in his care,
who, we see, was concerned for us before we were born?"[130] But just
such ingratitude was Adam's shame. The grateful piety (*grata pietas*)[131]
due in return to the father almighty, Maker of heaven and earth,

---

[126]   Ibid., 2.6.1 (1:341). The phrase *à laquelle nous sommes créez* was added in the
French version (1560).
[127]   *Inst.*, 1559, 1.4.4 (1:50). Calvin could have found a portrayal of this distorted
religion (and no doubt did) in Cicero. See Egil Grislis, "Calvin's Use of Cicero in the
Institutes" (1971), 5–37; esp. 15–16, 20.
[128]   Comm. Ps 23.5, CO 31:326. The metaphor of the table is not as common as the
metaphor of the theater in Calvin's utterances about creation, and in this particular
passage it is, of course, suggested by his text. Nevertheless, he regularly sees creation
under the image of the father's provision of food for his children (e.g., *Inst.* 1559, 1.14.2,
16.7 [1:162, 206]). Hence the continuity with the eucharistic table in the doctrine of
redemption is evident. Interestingly, Schleiermacher carried the old Calvinistic image
of the theater over to the theme of redemption, asserting that the world, as the product
of divine wisdom, is precisely the *Schauplatz der Erlösung* (*Der christliche Glaube*, § 169).
On the theological significance of this modification of the theater image, see my essay
"Nature and the Theater of Redemption: Schleiermacher on Christian Dogmatics and
the Creation Story," *Ex Auditu* 3 (1987):120–36.
[129]   *Inst.* 1536, OS 1:76; *Institution*, 66.
[130]   *Inst.* 1559, 1.14.22 (1:182).
[131]   "Talem patrem grata pietate ardentique amore sic colamus, ut nos totos eius
obsequio devoveamus, illum in omnibus honoremus " (*Inst.*, 1536, OS 1:76; *Institution*,
67).

became impossible when the fall of the first human took away true knowledge of God. If Adam's offspring want to get back to the God who framed and fashioned them, but from whom they have been estranged, so that he may begin again to be a father to them, then they must humbly embrace the cross.[132] And that is where the argument takes us next.

---

[132]   *Inst.* 1559, 2.6.1 (1:341). Cf. 1.2.1 (1:40): "Nemo iam in hac humani generis ruina Deum vel patrem, vel salutis authorem, vel ullo modo propitium sentiet donec ad eum nobis pacificandum medius occurrat Christus."

THREE _____

THE NEW HEIR AND THE
SACRAMENTAL WORD

> *Jesus Christ is the only food by which our souls are fed. But because this food is distributed to us by the word of the Lord, which he has appointed as the instrument for this purpose, the word too is called "bread" and "water."*

In the second chapter, I did not speak directly of the Eucharist. Rather, I tried to show that "man" in the theology of Calvin is "eucharistic man." Long before he arrives at the doctrine of the Lord's Supper, Calvin has made it clear that for him authentic humanity is constituted by the act of thanksgiving to the Maker of heaven and earth, whose goodness has prepared a table before us: that is the truth of our being, grounded in the creation. I borrow the description "eucharistic man" from Gregory Dix's great work *The Shape of the Liturgy.* He wrote in his preface: "Over against the dissatisfied 'Acquisitive Man' and his no less avid successor the dehumanised 'Mass-Man' of our economically focussed societies insecurely organised for a time, christianity sets the type of 'Eucharistic Man'—man giving thanks with the product of his labours upon the gifts of God, and daily rejoicing with his fellows in the worshipping society which is grounded in eternity."[1] Dix would be astonished to find in Calvin the idea that "eucharistic man" so fittingly expresses. (He had no understanding whatever of the Calvinist Supper.[2]) But in fact Calvin would agree with Dix that in the

_____

[1]   Dom Gregory Dix, *The Shape of the Liturgy* (Westminster: Dacre Press, 1945), xviii–xix.
[2]   Dix's sad travesty of Calvin's doctrine of the Lord's Supper (ibid., 632–33) rests on the assumption that Protestantism means individualism.

Eucharist the "only authentic conception of the meaning of *all* human life" finds its "realization."[3]

If, however, the first step to piety is to recognize God as father and to live in thankful devotion to him, it must be added next that, to Calvin's mind, there is no way for fallen humanity to take this step except through faith in Jesus Christ. Authentic, eucharistic humanity is a real possibility only through the grace of reconciliation. It is difficult to follow Calvin's thoughts here without getting our metaphors mixed. The rhetorical power of his theology arises largely out of his keen sense of vivid metaphor, but so also does much of its ambiguity. When one of his Lutheran critics, Tileman Heshusius (1527–88), took him to task for discovering a figure of speech in the words "This is my body," he gave a reply that tells us a great deal about his theological style— the only reply, he says, worthy of a theologian. He admits that figurative expressions may not present an object as simply as plain ordinary discourse, but they do, he insists, capture the attention and make their subject penetrate the heart.[4] He would have had little sympathy for Hegel's attempt to move from representation to pure concepts, or for Schleiermacher's attempt to rise above poetic and rhetorical language to the dialectically correct discourse of Christian dogmatics.

Perhaps his skillful use of the images of the fountain and the divine father vindicate his point: they get through to the religious imagination better than talk of absolute causality (Schleiermacher) or finite and infinite spirit (Hegel). But it need not follow that Calvin was therefore a better theologian than Schleiermacher or Hegel; it is a matter of different, but equally necessary, theological operations. And one problem with first-order discourse immediately confronts us as I move on to the christological starting point that I postponed in chapter two. I have to speak now of two images that are not easily put together: Christ as the "new heir" and Christ as the "food of our souls." Even to focus on these two images is selective, though not arbitrary (as I hope to show). But to take them out of a richer store of metaphors by no means resolves the embarrassment of metaphorical pluralism. This is not to imply that the two chosen images stand in logical contradiction to each other. That would be to misunderstand their nature as *orationis*

---

[3]   Ibid., xix (emphasis mine).

[4]   *Dilucida explicatio sanae doctrinae de vera participatione carnis et sanguinis Christi in sacra coena ad discutiendas Heshusii nebulas* (1561), CO 9:514; TT 2:567.

lumina[5] ("lanterns of style"): they adorn style and flash rays of light on the subject matter, so that one can see it more vividly illustrated. And of particular interest to anyone who is looking for the systematic cohesion of Calvin's theology is the light his favorite images shed on the bond between the two themes of creation and redemption.

My task in this chapter is, accordingly, to document and to explicate (as far as I can) three cardinal propositions that link creation and redemption in the Calvinistic scheme. First, the meaning of Christ's work is that he alone, as the new "heir," or the only son of God by nature, can open up access to the father and fountain of good, from whom our ingratitude has estranged us. Second, faith in Christ is the renewal of the grateful piety that perished with Adam's disobedience, and so intimate is the union faith establishes between Christ and ourselves that his very life flows into us; we may even say that his flesh becomes the "food of our souls." Third, the means by which the gift of faith is given and union with Christ is both begun and nurtured is the word of the gospel, to which a kind of sacramental efficacy is ascribed; and because it is the means by which Christ the bread of life is given to us, the word too is called "our food and drink." Obviously, though further discussion must wait, I shall be exploring the links not only retrospectively with creation, but also prospectively with Calvin's sacramental theology in general and his doctrine of the Eucharist in particular.

THE FATHER'S ONE TRUE SON

The way back to the father is not simple. Fallen humanity's religion of servile dread, though it is a frightful distortion of genuine piety, is not a total misunderstanding. The heavenly father is really displeased with his children's disobedience. "God will never listen to us unless he is well disposed to us. But he must first be reconciled, because our sins make him angry with us."[6] Not that the father has ceased to love his children. On the contrary, it is because of his love that he finds a way to reconcile us to himself. God's love is the supreme cause or source of salvation: he established a means of reconciliation in Christ, so that nothing might stand in the way of his love. Through this reconciliation God began actually to embrace with his goodwill those he had loved

---

[5]   Calvin may have in mind Quintilian's discussion of *sententiae* ("apothegms"). "Ego vero haec lumina orationis velut oculos quosdam esse eloquentiae credo" (Quintilian, *Institutio oratoria*, VIII.v.34).

[6]   Comm. Heb. 8.3, CO 55:97–98.

already before the creation of the world.[7] It follows that when the Bible speaks of God's enmity toward us, or God's anger, the language must be "accommodated," designed to impress on us, by a manner of speaking that is admittedly improper, the seriousness of our condition. Our minds cannot accept life from God's mercy with the gratitude they owe unless they are taught that apart from Christ God is, in a way, opposed to us (*quodammodo infestus*). In Christ alone we are to embrace God's benevolence and fatherly love, and when we want reassurance that God is favorably disposed to us, we must fix our eyes and minds on Christ.[8]

If we ask how exactly Calvin understood the person and work of Christ, we find ourselves, unfortunately, in a morass of disputed questions. In the chapter on the two natures of Christ in the 1559 *Institutes*, he tries to offer a simple statement of Chalcedonian orthodoxy that steers firmly between the Nestorian and the Eutychian heresies. When we read that "the Word became flesh" (John 1:14), we are not to suppose that he was changed into flesh, or mixed with flesh. The Son of God became Son of Man not by confusion of substance, but by unity of person. "We assert that his divinity was so joined and united with his humanity that the property of each nature remains whole, and yet from these two natures one Christ is constituted."[9] Equipped with this impeccable formula, Calvin can readily dismiss the error of Nestorius, who separated what he should have distinguished and ended with two Christs; and he can warn us against the madness of Eutyches, who so stressed the unity of Christ's person as to destroy both of his two natures. It is no more permissible to confuse the two natures in Christ than to pull them apart.[10]

---

[7]   *Inst.* 1559, 2.17.2 (1:530). Here and in the closely parallel passage in 2.16.4 (1:506–7) Calvin is following Augustine's expositions of the Fourth Gospel (MPL 35:1923; NPNF 7:411).

[8]   *Inst.* 1559, 2.16.2–3 (1:504–6).

[9]   Ibid., 2.14.1 (1:482). The so-called "definition" of the Council of Chalcedon (451) stated that we apprehend the one Christ in two natures without either confusion or separation. Calvin appropriated the christological formula "distinction without separation" to describe the nature of the sacramental union of sign and thing signified. Indeed, this was one of the most distinctive features of his sacramental theology. By it he defined his position against the Zwinglians on the one side, and the Roman Catholics and Lutherans on the other. See p. 137 below.

[10]   Ibid., 2.14.4 (1:486–87). Cf. Comm. John 1.14, CO 47:13–14. I have discussed Calvin's views on the christological and trinitarian dogmas very briefly in *The Old Protestantism and The New* (1982), 205–7, with references to the studies by Benjamin B. Warfield (1909b), Jan Koopmans (1938), Antonio Rotondò (1968), and W. Nijenhuis (1972). See also E. David Willis (1966) and the studies and translations made by Joseph N. Tylenda (1973, 1977) of Calvin's controversies with Stancaro and Biandrata.

And yet, despite his formally correct assertions of Chalcedonian orthodoxy, Calvin has repeatedly been seen as moving close to the Nestorian limit: that is, as failing to do full justice to the union of the human and the divine natures in Christ's person. The issue becomes critical in the debates between Lutherans and Calvinists on the Lord's Supper. The Lutheran view of the Real Presence required belief in the ubiquity of Christ's body, and this the Lutherans defended on the grounds of the intimate personal union of Christ's two natures: by a communication of properties, the unlimited presence of his divinity was communicated to his humanity. Calvin, on the other hand, held that the communication of properties, which he recognized as a very ancient idea, was simply a manner of speaking (a *tropus*). To his mind, there was no possibility that the body of Christ might actually become ubiquitous by reason of its union with his divinity. True, the Scriptures do sometimes ascribe to one of Christ's natures what properly belongs only to the other. We are told, for example, that God purchased the church with his blood (Acts 20:28). But God does not have blood, and the assertion is only a bold manner of speaking warranted by the intimacy of the personal union.[11] There can be no question of such an actual exchange of properties as the Lutheran doctrine of the ubiquity of Christ's body requires.[12] Clearly, the eucharistic debate between the Lutherans and the Reformed was at the same time a

---

[11]   *Inst.* 1559, 2.14.1–2 (1:482–84). Calvin suggests the analogy of the two elements in a human being, body and soul. Each retains its own distinctive nature, and yet there is only one person. Sometimes we predicate of the soul what properly belongs to the body, or *vice versa*; and sometimes we predicate of the whole person what cannot belong to either body or soul separately. The analogy was an ancient one. Joseph N. Tylenda argues that for Calvin the *communicatio* does not consist in predicating of one nature *in the abstract* what properly belongs only to the other, but rather in assigning an attribute of one nature to the *person* of Christ while designating him by his other nature ("Calvin's Understanding of the Communication of Properties," 1975–76). Zwingli, by contrast, "seems to have relegated the communication of idioms to a mere manner of speaking about the two natures" (63, n. 21). Tylenda makes an acute case and introduces some important quotations from Calvin, especially the letter of 23 January 1548 to Viret. (He omits one interesting passage that would lend support to his argument. See p. 182, n. 78, below: the second point). The difficulties in his interpretation, it seems to me, are (1) that Calvin does, after all, describe the *communicatio* as an interchange of properties between the two natures; (2) that he too, not only Zwingli, calls this interchange a *tropus* or manner of speaking; and (3) that if the interchange meant attributing a property of one nature to the divine-human person, then it would not be (as Calvin calls it) "improper." However these difficulties are to be resolved, Tylenda shows clearly that Calvin meant something quite different by the *communicatio idiomatum* from what Luther meant.

[12]   For the Lutherans the exchange of properties, though carefully qualified, was a *realis communicatio*, not merely *verbalis: Konkordienformel* (1577), solida declaratio, art. VIII, sec. 63 (BELK, 1037–38; BC, 603).

christological debate: the Reformed accused their opponents of a Eutychian confusion of Christ's natures, and they were in turn accused of a Nestorian separation.[13]

When we turn from Christ's person to his work in Calvin's theology, we again enter controversial territory. During Calvin's lifetime, the nature of the atonement was not, strictly speaking, a matter of church dogma. When the Protestant reformers accused their Roman Catholic opponents of denying the work of Christ, they meant denial not in principle but in practice: permitting the demand for works or the appeal to the merits of the saints to make the grace of Christ of no effect.[14] Later in the sixteenth century, the idea of Christ's satisfaction for sin did come under sharp attack in the acute treatise by Faustus Socinus (1539–1604), *Concerning Jesus Christ the Savior*. Socinus argued that satisfaction for sin is neither necessary, since God can and does forgive without it, nor possible, since satisfaction and forgiveness are mutually exclusive concepts and in any case no one can endure eternal death for anyone else.[15] One can well imagine the horror with which Calvin would have read the treatise. But he passed from the scene long before it was completed (1578) and published (1594). Written in response to one of Calvin's followers, Jacques Couvet, Huguenot minister in Paris, it helped to make Calvin's theory of atonement posthumously controversial. Protestant orthodoxy tended to rally around the controverted points, narrowing the doctrine of atonement precisely to the ideas of satisfaction and substitution that Socinus had rejected. And the question of recent Calvin scholarship is whether, in so doing, they misrepresented Calvin himself, whose utterances on the work of Christ appear to be much more rich and varied, even if the ideas of satisfaction and substitution are unquestionably present.[16]

---

[13]   On the ubiquity of Christ's body see pp. 174-75 below.

[14]   Calvin's *Supplex exhortatio ad invictiss. Caesarem Carolum Quintum* (1543) abounds in christological accusations of this kind. He published it *eorum omnium nomine . . . qui Christum regnare cupiunt* (CO 6:453; TT 2:121).

[15]   Part three of the treatise contains the critique of satisfaction. Part four includes a critique of the view that Christ's satisfaction and righteousness are "imputed" to believers. See John Charles Godbey, "A Study of Faustus Socinus' *De Jesu Christo Servatore*," 2 vols. (Ph.D. diss., University of Chicago, 1968). Godbey is mainly concerned to show that the treatise, taken as a whole, is not merely critical but presents a positive interpretation of Christ's work.

[16]   Calvin did engage in an exchange of letters with Faustus's uncle, Laelius Socinus (1525–62), that induced him to make some additions to the 1559 *Institutes*. See David Willis, "The Influence of Laelius Socinus on Calvin's Doctrines of the Merits of Christ and the Assurance of Faith" (1965). Of the several studies of Calvin's teaching on the work of Christ, Paul Van Buren (1957) concentrates on the substitutionary motif, John Frederick Jansen (1956) and Klauspeter Blaser (1970) on the "threefold office."

Once again, the controverted issues are not without pertinence to the doctrine of the Eucharist. We shall find that Calvin perceived the Lord's Supper not simply as a remembrance of Christ's death in our place, but above all as a means of nurturing communion with Christ, apart from which his death is of no avail. If one looks back from Calvin's discussion of the Lord's Supper in the 1559 *Institutes* to his earlier chapter on the work of Christ, one is less likely to overlook important ideas often buried by the debates over substitutionary atonement. The Eucharist certainly attests a finished, vicarious work of Christ on the cross. But it also fosters a daily communion with the living Christ, and it draws the church into participation in his continuing priestly office. These are elements in Calvin's eucharistic theology that must be taken up as we proceed, and they are firmly grounded in his doctrine of atonement.[17] For now, however, I want to ask the good Calvinistic question not *how*, but *to what end* Christ is our Savior. It was with just such a question that Calvin tried to rise above the morass of controversy on the Real Presence. A similar approach may help us through the controversies over his doctrines of Christ's person and work—or, at least, give us a sound approach to them.

Calvin himself remarks that "scripture uses a variety of metaphors (*translationibus*) to express the grace of Christ toward us." When the Letter to the Hebrews states that the builder has more honor than the building (Heb. 3:3), it may be objected that Christ himself is only a part of the building since he is its foundation; he is simply one of us, his

Charles A. M. Hall (1968) has a section on Christus Victor. (Also pertinent to Calvin's teaching on the threefold office is Gerald W. McCulloh, *Christ's Person and Life-Work in the Theology of Albrecht Ritschl with Special Attention to Munus Triplex* [Lanham, MD: University Press of America, 1990], especially 113–35, 151–56.) Robert A. Peterson (1983) endeavors to include all Calvin's pertinent ideas and images, and one might say that with his able review the problem of Calvin's doctrine of atonement moves from the old reductive dogmatism to an inclusiveness that verges on dogmatic disarray. For one must surely ask what exactly Jesus did that can be represented by such a wealth of metaphors.

[17]   It is not easy to harmonize all Calvin's thoughts on the work of Christ, partly because he holds to a substitutionary atonement that is nonetheless ineffectual until we are united with Christ. Similarly, he teaches a forensic justification, yet one that is given only through union with Christ. See my article "Atonement and 'Saving Faith'" (1960) for some reflections on the dogmatic problem of this tension between substitutionary and participatory categories. I there suggested that perhaps the "happy exchange" could be taken as the regulative conception of Calvin's thoughts on the atonement (see, e.g., *Inst.* 1559, 1.12.2 [1:465–66]; cf. 4.17.2 [2:1362] on the Eucharist). The priestly work into which Christ receives us as his companions is the third of his three offices (2.15.6 [1:502]). But it clearly does not exclude a work done wholly in our place: our guilt was transferred to his head (2.16.5 [1:509–10]).

brethren—that is, not the builder but himself made by God. The solution is easy. Christ is the foundation of our faith in such wise that he is still our governor, our brother without ceasing to be our Lord.[18] The metaphors are not contradictory but complementary. And I think it can further be safely said that for Calvin all the complementary descriptions of Christ serve to present him to us as the one who has opened up access to God. In this way he is the Savior who solves the human dilemma. On Hebrews 7:25 ("He is able for all time to save those who draw near to God through him") Calvin offers this commentary, which seems to me to disclose the heart of his thinking on Christ's person and work:

> [The Apostle] is pointing out what faith should look for in the mediator. The highest good of humans is to be united with their God, with whom is the fountain of life [Psalm 36:9] and of all good things. But their own unworthiness drives everyone away from access to him. The proper function (*proprium officium*) of the mediator is to come to our assistance at this point and to reach out his hand to lead us to heaven . . . . Relying now on Christ the mediator, we pass right through to heaven by faith (*fide in coelum usque penetramus*). For there is no longer any veil in our way, but God appears openly to us and invites us warmly to approach him intimately.[19]

It is, of course, true that Calvin's language in this passage is shaped by the text he is commenting on.[20] But it is also characteristically modified by his own favorite themes. In the first place, the access opened up by Christ is *access to the fountain*, and one could assemble a multitude of parallel passages, in others of Calvin's writings, where the saving work of Christ is similarly expressed and a link is forged between Christology and the doctrine of God as fountain of good. "It is true that the fountain of life, righteousness, virtue, and wisdom is with God, but the fountain is hidden and inaccessible to us. The abundance of all these things is opened to us in Christ so that we may seek it from him . . . . Outside of Christ we should not look for any good thing at all."[21]

---

[18]   Comm. Heb. 3.3, CO 55:36–37. Calvin goes on to make the quite different point that Christ, as human, was made by God, but, as himself eternal God, gives life and renewal to all things by his Spirit.

[19]   Comm. Heb. 7.25, CO 55:94. The phrase *ad familiarem accessum* perhaps retains in Calvin's mind the specific sense of "family" or "household access."

[20]   Cf. Comm. Heb. 10.20, CO 55:129: "Nec quisquam Deum inveniet, nisi cui via et ostium erit homo Christus." Other important "access" or "way" passages in the New Testament are John 14.6 and Romans 5.2; for Calvin's comments on them see CO 47:323–25, 49:89.

[21]   Comm. John 1.16, CO 47:16–17. Cf. Comm. Col. 1.19, CO 52:87.

"From him we draw whatever spiritual goods we have as if from the sole fountain."[22] "In him we have the fountain of all good things."[23] "We glory that God is ours: whatever good can be imagined or desired follows and flows from this fountain. For God is not only the highest of all goods but contains the sum of them and every part in himself. And he is made ours through Christ."[24]

The point could be documented many times over: God is the fountain, and the fountain is opened to us in Christ alone. Two further passages may suffice. In his *Humble Exhortation* to the emperor, princes, and other delegates to the Diet of Speyer (1544) Calvin wrote:

> Not even our opponents can deny how untiringly we urge people to look to no other source but God for whatever good they desire, to trust in his power, to rest in his goodness, to depend on his truth, to turn to him with wholehearted devotion, to repose upon him with full hope, to seek him in need (which means, at every moment), to ascribe to him all the good things they receive and to prove they do so by giving voice to their praise. And so that they may not be frightened away by the difficulty of access, we show them the fountain of all good set before us in Christ, so that we may draw from it whatever we need.[25]

Similarly, in his commentary on John 6:11 Calvin remarks:

> Further, Christ makes it clear that he not only bestows spiritual life on the world but was appointed by the Father to nourish the body. For the abundance of all good things is given into his hand that he may pour them out into us like a channel. But it is not quite right to call him a channel: he is rather a living fountain gushing from the eternal Father.[26]

Later in the *Commentary on the Gospel of John*, the image of the fountain leads Calvin to a general conclusion about theology:

---

[22]   *Catechismus ecclesiae Genevensis* (1545), OS 2:80; TT 2:43. Cf. *Inst.* 1536: "dum omne nostrum bonum in ipso esse agnoscimus" (OS 1:41; *Institution*, 24).

[23]   Comm. 1 Cor. 3.11, CO 49:354. Christ is the foundation of the church "quia in eo Deum patrem cognoscimus, quia in ipso habemus bonorum omnium fontem." The construction appears to identify "God the Father" as "the fountain of good," rather than naming Christ himself the fountain. But see the following note.

[24]   Comm. Rom. 5.11, CO 49:94. Cf. Comm. John 5.24, CO 47:116, where the *fons vitae inexhaustus* seems to mean Christ himself, into whom the faithful are engrafted (*insiti*). Peter Brunner remarks: "Darum gilt die Aussage, Gott sei der Quell aller Güter für den Mangel der Menschen, jetzt auch von Christus" (*Vom Glauben bei Calvin* [1925], 81). Among other passages, Brunner goes on to cite *Inst.* 1559, 2.16.19 (1:528) and 3.20.1 (2:850), in both of which it is Christ who is the fountain. The echo of John 1:16 and Col. 1:19 is clear in the second passage (cf. n. 21 above). See further p. 132 below.

[25]   *Supplex exhortatio*, CO 6:474; TT 1:147. The relative *ex quo* in the last clause could be translated "from him [Christ]."

[26]   Comm. John 6.11, CO 47:133. In the same passage Calvin also speaks of Christ as God's *oeconomus* ("steward").

Christ says he is the life because God, with whom is the fountain of life [Psalm 36:9], is not promised anywhere else but in him. Hence all theology outside of Christ is not only confused and worthless but mad, deceitful, and counterfeit. For although the philosophers sometimes let fall excellent utterances, all they have is fleeting and mixed up with perverse mistakes.[27]

In the second place, the access opened up by Christ is *access to the father.*[28] This is by no means to be taken in a merely conventional sense as though "father" meant simply "God." The language is expressly familial, grounded in the eternal relationship of the Son to the Father, who would never have been called "father" at all but for this relationship.[29] "Father," in Calvin's thinking, is not just a name but a description, and he perceives the coming of Christ as the incarnation of a fatherly love that had always been active in the world. When Jesus wept over Jerusalem, he testified that the spirit of fatherly love had been transfused into human nature.[30] God had never been father to humans and angels except because of his only begotten Son; but after the Son was brought into the world, the heavenly fatherhood became more clearly known.[31] In former times God testified that he is a father through the Old Testament rituals, and he was certainly known in the same image in which he now appears to us. Now, however, he appears in full splendor. "For today the grace of which the prophets have written is placed intimately before our eyes, and whereas they had only a modest taste, we are offered a richer enjoyment of it."[32]

It followed, for Calvin, that the language of reconciliation had to be used circumspectly: there must be no suggestion that God was not good or loving before Christ came into the world, as though Christ

[27]   Comm. John 14.6, CO 47:324–25. Cf. Calvin's preface to Olivétan's New Testament (1535, 1543): "Et mesme tout ce qui se pourroit penser ou desirer de bien est trouvé en ce seul Iesus Christ . . . . Voila ce qu'il nous fault en somme cercher en toute l'Escriture. C'est de bien congnoistre Iesus Christ, et les richesses infinies lesquelles sont comprinses en luy: et nous sont par luy offertes de Dieu son Pere" (CO 9:813, 815; LCC 23:69–70). It is a fundamental point of Calvin's understanding of the Bible that even the "holy men of old" who lived before the incarnation drank from the fountain of God's eternal Wisdom (i.e., Christ). See, e.g., *Inst.* 1559, 4.8.5 (2:1153).

[28]   " . . . per eum accessus nobis patefactus est ad patrem" (*Catechismus,* OS 2:80; TT 2:43).

[29]   " . . . neque Deum Patrem ita fuisse vocatum ab initio, nisi mutua iam tunc fuisset ad filium relatio" (*Inst.* 1559, 2.14.7 [1:491]).

[30]   Comm. Luke 19.41, CO 45:576.

[31]   *Inst.* 1559, 2.14.5 (1:488).

[32]   Ibid., 2.9.1 (1:423). Perhaps the phrase *in eadem imagine* means "in the same *paternal* image," though later in this section *in hac sua imagine* refers to Christ. Either way, the main point is the same.

initiated his love. Titus 3:4 reads, "When the goodness and loving
kindness of God our Savior appeared . . . ." Does this mean that the
goodness of God was unknown before the appearance of Christ in the
flesh? Not at all. The incarnation was not the first *manifestation* of his
fatherly love, but the *pledge* of it. "That the world was reconciled to
God by the death of Christ is the familiar way of speaking in the
scriptures, although we know that he was a kindly father throughout
the ages. But . . . not without reason is God the Father said to have
displayed his goodness to us in Christ."[33]

To be reconciled to God through Christ means, in short, to "have in
heaven instead of a judge a kindly-disposed father."[34] There is no other
way for God to be well disposed to us, when we approach him, than
by laying aside his judicial person and freely forgiving our sins.[35] In
the precepts of the law God is only the rewarder of perfect righteousness and the severe judge of evildoing, but in Christ God's face shines
full of grace and mildness even on poor, unworthy sinners.[36] The work
of Christ is, quite simply, to give us access to a gracious, fatherly God.
This does not, of course, render all the debates about atonement in
Calvin's theology spurious and unnecessary. Atonement, in his eyes,
is not a mere change in our own subjective consciousness by which we
come to realize that God is not, after all, a judge but only a father. If God
casts aside his judicial person for us, that is only because justice has
been done by another.[37] Nevertheless, there really is a sense in which
the legal language of justification by faith "self-destructs": the point of
the doctrine is to move us out of the legal domain into the world of
family relationships, and it is just this point that so often gets lost in
theological controversy over satisfaction, substitution, and imputation.

Calvin certainly held that God is a just judge who cannot cast aside
his governance of the universe. And yet he also held that it is not God's
judicial person but God's fatherly person that determines the life of
true piety. The familial imagery runs alongside the forensic imagery

---

[33]   Comm. Tit. 3.4, CO 52:428; my emphasis. Remarkably, Calvin goes on to argue
that the "epiphany" intended in this verse is not the incarnation but the proclamation
of the gospel. Cf. *Inst.* 1559, 3.2.6 (1:548).
[34]   " . . . ut eius innocentia Deo reconciliati, pro iudice iam propitium habeamus
in caelis Patrem" (*Inst.* 1559, 3.11.1 [1:725]).
[35]   Comm. Ps. 143.2, CO 32:400.
[36]   *Inst.* 1559, 2.7.8 (1:357). Calvin does not expressly use the paternal title for God
here, but the thought of what he elsewhere describes as paternal kindness is clearly
present.
[37]   See, e.g., ibid., 2.15.6 (1:501).

and finally supplants it. In the end, Christ saves us, reconciles us, justifies us as God's Son who takes us for his brothers and sisters.[38] Calvin reads Christ's story in consistently filial terms—even where the text hardly warrants it. He is so sure that Christ's affliction was the affliction of an obedient son that he has him cry out on the cross: "Father, father, why have you forsaken me?"[39] (The text says, "My God, my God . . . .") Of course, Calvin cannot allow that the Father was ever really angry with his beloved Son, in whom he was well pleased.[40] Quite the contrary, the meaning of our reconciliation is that we are drawn, as Christ's brothers and sisters, into the Father's delight in his one true Son: Christ holds the name of "son" by right, but he shares this honor with us,[41] and God will recognize as his sons and daughters those who have received his only-begotten Son[42]. The Son of God holds out to us the hand of a brother and takes us into the presence of the Father.[43] Whatever is his by nature then becomes ours by grace.[44] Thus Christ, the new heir, restores to humanity what was lost in the first son of God, Adam.

The name "heir" is bestowed on Christ manifested in the flesh. He received the title (haereditatem hanc) by being made human and putting on the same nature as we have, to recover for us what we had lost in Adam. For in the beginning it was humanity (hominem) that God (so to say) appointed as his son and the heir of all the good things that were his. But by sinning the first humans (primus homo) were estranged from God and deprived themselves and their posterity both of God's blessing

---

[38] Wherever possible. I have avoided sex-specific language because it was clearly not Calvin's intention to be exclusive. See p. 88, n. 3, below.

[39] Inst. 1536, CO 1:83; Institution, 74–75. In subsequent editions Calvin changed pater, pater to Deus meus, Deus meus (Inst. 1559, 2.16.11 [1:517]). See Matt. 27:46, Mark 15:34. Cf. Ps. 22:1.

[40] "Neque tamen intelligendum est, patrem illi unquam iratum fuisse (Matth. 3). Quomodo enim dilecto filio, in quo illi complacitum est, irasceretur?" (Inst. 1536, CO 1:83; Institution, 74).

[41] "Caeterum hoc nomen iure Christus obtinet quia unicus est natura filius. Nobiscum vero hunc honorem adoptione tunc demum communicat, quum inserimur in eius corpus" (Comm. John 3.16, CO 47:65). On Christ as brother see further Inst. 1536, CO 1:78 (Institution, 69); Inst. 1559, 2.12. 2, 14.6 (1:465, 489); ibid., 3.20.21, 20.36 (2:879, 899); Comm. John 11.33 (CO 47:265), Comm. Heb. 2.16 (CO 55:34), Comm. 1 John 4.2 (CO 55:349), etc. Calvin's main scriptural warrants for the brotherhood of Christ are John 20:17, Rom. 8:17, and Heb. 2:17.

[42] Inst. 1536, CO 1:88; Institution, 81. The allusion is to John 1:12.

[43] Comm. 1 Tim. 2.5, CO 52:270.

[44] "Qui cum verus sit filius, nobis in fratrem ab ipso [sc. deo] datus est, ut quod natura ipse proprium habet, adoptionis beneficio nostrum fiat, si tantam beneficentiam certa fide amplectimur" (Inst. 1536, CO 1:105; Institution, 103). What is his by nature (natura) is made ours by grace (gratia: Inst. 1559, 2.12.2 [1:465]) or as a gift (dono: 2.14.6 [1:489]).

and of every good. Only then do we begin to enjoy by right the good things of God when Christ, who is heir of all things, admits us into his company. For he is heir to make us wealthy with his riches. The apostle crowns him now with this title so that we may know that without him we are destitute of all good things.[45]

FAITH, PIETY, AND THE
BREAD OF LIFE

So far, I have tried to present Calvin's thoughts on reconciliation strictly from the perspective of what Christ does: he opens up an access for us to the father and fountain of good. But we, of course, cannot remain passive spectators of his work: it is by definition an activity that draws us into itself. The heavenly treasure opened to us in Christ is ours only if we receive it by faith. Taught by faith that the fullness of God's bounty resides in Christ, we must continually draw from the fountain by prayer. "Otherwise," Calvin says, "to know that God is lord and bestower of all good things—who invites us to ask him for them—and yet not to go to him, and not to ask, would be useless. It would be as if treasure were pointed out to someone, and he left it hidden and buried in the ground."[46] "Faith," as the vessel that receives the grace of Christ, is the master term in Calvin's portrayal of the Christian life:[47] it controls his thoughts on obedience, prayer, and

---

[45]   Comm. Heb 1.2,CO 55:11. In itself, Calvin thinks, the title "Son of God" could inspire fear. But the mediator in the Letter to the Hebrews is one of us (Comm. Heb. 4.15, CO 55:53–54). Frequently, when contrasting Christ and Adam, Calvin emphasizes the obedience of Christ (see, e.g., *Inst.* 1559, 2.12.3 [1:466]).

[46]   *Inst.* 1536, OS 1:40–41, 96; *Institution*, 24, 92.

[47]   "Fidem vero quasi vasi conferimus, quia nisi exinaniti ad expetendam Christi gratiam aperto animae ore accedimus, non sumus Christi capaces" (*Inst.* 1559, 3.11. 7 [1:733]). Calvin goes on to call faith the *instrumentum percipiendae iustitiae.* Cf. the dedicatory preface to the King: "Quid enim melius atque aptius fidei convenit, quam agnoscere nos omni virtute nudos, ut a Deo vestiamur, omni bono vacuos, ut ab ipso impleamur," etc. (OS 1:24, *Institution*, 4). In *The Nature and Function of Faith in the Theology of John Calvin* (1983), Victor A. Shepherd deals with Calvin's concept of faith much more comprehensively than I can in the following brief section. But I should record my dissent from some of Shepherd's criticisms of his predecessors. If Doumergue (1910) and Stuermann (1952) could answer back, Doumergue would no doubt point out that Shepherd has missed the pivotal importance of the fatherhood of God in Calvin's faith, and Stuermann that the distinction between faith itself and its effect—union with Christ—is not his but Calvin's (see Shepherd, 229–30). These are the two themes that I need to address here. The most important of the older studies of Calvin's concept of faith, S.P. Dee (1918) and Peter Brunner (1925), do not provide much help on the first of these themes, but Dee has some interesting reflections on the second theme, on which there is also an admirable study by Wilhelm Kolfhaus (1939).

worship. Following Calvin himself, we need to ask, first, what faith is; second, what faith effects. To anticipate: faith is knowledge of God's fatherly goodwill, and as such coincides with piety; what faith effects is a living union with Christ, the "food of our souls." The functional equivalence of faith and piety takes our minds back to Eden, and the theme of union with Christ will lead us on—directly into Calvin's sacramental theology.

Faith and The Fatherhood of God

Calvin's well-known definition of faith appears in book three, chapter two, of his 1559 *Institutes:* "Now we can agree on the right definition of faith if we say that it is firm and certain knowledge of the divine goodwill (*benevolentiae*) toward us, based on the truth of the free promise in Christ, and both revealed to our minds and sealed on our hearts through the Holy Spirit."[48] Calvin's assignment of faith to the domain of knowledge (*cognitio*) has often been perceived as a contrast between him and Luther, whose emphasis was rather on faith as confidence or trust (*fiducia*). The contrast is easily overdone.[49] But it is certainly true that there has been a marked tendency throughout the history of the Reformed tradition, from Zwingli to Karl Barth (1886–1968),[50] to frame the cardinal theological question in cognitive terms. Calvin is no exception. Gustaf Wingren, indeed, accused Barth of exchanging the Reformation question of righteousness for the modern question of knowledge. But this is to identify the Reformation with Martin Luther. Among the Reformed, it was a question of knowledge from the very first.[51]

---

[48]   *Inst.* 1559, 3.2.7 (1:551).
[49]   For documentation I can refer to my essay "John Calvin on Luther" (1968), reprinted as "The Pathfinder: Calvin's Image of Martin Luther" in *The Old Protestantism*, chap. 2; see 44–45.
[50]   The regulative importance of "knowledge" in Barth's *Church Dogmatics* needs no special proof; cf. his Gifford Lectures, *The Knowledge of God and the Service of God according to the Teaching of the Reformation*, trans. J.L.M. Haire and Ian Henderson (London: Hodder & Stoughton, 1938). Zwingli expressly launches his treatise on true and false religion with the proposition that "fieri nequit, ut rite de religione tractetur, nisi ante omnia deum agnoveris, hominem vero cognoveris" (*De vera et falsa religione commentarius* [1525], SW 3:640; LWZ 3:58).
[51]   Gustaf Wingren, *Theology in Conflict: Nygren-Barth-Bultmann*, trans. Erich H. Wahlstrom (Philadelphia: Muhlenberg Press, 1958), 26. Cf. Gerrish *The Faith of Christendom: A Source Book of Creeds and Confessions* (Cleveland: World Publishing Co., 1963), 138–39. Wingren's critique has more recently been taken up by Alister E. McGrath, who (mistakenly, in my opinion) discovers in Barth's alleged "epistemologically reduced concept of salvation" an "inverted liberalism." See McGrath, "Karl Barth and the Articulus Iustificationis: The Significance of His Critique of Ernst Wolf Within the Context of His Theological Method," *Theologische Zeitschrift* 39 (1983): 349–61.

It would be a mistake, however, to take "knowledge" in Calvin's definition of faith to denote mere acquaintance with information provided. Faith is a matter of the heart, not just of the brain.[52] Perhaps the initial moment in faith, as Calvin sees it, can best be termed in English "recognition":[53] it has to do, above all, with recognizing God in his true character, seeing God for who he is. No principle is more fundamental to Calvin's theology than what he calls his "rule of piety": to be clear about who the God we worship is.[54] From this rule it follows that only the firm and certain knowledge of God that is faith can draw the line between true worship and idolatry or superstition. There is no religion where truth does not reign: if the end of life is to serve God's glory, knowledge of God must come first.[55] Calvin by no means belittles confidence in God, or love for God either; rather, he holds tenaciously to the axiom that there cannot be either one where the character of God is misperceived. Faith must lead the way. Thus the apostle (in Ephesians 3:12) derives confidence from faith, and boldness, in turn, from confidence.[56] We can certainly distinguish three stages here—faith, confidence, boldness—but faith can no more be separated from confidence than heat or light can be taken away from the sun.[57] Similarly, as we have seen in the passage from which Erich Fromm took his small fragment,[58] Calvin rejects the scholastic doctrine that love has precedence over faith. Faith engenders love: that is to say, love can arise only when we first are clear about who God is. It is a matter of plain psychology.

---

[52]   "Restat deinde ut quod mens hausit, in cor ipsum transfundatur" (*Inst.* 1559, 3.2.36 [1:583]; cf. 3.2.8, 33 [552, 581]). Neither does *cognitio* mean *comprehensio:* rather *persuasum habet quod non capit.* Persuasion of divine truth, though it is certitude, is not rational demonstration (3.2.14 [1:559–60]). Cf. Serm. 2 Thess. 1.6–10, CO 52:227–28.

[53]   ". . . optima ratione fides subinde in Scripturis agnitio vocatur" (*Inst.* 1559, 3.2.14 [1:560]).

[54]   "Nam haec demum vera pietatis regula est, distincte tenere quisnam sit Deus quem colimus" (Comm. Acts 17.24, CO 48:410).

[55]   Comm. Heb. 11.6, CO 55:148–49. In this passage Calvin expressly locates faith in the heart, and virtually equates it with the sense of divine goodness: "Quod si vera Dei cognitio cordibus nostris insideat, fieri non poterit quin nos afficiat reverentia et timore . . . . Nemo enim, nisi percepto divinae bonitatis sensu, ita ut salutem ab eo speret, ad eum quaerendum erit animo comparatus."

[56]   *Inst.* 1559, 3.2.15 (1:561).

[57]   Comm. Eph. 3.12, CO 51:183. Note that in this passage Calvin tends, in differentiating the three terms (*fides, fiducia, audacia*), to narrow *fides* to believing the promises. It is more characteristic of him to represent faith as grasping the divine will *in* the promises.

[58]   *Inst.* 1559, 3.2.41 (1:589). See p. 23 above.

But now, what we need to know of God, if we are to trust and love him, is that he means well to us, and it would be mere rashness on our part to conclude that he is well disposed to us unless he himself gives us the evidence. This is what Calvin means by asserting that faith is "based on the truth of the free promise in Christ." Christ is the evidence, the sole pledge, of God's love; without him, it is the tokens of wrath that we would notice.[59] He was anointed by the Spirit to be herald and witness of the Father's grace.[60] Faith, accordingly, is *fides Christi*—faith in Christ—because everything faith should consider is exhibited in him. "From this it follows," Calvin concludes, "that a bare and confused knowledge about God must not be mistaken for faith, but only such knowledge as is directed to Christ and seeks God in him. And this happens only when the worth and work of Christ (*Christi virtus et officium*) are understood."[61] It is, of course, true that such faith is often assailed by doubt, but that cannot change the definition of faith: it remains in essence a firm knowledge of God's goodwill, based on the evidence of God's love in Christ, even if its assurance is sometimes shaken.[61] And to know God's goodwill is, we would now expect, to know God as the source of good and our heavenly father.

The connection of faith with Calvin's two favorite images of God may be illustrated from his Catechism. Honoring or worshipping God, which is the overall theme of the Catechism, is divided into four elements: placing all our confidence in God, serving him with obedient lives, calling upon him in every need, and acknowledging him with heart and mouth as the sole author of all good.[63] Under these four divisions Calvin presents, in turn, faith, the law, prayer, and the word and sacraments. But the themes are not kept wholly distinct: they are woven tightly together. Hence, for example, the obedience required by the law (the First Commandment) is to place all our confidence in God, which belongs to faith, and to call upon him, which is prayer.[64] It becomes clear that faith, understood as the knowledge of God's fatherly goodwill, is the regulative term on which everything else depends.[65] We place our confidence in God only when we are convinced (by faith) that he loves us and wants to be our father, which

---

[59]   *Inst.* 1559, 3.2.7 (1:550–51).
[60]   Ibid., 2.15.2 (1:496). This was Christ's prophetic office.
[61]   Comm. Eph. 3.12, CO 51:183.
[62]   *Inst.* 1559, 3.2.17–19 (1:562–65).
[63]   *Catechismus*, OS 2:75; TT 2:38.
[64]   Ibid., OS 2:97; TT 2:57.
[65]   "Sic autem [fidem] definire licet, ut dicamus certam esse ac stabilem cognitionem paternae erga nos Dei benevolentiae" (ibid., OS 2:92; TT 2:53).

means, only as we know him in Christ.[66] To love God as the summary of the law requires is to recognize him as our lord, father, and savior (and this again is faith).[67] Genuine prayer flows from faith (Rom. 10:14) because no one will duly call upon God who does not first rest confidently on God's goodness, and this is why we are taught to address God as "father."[68] Finally, to praise God is simply to acknowledge him thankfully as author of all that is good.[69] Everything in the Catechism turns around correctly identifying God, which is what faith does.

It is particularly striking how often Calvin simply identifies believing in God with recognizing God's fatherhood. To find examples of this identification, there is no need to go beyond the great chapter on faith in the 1559 *Institutes*. Against the Roman church's notion of implicit faith, for instance, Calvin writes in section two:

> Is that all it means to believe: to understand nothing, and to surrender our mind obediently to the church? Faith does not rest on ignorance but on knowledge— knowledge not simply of God, but of God's will. We attain salvation not because we are ready to embrace as truth whatever the church has prescribed, or because we delegate to the church the duty of inquiring and learning, but rather *when we recognize that God is a father who is well disposed to us*—now reconciliation has been brought about through Christ—and that Christ has been given to us as our righteousness, sanctification, and life. It is by this knowledge, I say, not by surrendering our minds, that we obtain access to the kingdom of heaven.[70]

In a later section in the same chapter (section 16), when he is commenting on the assurance of faith, Calvin gives a virtual definition of what it means to be a "true believer" (*vere fidelis*): "In short, they alone are truly believers who, *persuaded and firmly convinced that God is a kindly and well-disposed father to them,* promise themselves everything because of his generosity, and who, relying on the promises of God's

---

[66]   Ibid., OS 2:75–76; TT 2:38. The Catechism describes the heavenly father as not only supremely good, but goodness itself (OS 2:120, TT 2:75).

[67]   Ibid., OS 2:110; TT 2:67.

[68]   Ibid., OS 2:116, 119; TT 2:73, 75.

[69]   Ibid., OS 2:127; TT 2:81. Calvin expressly notes that when he takes up the theme of "acknowledging God," he is drawing the implications from the previous sections. Cf. Comm. Heb. 11.6, CO 55:148–49, quoted in part in n. 55 above.

[70]   *Inst.* 1559, 3.2.2 (1:545; my emphasis). In one place Calvin admits that we might sometimes speak of a kind of *fides implicita:* that is, a faith that lacks clear and distinct knowledge of sound teaching. Even so, it would still be faith "born of the word of God" and would therefore be connected with *some* light of knowledge (Comm. Mt. 15.22, CO 45:456–57).

goodwill toward them, presume that they can await salvation without doubting."[71]

Not only is faith virtually equated in these two passages with the recognition of God's fatherhood, but the recognition of God's father-hood is in turn virtually synonymous with salvation. Calvin some-times supported this double equation from John 17:3, with which he took some formal liberties—though, arguably, not departing from the sense intended. The verse reads: "And this is eternal life, that they know thee the only true God, and Jesus Christ whom thou hast sent." Calvin assumed these words to be an integral part of Jesus' prayer, not an editorial comment, and he could only take them to mean that eternal life is to know that God is father. Hence he quotes the text in this form: "This is eternal life, to know that the father is the one true God . . . ." And he uses it to establish that the Maker, from whom we have been estranged, can become a father to us again only through the mediation of Christ.[72] The word "father," inserted by Calvin into the text, has to be given its full descriptive weight. As he puts it elsewhere: our salvation consists in knowing God's fatherly favor toward us.[73] One must, of course, be careful not to construe this assertion reductively, as though salvation were simply a novel conception of God. (That is the way Ernst Troeltsch [1865–1923], for instance, understood authen-tically modern faith.)[74] For Calvin, the fatherhood of God was bound up with the deed of reconciliation; and if salvation is given with the

---

[71]   Ibid., 3.2.16 (1:562); my emphasis. Cf. 3.2.12,13 ("Fides . . . qua Deum invocamus patrem"), 26, 39, 42 ("Fides credit [Deum] nobis esse patrem"); 1:557, 559, 572, 586, 590. In a later chapter Calvin writes: "Neque enim . . . vera est fides nisi dictet et suggerat suavissimum illud patris nomen" (3.13.5 [1:768]). The filial-paternal relationship does not exclude the language of service to God. (How could it if Calvin wished to be a biblical theologian?) Rather, the meaning of servanthood is *determined by* "sonship." Correspondingly, Calvin distinguishes two types of fear: a merely servile dread of God and the reverence for God that fits those who are *both* servants *and* children. The difference between the two types is plain from the fact that whereas those who lack piety (the *impii*) are frightened by the thought of divine vengeance, *fidelium timor* is fear, not of punishment, but of giving offense to the heavenly father (3.2.26–27 [1:572–73]). See further chapter four, pp. 95-102.

[72]   *Inst.* 1559, 2.6.1 (1:341). Cf. the Catechism: " . . . hanc esse vitam aeternam, unum verum Deum nosse patrem . . . utque nobis non Dominus tantum sit, sed etiam pater ac servator, nosque illi vicissim filii simus et servi" (OS 2:128; TT 2:82). In his commentary on John 17:3 Calvin identifies this knowledge with faith (CO 47:376).

[73]   Spiritual perception includes three things: "Deum nosse, paternum erga nos eius favorem, in quo salus nostra consistit, et formandae secundum legis regulam vitae rationem" (*Inst.* 1559, 2.2.18 [1:277]). Cf. Serm. Deut. 32.28–31, CO 29:30.

[74]   See, e.g., *Ernst Troeltsch: Writings on Theology and Religion*, trans. and ed. Robert Morgan and Michael Pye (1977; reprint ed., Louisville, KY: Westminster/John Knox Press, 1990), 184.

recognition of God's fatherhood, that is because God's fatherly goodness is the guarantee of everything we need.

> Now we understand that in the divine goodwill, which faith is said to
> look to, the possession of salvation and eternal life is obtained. For if no
> good thing can be lacking as long as God is well disposed, we are more
> than sufficiently assured of salvation when he himself assures us of his
> love. "Let him show his face," says the prophet [Psalm 80:3], "and we
> shall be saved." . . . Once it has grasped the love of God, faith has the
> promises of the present and the future life and a firm guarantee of every
> good thing . . . . Thus, when we wanted to express the sense of
> blessedness, we affirmed the grace of God, the spring from which good
> things of every kind flow to us . . . . If God's fatherly face shines upon
> us, even our afflictions well be blessed, because they will be turned into
> aids to salvation.[75]

One cannot fail to notice that the language of faith, as we have now
explored it, echoes the language of piety, which is "the reverence
joined with love for God that knowledge of his benefits induces."
"For," as Calvin says in explanation of his definition of piety, "until
people sense that they owe everything to God, that they are cherished
by his fatherly care, that he is the author of their every good, so that
they should ask for nothing apart from him, they will never bow to
him in willing reverence. No, unless they fix their happiness in him,
they will never devote themselves wholly, truly, and sincerely to
him."[76] It is piety that does all these things; insofar as faith does them,
it is the functional equivalent of piety. Hence, as Calvin admonishes
us: "Faith is in no way to be detached from a pious disposition (*a pio
affectu*)."[77] Although it is knowledge, it is not bare intellectual assent to
truths proposed. The assent of faith is more of the heart than of the
brain, more of the disposition than of the understanding; it consists
precisely in a "pious inclination" (*pia affectione*).[78]

We might even venture to say that faith consists in *the* pious
inclination. For, like the piety that is induced by the sense of God's
benefits, faith is built on the goodness, benevolence, or mercy of God.
Believers certainly accept all the words of God, including his threats
and commandments, but they rest solely on the word of God's mercy
or goodwill. "For in God faith seeks life, which is not to be found in
commandments or the pronouncement of penalties, but in the promise of mercy—and only a free promise."[79] Calvin's restrictive defini-

---

[75]   *Inst.* 1559, 3.2.28 (1:574).
[76]   Ibid., 1.2.1 (1:41). See p. 26 above.
[77]   Ibid., 3.2.8 (1:553).
[78]   Ibid., 3.2.8 (1:552).

tion of the proper object of faith (not every word of God, but only the free promise) ran into sharp criticism.[80] But he stood by it, and his reflections clearly bring his notion of faith into line with his notion of piety. The pious mind, as we have seen, acknowledges that God is a just judge, but it is a pious mind only because it has tasted the father's goodness. The believing mind, too, holds many things to be true that do not strictly make it a believing mind: only the fact that it reposes on the fatherly goodness of God makes it what it is.

There is, of course, one important difference between the prelapsarian piety of Adam and Eve and the pious disposition of the Christian: the sense of divine goodness is now differently mediated, and this carries other differences with it. In God's original design, the very fabric of the universe was to have been the school in which we were to learn piety. But now, since the Fall, faith directs us to God the father in Christ: we cannot any longer infer that God is a father simply from contemplating the universe.[81] It follows that although the goodness of God is still the actual object of devotion, it is now his pardoning, reconciling goodness. Thus Calvin asserts that "the proper object of faith is the goodness of God *by which sins are forgiven*,"[82] and he admits that it is one thing to feel the support of the Creator, another thing to embrace the grace of reconciliation offered us in Christ. The goodness of God is now God's grace.[83]

---

[79]   Ibid., 3.2.29 (1:575).

[80]   Ibid., 3.2.30 (1:576). The chief critic was the Roman Catholic theologian Albert Pighius (ca. 1490–1542).

[81]   Ibid., 2.6.1 (1:341). It should be noted in this passage that according to Calvin, following John 1:4, life was in Christ from the beginning: i.e., it was always mediated by the Word. This is in harmony with his conviction that the incarnation of the Word does not make God benevolent but *manifests* God's benevolence (see above, pp. 59-60; cf. *Inst.* 1559, 3.2.6 [1:548]).

[82]   Ibid., 3.3.19 (1:614, emphasis mine); cf. 2.6.4 (1:346–48).

[83]   Ibid., 1.2.1 (1:40). In Calvin's usage, the word *gratia* denotes both the disposition of the heavenly father (God's "favor") and, by transference, what he gives out of this disposition to his children (God's "gift" or "gifts," the *dona gratuita . . . quia effectus sunt gratiae;* Calvin to Bullinger, 25 February 1547, CO 12:483). In the former sense, it can be used interchangeably with God's "love" (*amor Dei*), but it always carries the associations of its cognate forms *gratuitus* ("free," "unmerited") and *gratis* ("for nothing": see especially *Inst.* 1559, 3.13.5 [1:767–68]). Hence it is linked closely with forgiveness or, more technically, the free imputation of righteousness on account of Christ (2.17.1–4 [528–32]; 3.11.15, 15.3 [745, 790–91]). It is thus specifically God's grace in Christ (4.1.26 [2:1038–39]) or simply the grace *of* Christ (as in the title to book three), and in this usage approaches the second meaning, "gift," often in the plural (*duplex gratia:* 3.11.1, 11.6 [1:725, 732]; *gratiis omnibus: Secunda defensio piae et orthodoxae de sacramentis fidei, contra Ioachimi Westphali calumnias* [1556], CO 9:88 [TT 2:302], where *gratiae, gratuita beneficia,*

At the very least, then, we must say that for Calvin redemption is not only the restoration of piety, but also a deepening of it. Nevertheless, the Creator's love and the Redeemer's love are not two loves, any more than the Creator and the Redeemer are two Gods. Creation and redemption are works of the one true God who wants us to know him as father, and it would not be incorrect to say that, in Calvin's thinking, the significance of faith is that it makes piety a possibility once more. The first step to piety is to recognize God as father, but apart from faith in Christ this knowledge is no longer open to us.[84] Only the recognition of faith can evoke the attitude of piety. This is why piety is instilled into the breasts of believers alone,[85] and why faith can be called the "root of true piety" (*verae pietatis radix*): because it is faith that "teaches us to expect and to desire all good things from God alone and disposes us to obey him."[86]

It was evidently important to Calvin to view salvation in terms of restoration and renewal, even while affirming the richer grace that gives to us a deeper understanding of the divine goodwill than was open to the first human pair before their disobedience. In particular, he liked to speak of salvation as recovery of the lost or disfigured image of God in humanity, which he interpreted, as we have seen, in line with his notion of piety. The sole aim of regeneration is that the image of God, disfigured and almost wiped out through Adam's transgression, might be formed in us again,[87] and this is brought about through the increasing conformity of the regenerate with Christ. Here is perhaps Calvin's best summary statement on the restoration of the image:

> The recovery of salvation begins for us in the renewal we obtain through Christ, who is also called the "Second Adam" because he restores us to true and complete integrity. By contrasting the life-giving spirit that Christ bestows on believers with the living soul with which Adam was created (1 Cor. 15:45), Paul commends the richer measure of grace in regeneration. Still, he does not annul the other main point: that the goal of regeneration is for Christ to form us again in the image of God. . . .

---

gratuita dona, and *bona* are all used synonymously). Correspondingly, the *pietas* that answers to the divine disposition is also closely linked with forgiveness: justification by faith is *pietatis totius summa* (*Inst.* 1559, 3.15.7 [1:794]; cf. 3.4.2, 11.1 [625, 726]). With Calvin's use of the term *gratia* compare Thomas, ST IaIIae, Q. 110, a. 1.

  [84]   *Inst.* 1559, 2.6.4 (1:347); cf. 1.2.1 (1:40), 2.6.1 (1:341), 3.6.3 (1:686).
  [85]   " . . . quae solis fidelium pectoribus instillatur pietas" (ibid., 1.4.4 [1:50]).
  [86]   "Fides ergo verae pietatis radix est, quae bona omnia ab uno Deo sperare et expetere docet, ac nos in eius obsequium format" (Comm. Ps. 78.22, CO 31:729). I am indebted to Barbara Pitkin for drawing my attention to this passage.
  [87]   *Inst.* 1559, 3.3.9 (1:601); cf. 17.5 (807). See Comm. 2 Cor. 3.18, CO 50:47.

We see now that Christ is the most perfect image of God: if we are formed in this image, we are so restored that by true piety, righteousness, purity, and understanding we bear the image of God.[88]

From this passage on conformity to Christ, we can readily make the transition to the other aspect of faith: not what it is, but what it effects.

Faith and Union with Christ

Calvin's location of faith in the domain of cognition might seem, at first sight, to imply a purely external relationship with Christ. But his reflections on the "effect" of faith occasion some remarkable utterances on the intimate union between Christ and ourselves. In his formal definition, faith is knowledge that rests on the promise in Christ. However, Calvin can also say that true knowledge of Christ is to receive Christ himself clothed with his gospel,[89] and he can trace the confidence of faith to the intimate communion we have with him.[90] He insists that faith does not merely look at Christ in the distance, so to speak, but embraces him so that he may become ours and dwell within us. "It makes us grow into his body, have life in common with him, in short become one with him."[91] We "put on Christ," are "engrafted in Christ," and so on.[92]

Calvin took care to insist that "believing in Christ" and "communion with Christ," though connected, are not the same thing. In part, his reasons were exegetical: he read in the Letter to the Ephesians (Eph. 3:17) the prayer "that Christ may dwell in your hearts through faith" (*per fidem* in the Latin version, διὰ τῆς πίστεως in the Greek), and he apparently took the instrumental language to imply a distinction between what faith is and what it effects. Or perhaps he found in the language of Ephesians only the warrant for a distinction that he needed to make on theological grounds, not least in his doctrine of the Eucharist. In his commentary on Ephesians 3:17, he writes:

> Paul, therefore, aptly designates those in whom Christ dwells as "strengthened by the spiritual might (*virtute*) of God." He also points

---

[88]   *Inst.* 1559, 1.15.4 (1:189–90). Calvin held that Christ was the source of the divine image even in Adam (2.12.6 [1:471]). He also speaks of Christ as the "mirror" or "image" of the invisible God (Comm. John 6.47, CO 47:151), the "mirror of God's inestimable grace" (*Inst.* 1559, 2.14.5 [1:487]), and so on.

[89]   *Inst.* 1559, 3.2.6 (1:548); cf. 2.9.3 (1:426).

[90]   Ibid., 3.2.24 (1:570).

[91]   Comm. John 6.35, CO 47:145.

[92]   *Inst.* 1559, 3.1.1 (1:537). "Verbum enim fidei insculptum est sacramentis" (Calvin to Bullinger, 25 February 1547, CO 12:487).

out the location where Christ rightly dwells, in the heart, to make us aware that it is not enough if he lodges on our tongues or flits in our brains. Further, he describes the manner in which so great a benefit (*bonum*) is attained. "He dwells," he says, "through faith." What a tribute to the excellence of faith that by it the Son of God is made ours and makes his home in us [John 14:23]! By faith we do not only acknowledge that Christ suffered for us and was raised from death for us; we also receive him as he offers himself to us, to be possessed and enjoyed. This should be noted carefully. Most people regard partaking of Christ (*Christi esse participem*) and believing in Christ as the same thing. But our partaking of Christ (*participatio quam habemus cum Christo*) is rather the effect of believing (*fidei effectus*). In short, Christ is not to be looked at by faith from a distance, but so received by the embrace of our souls as to dwell in us. And this is how it happens that we are filled with the Spirit of God.[93]

Calvin's theme here is what he elsewhere calls the "mystical union" of believers (or the church) with Christ,[94] a pivotal theme in his doctrine of the Lord's Supper.

Comparison of Calvin's language with the language of such medieval mystics as Bernard of Clairvaux (1090–1153) reveals a striking affinity between the reformer and the mystic. The common assumption that there is only a sharp antagonism between the mystical tradition and Reformation theology has been shown to rest on so narrow a definition of a "mystic" that it disqualifies Bernard as well as Calvin.[95] Nevertheless, I am inclined to think that, whatever the linguistic and even material kinship between Calvin and Bernard, Calvin meant no more by the actual word *mysticus* than simply

[93]   Comm. Eph. 3.17, CO 51:186–87. *Particeps* sometimes means "partner" or "comrade." But the verb *participare* means "to share in, partake of, participate in," and is important in Calvin's eucharistic vocabulary. It was, I think, misleading when S. P. Dee, after citing such passages as Calvin's comments on Eph. 3:17, concluded: "Uit het voorafgaande blijkt allereerst, dat, wanneer Calvijn tusschen geloof en unio mystica onderscheid maakt, hij daarmede een bloot logische distinctie bedoelt. In werkelijkheid vallen beide saam" (*Het Geloofsbegrip van Calvijn*, 190). Dee was concerned to avoid any suggestion of a temporal sequence or break (first faith, then union): for Calvin, union is the immediate consequence of faith, and faith in turn remains dependent on the mystical union. (A similar blurring of Calvin's distinction between faith and its effect appears in Werner Krusche, *Das Wirken des heiligen Geistes nach Calvin* [1957], 270). Nevertheless, Calvin is plainly struggling to express a *real* distinction in the elements that make up the experience of the Christian, not, as the word "logical" might be taken to imply, a distinction only in the mind of the theologian who is trying to interpret Christian experience. Dee's interest was largely in the intriguing debates over faith–union and forensic justification in Calvin, and I do not need to delve into the debates here.

[94]   *Inst.* 1559, 2.12.7 (1:473), 3.11.10 (1:737).

[95]   Dennis E. Tamburello, "Christ and Mystical Union: A Comparative Study of the Theologies of Bernard of Clairvaux and John Calvin" (1990).

"mysterious." Hence he can equally well use the adjective "secret" or "wonderful" to characterize our communion with Christ.[96] "Mystical" was perhaps suggested to him by his favorite biblical proof for union with Christ: Ephesians 5:28–33, the passage that compares the marriage bond to the relationship between Christ and the church. Calvin was fascinated by the notion of a sacred wedlock that makes us flesh of Christ's flesh and bone of his bone, and he noted that verse 32 says: "This is a great mystery, and I take it to mean Christ and the church."[97] In his commentary on Ephesians 5:28–33, he calls it a "remarkable passage on the mystical communion (*de mystica communicatione*) that we have with Christ." It means, he explains, that through the communication of Christ's substance we grow together into one body. Paul is describing the spiritual union with Christ by which we become bone of his bone and flesh of his flesh—not just because he is a human like ourselves, but because he engrafts us into his own body by the power (*virtute*) of his Spirit, so that we may draw life from him. But Paul adds that this is a great mystery (*magnum esse arcanum*), implying that no words can explain all that the grandeur of the matter demands. We should strive to feel Christ living in us rather than to explain the way the communication happens. It is a great mystery how Christ breathes his life and power (*virtutem*) into the church.[98] This, I think, is all Calvin means by calling our union or communication with Christ "mystical."

However severely cognitive Calvin's notion of faith may seem to be, then, faith was inseparable in his mind from its effect: a union with Christ that eludes our understanding. When Christ gives us the light of faith, he at the same time (*simul*) engrafts us into his body to make us partakers of every good thing.[99] Again and again, Calvin tells us not to think of Christ as standing far off. He dwells within us, makes us participate not only in the good things that are his but in his very self, so that his righteousness overwhelms our sins, and by a wonderful

---

[96]   *Arcana unio* (*Inst.* 1559, 4.17.1 [2:1361]), *mirabilis communio* (3.2.24 [1:570]), *mirifica corporis et sanguinis eius communio* (4.17.26 [2:1394]), *sacra coniunctio* (2.17.7 [1:473]). Of course, Calvin often uses the idea of communion with Christ (*communicatio, societas, participatio*) with no adjectival qualifier (e.g., 3.8.1, 14.4, 15.5 [1:702, 771, 793]; 4.17.7 [2:1367]), and sometimes he writes of union with God rather than Christ (e.g., 2.8.18, 15.5 [1:385, 500]; 3.25.2 [2:988]; 4.17.33 [2:1408]).

[97]   "...sacrum illud coniugium quo efficimur caro de carne eius, et ossa ex ossibus" (*Inst.* 1559, 3.1.3 [1:541]). "Tandem epiphonema subnectit: Magnum hoc mysterium" (4.19.35 [2:1482]).

[98]   Comm. Eph. 5.28–33, CO 51:225–28. I shall return later to Calvin's assertion that we have a *symbolum et pignus* of union with Christ in the Sacred Supper.

[99]   *Inst.* 1559, 3.2.35 (1:583).

communion that is more than just fellowship (*societas*) he grows into a single body with ourselves.[100] Because this mysterious union is so hard to understand, we have to resort to images or metaphors. One image is marriage. In John 6 Calvin finds another: eating in order to live.

On the Lord's strange words, "I am the bread of life" (John 6:35), Calvin remarks in his commentary that it was the mention of the Old Testament manna and daily food that suggested the metaphor or figure of bread, which was more suitable than plain speech for instructing the uncultured crowd. God could very well impart a hidden strength (*arcanam virtutem*) to feed our bodies without bread; but eating bread shows more clearly both our own weakness and the power of God's grace. Similarly, it penetrates our heads better if we are told, by analogy, that Christ is the bread by which our souls are fed, not simply that he is our life. In one respect, it is true, the comparison falls short: Christ does not only sustain our life but also initiates it. But the point (the "simple doctrine"), expressed in language that arose out of the previous discourse, is this: "Our souls do not live by their own intrinsic strength (*intrinsica virtute*), so to speak, but borrow life from Christ."[101] Then how do we eat this food? As we receive Christ by faith. The text says, "He who comes to me . . . . " To come and to believe, Calvin admits, have more or less the same meaning. But it is the feeling of hunger that drives us to Christ, and in this sense coming to Christ is the effect of faith.

> Moreover, those who infer from this passage that eating Christ is nothing but faith are not arguing quite correctly. I certainly admit that there is no other way for us to eat Christ than by believing, but the eating is itself the effect or fruit of faith rather than faith. For faith does not merely look at Christ as if in the distance, but embraces him that he may become ours and dwell in us. It makes us grow together (*coalescamus*) into his body, have life in common with him, in short become one with him. So it is true that we eat Christ by faith alone, provided we grasp at the same time how faith unites us with him.[102]

---

[100]   Ibid., 3.2.24 (1:570–71). The idea of an "exchange" consequent on union with Christ—his righteousness for our sin— is already grounded in the incarnation (2.12.2 [1:465]). But it requires also the mystical union. The Eucharist is a pledge of the *mirifica commutatio* (4.17.2 [2:1362]).

[101]   Comm. John 6.35, CO 47:144.

[102]   Ibid., CO 47:144–45; cf. on v. 47, CO 47:151 ("Quare manducatio effectus est aut opus fidei"). The main adversary here is certainly Zwingli: see, e.g., his *De vera et falsa religione commentarius* (1525), SW 3:776–77; LWZ 3: 201–2.

Calvin's reflections on John 6 will, of course, need to be taken up again when we turn directly to the Lord's Supper. The distinction between faith and faith's effect then takes on a sharply polemical significance. I am not sure that I would wish to defend the distinction as a piece of exegesis. But theologically it is interesting. It shows Calvin trying to affirm simultaneously two points that were of immense importance to him, yet hard to combine. He held firmly that the initial psychological moment in faith is perception or recognition, seeing God as God is. The fact that the cognitive process of faith cannot occur at all without the mysterious activity of the Holy Spirit on the mind and the heart cannot alter faith's location on the psychological chart. Neither does it make any difference to the concept of faith itself whether we distinguish its object as God, God's will, or Christ. Speaking of belief in Christ, Calvin asserts that "faith flows from *knowledge* of Christ . . . because, if we are to trust him, we must perceive who he is and what he brings us."[103] We might call this appropriately, if a little impolitely, the "anti-papist" strand in Calvin's concept of faith: he thought the church of Rome put resignation to ecclesiastical authority in the place of a clear perception of God's will in Christ, leaving its adherents in a fog of ignorance about God's character and intentions. [104]

The other strand in Calvin's concept of faith is largely anti-Zwinglian and is represented by the theme of faith's effect. Faith in Christ entails much more than simply believing that he won certain benefits for us by his death: it brings us into relationship with Christ himself, and it includes much that we rather feel than understand. Now Calvin certainly held that there is more to faith itself than what the Lutherans stigmatized as *fides historica:* mere assent to the gospel story, which, he says, is all that most people understand when they hear the word "faith."[105] But even when faith is deepened by the notion of confidence in God's goodwill, based on the promise in Christ, it still does not in itself contain as much as Calvin wished to affirm about being a believer in Christ. And he was anxious not to lose the mysterious more by permitting a reduction of "feeding on Christ" to simply "believing in him." Only by differentiating between faith and faith's effect can we be sure not to diminish the rich meaning of the metaphor: Christ the

---

[103]   " . . . fidem ex Christi notitia fluere . . . quia si Christo fidamus, qualis sit et quid nobis afferat sentire nos oportet" (Comm. John 6.40, CO 47:148). My emphasis.
[104]   See, e.g., *Inst.* 1559, 3.2.2–3 (1:544–46).
[105]   Ibid., 3.2.1 (1:543).

food of our souls. At this point, Calvin's alleged intellectualism vanishes into a devotion of the heart that is repelled by rationalism.

THE WORD AS MEANS OF GRACE

My third and last theme in this chapter—the word as means of grace—moves us back, at least initially, from the mystical to the cognitive pole in Calvin's theology.[106] The very definition of faith as "firm and certain knowledge" makes it dependent on the communication of truth ("doctrine"), even if the truth conveyed by the word or promise is of no avail without the mysterious operation of the Spirit. But as one looks more closely, a two-sidedness appears in Calvin's reflections on the word, and it parallels his distinction between faith and the effect of faith. The word is not simply information about God; it is the instrument through which union with Christ is effected and his grace is imparted. The word of God, in Calvin's thinking, assumes the function that medieval theology ascribed to the sacraments. In this sense, it is the sacramental word.

The Word as Doctrine

To begin with, then, if faith is a kind of knowing, it necessarily requires the provision of truth, and this is to be sought nowhere else but in God's word. Faith is born from the word,[107] or, what is the same thing, from obedience, which is turning an attentive ear to God's express pronouncements in Scripture. Hence, in his chapter on the need for

---

[106]   By speaking of two "poles," I wish to suggest the extremities between which Calvin's thoughts on faith and the word are situated. I understand them to be purely imaginary limits: the cognitive strand in Calvin's concept of faith never excludes mystery, nor does the mystical strand leave him speechless. Calvin's notion is that faith, even as cognition, is somehow enabled to go beyond the normal limits of human knowing, but that the result is nonetheless knowledge even if it is not comprehension (*Inst.* 1559, 3.2.14 [1:559–60]). I have discussed Calvin's doctrine of the word of God in "Biblical Authority and the Continental Reformation" (1956), revised and reprinted as "The Word of God and the Words of Scripture: Luther and Calvin on Biblical Authority" in *The Old Protestantism*, chap. 3. See further H. Jackson Forstman (1962) and on the related theme of preaching, as Calvin understood it, Erwin Mülhaupt (1931), T.H.L. Parker (1947), Richard Stauffer (1977), and John H. Leith (1990). Leith rightly says: "For Calvin, preaching is sacramental in the context of the order of salvation and as a means of grace, and not in the more general sense by which all creation may be sacramental" ("Calvin's Doctrine of the Proclamation of the Word and Its Significance for Today," 211).

[107]   Comm. Luke 16.30, CO 45:413. Cf. Comm. Ps. 106.39, CO 32:132: "spiritual chastity" means cleaving wholly to the word of God.

Scripture to direct us to the Creator, Calvin makes his famous remark that "all right knowledge of God is born from obedience." Not that humans since the Fall no longer need to turn their eyes to contemplation of God's works; it still remains true that they have been placed in this glorious theater as spectators. But if they are to profit from seeing, they must first prick up their ears to the word.[108] In Calvin's reading of the story of Adam and Eve, sin entered through their ears, not their eyes: their shame was not that they fancied a delicious-looking fruit, but that they spurned the word of God. Unfaithfulness opened the door—contempt for what God had said. And just as the ears, when they were opened to Satan, were the corridors by which death was let in, so, as Bernard of Clairvaux rightly taught, the door of salvation is opened to us when we receive the gospel with our ears.[109]

The word of God, in Calvin's theology, is by no means simply equated with the Bible. It is true that he treats the words of the Old and New Testaments as oracles from the very mouth of God.[110] "Scripture says" and "the Holy Spirit says" are used synonymously throughout his *Institutes* and commentaries, and the human authors are regarded as only the instruments or secretaries of the Spirit.[111] The scholarly literature on Calvin still puzzles over the question how he can nevertheless—as he plainly does—admit that there are errors in the Bible.[112] But more important for my present purpose is the fact that reverence for Scripture did not prevent Calvin from seeking a word *within* the words, nor from identifying *this* word as the actual object of faith. For Calvin the Bible was not a mere compendium of supernaturally communicated information; it was the medium of a divine message. Life eternal, says the Catechism, following John 17:3, is to know God the Father and Jesus Christ whom he has sent. "By what means can we attain to so great a good? For this end God left us his sacred word . . . . Where are we to look for this word? In the holy scriptures, in which it is contained." [113]

Sometimes, we have seen, Calvin identifies the sacred word in the Bible as the promise. While it is certainly the part of wisdom to

---

[108]   "Neque enim perfecta solum, vel numeris suis completa fides, sed omnis recta Dei cognitio ab obedientia nascitur" (*Inst.* 1559, 1.6.2 [1:72]). Cf. 2.8.5 (1:372): "...cuius legitimus cultus sola constat obedientia."

[109]   Ibid., 2.1.4 (1:246).

[110]   See, e.g., ibid. 1.6.1, 7.5 (1:70, 80); 2.8.12 (1:379).

[111]   Ibid., 4.8.9 (2:1157); Comm. 2 Tim. 3.16, CO 52:383; Comm. 2 Pet. 1.21, CO 55:458.

[112]   See Gerrish, *The Old Protestantism*, 63, and the literature there cited, especially Krusche (1957) and McNeill (1959).

[113]   *Catechismus*, Q. 300, OS 2:128; TT 2:82.

embrace whatever is taught in Sacred Scripture,[114] nevertheless a person's heart is not aroused to faith by every utterance of God (*ad vocem Dei quamlibet*); some of God's utterances are more likely to shake or alarm faith. We need the promise of grace or mercy to testify that the father is well disposed to us. On this promise alone can the heart rest; it is what faith properly looks to in the word.[115] In short the word of faith, as the apostle says (Rom. 10:8), is the gospel, which offers us salvation because of our misery, not because of our worth. Nothing else can give that recognition of God's goodwill that faith requires, for the gospel is a free, wholly unconditional promise that does not throw us back on our own ambiguous achievements. Faith and the gospel are correlative terms: they belong together.[116]

At other times, without any real change of meaning, Calvin points to Christ clothed with the gospel as the object of faith, or Jesus Christ himself as the content of the whole Scripture. "This is the true knowledge of Christ: if we take him as he is offered by the father, namely, clothed with his gospel. For as he himself has been designated the goal of our faith, so we shall not run straight to him unless the gospel leads the way."[117] Calvin applies to Christ the Latin word *scopus* (borrowed from the Greek σκοπός), which means the mark on which one fixes the eye—the goal or target. Here Christ is *the goal of faith*. In his commentary on John 5:39 ("Search the scriptures . . . it is they that bear witness to me"), Calvin uses the same word to put forward a Christian understanding of the Old Testament. Christ does not reproach his opponents ("the Jews") for seeking life in the Scriptures; that is precisely the purpose for which the Scriptures were given.[118] But they smothered the light of life that the Scriptures contained. For how can the law bestow life without Christ? Calvin goes on to infer from the text, first, the principle that knowledge of Christ can be obtained only

---

[114]   *Inst.* 1559, 1.18.4 (1:237).

[115]   Ibid., 3.2.7 (1:550).

[116]   Ibid., 3.2.29 (1:575). Cf. 3.2.6 (1:548): "Principio admonendi sumus perpetuam esse fidei relationem cum verbo." Dowey has argued that Calvin was left with a dissonance between two interpretations of faith, one Bible-centered, the other Christ – or gospel-centered: "We must conclude, in fact, that two 'interpretations' exist side by side in Calvin's theology concerning the object of the knowledge of faith, because he never fully integrated and related systematically the faithful man's acceptance of the authority of the Bible *en bloc* with faith as directed exclusively toward Christ" (*The Knowledge of God in Calvin's Theology* [1952], 161–62).

[117]   *Inst.* 1559, 3.2.6 (1:548).

[118]   Calvin took the verb ἐρευνᾶτε to be an imperative (the RSV translates it as the indicative, "You search").

from the Scriptures, but also, second, a principle for interpreting Scripture.

We learn from this passage that knowledge of Christ should be sought from the scriptures. For those who imagine whatever they please about Christ will have nothing but a shadowy apparition instead of him. First, then, we must grasp that Christ cannot be rightly known from anywhere else but the scriptures. If this is so, it follows that the scriptures are to be read with the intention of finding Christ in them. Any who shall turn aside from this goal (ab hoc scopo deflectet) will never arrive at knowledge of the truth, however much they wear themselves out with learning their whole life long.[119]

Christ is the goal of faith; he is also *the goal of Scripture,* or of the devout reader of Scripture.

A similar passage was inserted into the preface Calvin wrote for Olivétan's French translation of the New Testament. There it is asserted emphatically that what we should look for in the whole of Scripture (that is, presumably, not in the Old Testament only) is "to know well Jesus Christ and the infinite riches that are contained in him." There cannot be any question at all of having any other goal or destination (French: *but ny adresse*), so that our understanding should come to a stop at the point where we learn in Scripture to know Jesus Christ alone.[120] As Calvin says elsewhere: even the letter of the law is the word of life if, through the Spirit, it offers (*exhibet*) Christ.[121] This hermeneutic principle, as we may perhaps call it, was grounded in his doctrine of revelation: Christ is not only the mark toward which the Scriptures draw us, but also, as God's eternal Word or Wisdom, the actual wellspring (*scaturigo*) of all the oracles of God. When the "Word of God" is set forth in Scripture, we are not to imagine a fleeting utterance: rather, "Word" denotes the everlasting Wisdom of God from which the oracles and the prophecies all come forth.[122] It would clearly be an absurdity, in Calvin's view, if one read the words of Scripture and overlooked the Word from whom they sprang.[123]

---

[119]   Comm. John 5.39, CO 47:125.

[120]   *Prefationes bibliis Gallicis Petri Roberti Olivetani . . . praemissae* (1535), CO 9:815; LCC 23:70. Calvin added the passage referred to in 1543. Cf. n. 27 above. His commentary on John appeared in 1553.

[121]   "Verum si per Spiritum efficaciter cordibus [litera] imprimitur, si Christum exhibet, verbum est vitae" (*Inst.* 1559, 1.9.3 [1:95]). *Exhibere* is a key term in Calvin's eucharistic theology, as will be noted below.

[122]   Ibid., 1.13.7 (1:129).

[123]   "Ergo ut omnes divinitus profectae revelationes verbi Dei titulo rite insigniuntur, ita verbum illud substantiale summo gradu locare convenit, oraculorum omnium

The crucial principle "no word, no faith" (if we may so formulate it)[124] by no means reduces faith to the mere acceptance of propositions culled indiscriminately from the Bible. Nevertheless, Calvin saw no disharmony between faith and doctrine: on the contrary, he also took it as an unquestionable axiom that there is no faith without instruction. For an illustration of this axiom, we can turn to his comments on the story of the burning, fiery furnace in the Book of Daniel, particularly on Daniel 3:28–29. Amazed at the deliverance of the three Jews from the furnace, King Nebuchadnezzar blessed the God of Shadrach, Meshach, and Abednego, and decreed that any who spoke against this God would be cut in pieces, and their homes reduced to a dung-pit. Calvin grants that the king's blessing was no common confession, but he points out that later events proved it to have been impulsive and transient. Hence he can examine the king's confession more closely and expose its defects. Why did the king say, "Blessed be the God of Shadrach, Meshach, and Abednego," and not rather call him *his* God? Well, perhaps that would have been excusable had he renounced his former superstitions. But he did not. He should have cursed his idols, since the glory of the one true God cannot be extolled unless every idol is reduced to nothing. The king's confession was fraudulent.[125] Neither does Calvin allow the king any praise for issuing the edict. In itself, the edict was pious and commendable. But Nebuchadnezzar was carried away by a blind, uncontrolled impulse; piety did not strike a root in his heart.

Calvin applies the text to his own day: under the papacy, edicts demanding blood for the glory of God are flying all around us, and yet it is all madness with no ray of genuine knowledge. No law can be passed, no edict promulgated, about religion and the worship of God unless correct knowledge of God shines out. Despite the appearances, Nebuchadnezzar's edict concerning the God of Shadrach, Meshach, and Abednego actually deserves blame; he did not ask who that God is, so that a firm reason could induce him to promulgate the edict.[126] His problem was that his volatile confession did not rest on doctrine or instruction; it was evoked by mere amazement at a miracle. He

---

scaturiginem" (ibid. [1:130]). I have capitalized "Word" only where the reference is plainly to the second person of the Trinity.

[124]   Cf. ibid., 3.2.6 (1:154): "Tolle igitur verbum, et nulla iam restabit fides."

[125]   Comm. Dan. 3.28, CO 40:642.

[126]   "Non inquirit quisnam sit ille deus, ut possit firma ratione adduci ad promulgandum edictum" (Comm. Dan. 3.29, CO 40:645–46).

inferred the eminence of Israel's God from the display of his power. But that would not do for piety, either in his day or in ours. Calvin explains:

> Piety is always built on knowledge of the true God, and knowledge requires instruction (*doctrinam*). Nebuchadnezzar knew the God of Israel to be a high God. How did he know that? By his power. For he had such a spectacle set before his eyes as he could hardly discount, even if he wanted to. And so, he acknowledges that the God of Israel is a high God— because the miracle so taught him. But this, as I reminded you, is not enough for solid piety unless instruction (*doctrina*) is brought in also and, indeed, plays the leading role. I certainly admit that miracles prepare people to believe. But if naked miracles are displayed without the addition of knowledge from the very word of God (*ex sermone ipso Dei*), faith will be short-lived . . . . [King Nebuchadnezzar] kept his senses fixed on the miracle; content with a mere spectacle, he did not seek to know who the God of Israel is, or what is comprised in his law. He was not even anxious about a mediator. In short, he neglected the sum of piety as a whole and rashly seized on one part only . . . . To test our compliance to God, we must hold fast to the principle that nothing pleases him that does not come from faith [Rom. 14:23]. But faith cannot be produced by any miracle, or any sense of divine power; it requires instruction at the same time.[127]

Calvin's interpretation of these two verses in Daniel (Dan. 3:28-29) gives trenchant expression to a fundamental mark of the Calvinistic mind, which is why I have dwelt on it at some length. I mean the Calvinistic striving after clarity in the concept we should entertain of God. The other side of this endeavor, Calvinistic horror of idolatry, is also brought out sharply in this same passage: if the king had had the faith or piety to make a genuine confession, he would have cursed his old idols. But he had only a partial, fragmentary faith (*fides particularis*) acquired on impulse. Thus he could not give a strong reason for his edict, and therefore he deserved no credit for issuing it. What he needed was a steady regimen of instruction in the correct knowledge of God.

Plainly, the directive that we should seek Jesus Christ in all the Scriptures cannot be taken to justify any neglect of sound doctrine. Of course, in tracking the intellectualistic strand in Calvin's theology, we have to avoid any suggestion that faith or piety can be reduced to an intellectual grasp of dogmatic propositions. The point, rather, is that *we cannot grasp the character of God without instruction,* and therefore

---

[127]   Comm. Dan 3.28, CO 40:642–43. The phrase I have translated "is always built on" is in Latin *semper fundata est in. Fundata* is the same word Calvin uses in his definition of faith in *Inst.* 1559, 3.2.7 [1:551].

cannot, without instruction, give God the honor that is his due. In the
dedicatory letter he prefixed to his commentary on Daniel, Calvin
offers an a fortiori argument: if the prophecy of Daniel sustained the
spirit of the pious in those dark times, how ashamed we should be if
we are not raised up by the clarity of the gospel, in which God shows
us his fatherly face. But the gospel is not just the bare assertion that
God is in fact our father; it is rather the announcement that we are now
privileged to call God father because Christ has reconciled us and is
our advocate.[128] As Calvin says in a place I have already quoted:
knowing God in Christ requires an understanding of Christ's worth
and work.[129]

The Word as Sacrament

It is not too difficult to see how the cognitive strand in Calvinism could
lead to an arid intellectualism that turns the worshipping community
into a class of glum schoolchildren. Heavy didacticism has always
been the bane of Reformed worship, and sometimes the point of it—
to let God's fatherly face become visible—is less than obvious. But
there is also the other strand, which points to a mystery that defies
understanding: communion with Christ. For the word of God is not
only a reassuring doctrine but also a powerful instrument of the Spirit,
and it is both these things together.

Calvin felt no antagonism between what we may call the "pedagogical" and the "sacramental" functions of the word. One bridge
between the two functions of the word is to be found in his view of
preaching, which is the most potent form of the outward word. The
word is indeed spiritual doctrine, contained in sacred writings, and it
must be read and pondered with a teachable mind. But the Catechism
emphasises that it is not enough for each of us to read privately at
home (though we should, every day): all must gather together in the
assembly of believers to *hear* the doctrine of salvation whenever they
can.[130] The word of God thus takes on, for Calvin, the character of a
public event. Faith springs from the word of God, but, as the apostle
Paul says, by hearing. On Romans 10:17 Calvin remarks: "This is a
notable passage on the efficacy of preaching, because [Paul] testifies
that from it faith is born . . . . Where the Lord is pleased to work, it

[128]   *Calvinus piis Gallis*, 19 August 1561, CO 18:621, 623 (no. 3485).
[129]   Comm. Eph. 3.12, CO 51:183. See p. 65 above.
[130]   *Catechismus*, Qq. 300–5, OS 2:128–29; TT 2:82–83.

is the instrument of his power." Of course, the human voice cannot, by its own power, penetrate the soul, but that does not prevent God from acting efficaciously through the voice to create faith in us by such human means (*ministerio*).[131] In book four of the 1559 *Institutes*, Calvin asserts that Christ has given the very power of the keys not to his ministers but to his own word—the preaching of the gospel. No matter who does the preaching, the gospel of forgiveness, which opens the kingdom of heaven, is the promise and decision of God.[132] But the gospel does still more: it unites us in one body with Christ.

In 1 Corinthians 1:9 Paul states that "God is faithful, by whom you were called into the fellowship (εἰς κοινωνίαν) of his Son, Jesus Christ our Lord" (RSV). In the works of previous exegetes Calvin found the word for "fellowship" (κοινωνία) rendered as *societas* and *consortium* (Erasmus's choice), and he judged both these words to be totally inadequate renderings for what he himself perceived as a far deeper, mystical union. We do not "socialize with Christ," or "consort with Christ"; in some mysterious way we "participate in him." Calvin could not see the Christian as Christ's companion or partner, but only as made one body with him. In his commentary on 1 Corinthians 1:9, he states the issue linguistically: "I prefer to use the word *communio*, because that better expresses the force of the Greek κοινωνία."[133] But in the *Institutes* he simply appeals to Christian experience: "Believers know what the κοινωνία of Christ signifies . . . ."[134] The meaning of the text, then ("called to the communion of his Son"), is that communion with Christ, which every Christian knows from experience, is given by the gospel:

> For this is the purpose of the gospel, that Christ may become ours, and that we may be engrafted into his body. When the father gives him to us to possess, he also communicates himself to us in him, and thence flows participation in all good things. Paul's argument is this: "Because you have been admitted (*adsciti*) by the gospel, which you received by faith, into communion with Christ, there is no reason for you to be frightened by the danger of death, since you have been made partakers of him (*facti eius participes*) who arose as victor over death."[135]

---

131   Comm. Rom. 10.17, CO 49:206–7.
132   *Inst.* 1559, 4.11.1 (2:1212–13). To explain the power of the keys, Calvin brings together Matt. 16:19 and John 20:23.
133   Comm. 1 Cor. 1.9, CO 49:313.
134   *Inst.* 1559, 3.5.5. (1:675).
135   Comm. 1 Cor. 1.9, CO 49:313. The phrase *facti eius participes* is perhaps an echo of Heb. 3:14. In his commentary on this verse, Calvin states that we are admitted to this participation by faith (CO 55:43).

Calvin concludes that Christians should think of themselves as parts of Christ's body (his limbs or members), so as to make all Christ's good things their own.[136]

It is crucial to Calvin's interpretation that the gospel is not a mere invitation to fellowship with Christ, but the effective means by which communion with Christ is brought about.[137] In his elegant *Short Treatise on the Lord's Supper* (1541), he writes: "We must not suppose that there is life anywhere else than in God. But just as God has placed all the fulness of life in Jesus, to communicate it to us by means of him, so he has ordained his word as the instrument by which Jesus Christ, with all his graces, is dispensed to us."[138] The steps in the way back to the fountain of life, then, are two: Christ is the access to the father and fountain of good, and the word is our access to Christ and all his graces. This was Calvin's firm conviction already in the very first edition of his *Institutes*. There, in a section on indulgences, he asks who taught the pope to enclose in lead and parchment the grace of Jesus Christ, which the Lord willed to be distributed by the word of the gospel. Either the gospel of God or indulgences must be false. Calvin has no doubt which it is. "For Christ is offered to us by the gospel with all the abundance of heavenly goods, with all his merits, all his righteousness, wisdom, grace, without exception."[139] These words reappeared throughout subsequent editions of the *Institutes*; in 1559 Calvin added the sentence (already alluded to): "And believers know what the κοινωνία of Christ signifies, which, as the same apostle testifies [1 Cor. 1:9], is offered us in the gospel to enjoy." [140]

What is most remarkable about these utterances is that they ascribe to the proclaimed word of God the power and efficacy that the medieval church credited to the seven sacraments. It therefore makes good sense to us when we discover that in Theodore Beza's (1519–1605) edition of the *Geneva Catechism* the fourth part, on the sacraments, actually begins with the heading "On the *Word* of God."[141] The intimate bond this rightly implies between word and sacrament is—structurally, at least—not so clear in the 1559 *Institutes*. But we can surely say that the doctrine of the word of God in Calvin's theology

---

[136]   Comm. 1 Cor. 1.9, CO 49:313.
[137]   This is even clearer from *Inst.* 1559, 3.5.5 (1:675), to which I return below. See also n. 33 above.
[138]   *Petit traicté de la saincte Cene* (1541), OS 1:504–5; TT 2:166.
[139]   *Inst.* 1536, OS 1:192; *Institution*, 203–4.
[140]   *Inst.* 1559, 3.5.5 (1:675).
[141]   *Catechismus*, OS 2:127 (emphasis mine); cf. TT 2:81.

ought never to be taken from the first book of the *Institutes* alone, where it is part of the question of authority, but also from book three, where it is the foundation of faith, and book four, where it belongs to sacramental theology. God's word, for Calvin, is not simply a dogmatic norm; it has in it a vital efficacy,[142] and it is the appointed instrument by which the Spirit imparts illumination,[143] faith,[144] awakening,[145] regeneration,[146] purification,[147] and so on.

Calvin himself describes the word as *verbum sacramentale*, the "sacramental word." He means the word that constitutes, or makes, a sacrament. And his argument is that the word, in this sense, cannot be a magical incantation muttered by the priest over the earthly elements, while an uncomprehending people looks on. If we say with Augustine, "Add the word to the element, and it becomes a sacrament," we can only mean, as he did, the proclaimed word of faith, which works not because it is uttered but because it is believed. "Accordingly," Calvin concludes, "when we hear mention made of the 'sacramental word,' we must understand the promise, which, when proclaimed in a clear voice by the minister, leads the people by the hand to where the sign aims and where it directs us."[148] Since Calvin elsewhere so plainly assigns this proclaimed word of promise the very functions that the medieval church looked for in the sacraments, we may fairly extend

---

[142] *Inst.* 1559, 2.10.7 (1:434): " Ac pro confesso sumo, eam verbo Dei inesse vitae efficaciam, ut quoscunque Deus participatione eius dignatur, eorum animas vivificet."

[143] Ibid., 1.9.3 (1:96).

[144] "[Fides] peculiare donum est spiritus, et nascitur ex verbo. Denique proprium Dei munus est, nos ad se trahere, qui vult efficaciter per verbum suum operari" (Comm. Luke 16.30, CO 45:413). In another place, Calvin describes the faith that is born of the word (*fidem e verbo conceptam*) as the instrumental cause of justification (Comm. Rom 3.24, CO 49:61).

[145] *Inst.* 1559, 2.5.5 (1:322). Calvin's language in this section, with its fundamental distinction between inward and outward modes of divine working, through the Spirit and the word respectively, is strongly reminiscent of Luther's case against Carlstadt. See Luther, *Wider die himmlischen Propheten* (1525), WA 18.136.9–13; LW 40:146.

[146] Comm. 1 Pet. 1.23, CO 55:229 (where the divine agent is the "living God"). Cf. Comm. 1 Pet. 1.25: Peter attributes *vim et efficaciam* to the life-giving word, but only as the Spirit's instrument. ". . . verbum non alibi quam in praedicatione, quae nobis offertur, quaerendum esse . . . . Certum quidem est eos qui plantant et rigant, nihil esse: sed quoties Dominus benedicere vult eorum labori, spiritus sui virtute facit ut efficax sit eorum doctrina: et vox quae per se mortua est, vitae aeternae sit organum" (CO 55:230–31). Here, as Calvin remarks, is quite extraordinary praise of preaching ("hic non vulgari elogio externa praedicatio ornatur"). Cf. Comm. Rom. 10.17, cited above (n. 131).

[147] Comm. John 15.3, CO 47:340: "Vox ipsa purgationis organum est." Note that here *doctrina, praedicatio,* and *vox* are used as equivalents.

[148] *Inst.* 1559, 4.14.4 (2:1279–80).

his use of the term *verbum sacramentale* to denote a proclamation that not only *makes* a sacrament but also, as an efficacious means of grace, *is* a sacrament.

In chapter two we discovered that eucharistic patterns of thought appear already in Calvin's doctrine of creation. Humanity, in the Creator's design, is "eucharistic man," called to thankfulness to the heavenly father who, by the work of creation, spreads a table of good things before his children. We can now say much the same thing of Calvin's doctrine of salvation: it, too, is couched in eucharistic language. Jesus Christ, as the one true son, who opens up the sealed access to the father and fountain of good, is the bread of life, the only food of our souls. By transference, so to say, the same image of nourishment fits the preached word of God, by which Christ is made ours with all his graces. Calvin writes: "Now all of scripture tells us that the spiritual food by which our souls are sustained is the same word by which the Lord regenerated us. But it often adds the reason: because in it Jesus Christ, our only life, is given and administered to us."[149] The word, then, is also called "bread" and "water": that is, our food and drink.[150]

Communion with Christ, enjoyment of the bread of life, and the divinely ordained means of nurture: these are Calvin's themes long before he turns to the Eucharist. His doctrine of salvation is "eucharistic" in the double sense that it draws out the image of the bountiful table and reaffirms the call to thankfulness. For "the reason why God bestows everything on us in Christ is so that we shall claim nothing for ourselves, but ascribe everything to him."[151] The question we shall have to ask is how the holy banquet is related to that grateful feeding upon Christ that takes place, so it now appears, all the time—whenever the word is proclaimed and received in faith. But, first, we should look at the other sacrament, the sign of adoption into the family of God. Without Baptism, an indispensable piece would be missing from the overall pattern of Calvin's eucharistic theology.

---

[149]   *De la Cene*, OS 1:504; TT 2:166.
[150]   Ibid., OS 1:505; TT 2:166. This is the source of my epigraph for the present chapter. Cf. Comm. John 21.15 (CO 47:452): Christ alone is properly our "pastor" (i.e., the one who feeds the lambs) because he is himself the only food of the soul, but he *transfers* this title to ministers of the word or gospel.
[151]   Comm. 1 Cor. 1.31 (CO 49:332).

FOUR

CHILDREN OF GRACE

> *We need figures or mirrors to display spiritual and heavenly*
> *things to our sight in an earthly kind of way. Otherwise, they*
> *would be beyond our reach . . . . Baptism is like an entrance*
> *for us into the church: it gives us the testimony that we, who*
> *otherwise are strangers and aliens, are received into the family*
> *of God and included in his household.*

Calvin's first statement of evangelical faith was not his *Institutes* of 1536; it was the preface he wrote to Olivétan's New Testament. First published in 1535, the preface sets out the fundamental ideas that never ceased to determine his view of the Christian religion.[1] In form it is a sketch of the history of salvation, written with such grace and quiet passion that I am sorely tempted to quote from it at length. But to summarize our progress so far, I simply give some highlights before moving on to the next items on the agenda, which are: adoption and the Sacrament of adoption, Baptism.

God made humans in his own image and likeness for a parent's delight in a beloved child. Their well-being depended on acknowledging God alone as the source of good; instead, they sought their dignity in themselves and through ingratitude defaced the divine image. Yet God, though angry and displeased, continued in his infinite goodness to love those who deserved no love (for he *is* love), surrounding them with tokens of the divine presence. "For the little birds that sing, sing of God; the beasts call out for him; the elements fear him; the moun-

---

[1]   Cf. B.A. Gerrish, "John Calvin," in Gerrish, ed., *Reformers in Profile* (Philadelphia: Fortress Press, 1967), 152–53.

tains echo him; the streams and fountains flash glances at him; and the grass and flowers laugh before him."[2] But there is no need for a long quest: all could find God *in themselves,* since all are sustained by his power within them. And God was not content to teach everyone alike in this way; he made his voice especially heard by a chosen people, and finally he offered the new covenant of the gospel.

The gospel is good news "because in it is declared that Christ, the one true (*naturel*) and eternal son of the living God, has been made human to make us children of God his father by adoption."[3] "By knowledge of the gospel we are made children of God, brothers and sisters of Jesus Christ, fellow-townsmen of the saints, citizens of the kingdom of heaven, heirs of God with Jesus Christ."[4] Thus "the gospel is the word of life and truth . . . . The key to the knowledge of God, it opens the gates of the kingdom of heaven to believers by freeing them from sins."[5] "There is only one way to life and salvation: certain faith (*foy et certitude*) in the promises of God. It cannot be had without the gospel, for by hearing and understanding the gospel living faith is conferred along with sure hope and perfect devotion (*charité*) to God and fervent love (*amour*) for our neighbor."[6] The gospel presents Jesus Christ to us as the one in whom alone every good thing we could conceive or desire is to be found, so that we should look for nothing else in Scripture but truly to know him and the endless riches offered us through him by God his father. "The truth is that God has given himself from the beginning; now he gives himself again, to be beheld more clearly in the face of his Christ."[7]

It would be hard to imagine a more perfect summary of the themes we have been examining. There is no need to list them. But note in particular the last sentence quoted: the self-giving of God links creation and redemption because he has been giving himself to humanity from the beginning; in the incarnation he does what he has always done, only more clearly. Note, too, that Calvin intends the self-giving of God to be understood in cognitive terms: God has shown himself to

---

[2]   *Praefationes bibliis Gallicis . . . praemissae,* CO 9:795; LCC 23:60. An astonishingly lyrical, almost precious sentence!
[3]   Ibid., CO 9: 803; LCC 23:64. Calvin emphasizes the fact that we are called to the inheritance of God's children without respect of persons—male or female, little or great, servant or lord, master or disciple, cleric or lay—and he uses the convenient French expression *Chrestiens et Chrestiennes* (CO 9:807) to include male and female.
[4]   Ibid., CO 9:807; LCC 23:66.
[5]   Ibid.
[6]   Ibid., CO 9:807–9; LCC 23:67.
[7]   Ibid., CO 9:811–15; LCC 23:68–70.

our contemplation.[8] However, the point I want to focus on next is the way in which Calvin describes the gospel: it is, quite simply, the good news of adoption.

The gospel, according to Calvin, is that through Christ the children of Adam and Eve can become once more children of God. "His task was so to restore us to God's grace as to make children of God out of the children of humanity . . . . In this way, we are assured of the inheritance of the heavenly kingdom, for the only son to whom it wholly belongs has adopted us as his brothers and sisters." It follows that of all the good things God promises, adoption is the most important. "The promise by which God adopts us as his children is the foremost promise of all. But the cause and root of our adoption is Christ, because God is father only to those who are members—brothers and sisters—of his only-begotten son."[10] Or, to put it this time from the perspective of our vacillating faith rather than God's unfailing goodwill: "If we had not been adopted in Christ as children of grace, with what assurance would anyone have called God 'father'?"[11] The quotations could be multiplied almost ad infinitum.[12]

---

[8]   The Latin has *intuendum praebuisse* (CO 9:816).

[9]   *Inst.* 1559, 2.12.2 (1:465–66). Once again, while recognizing that some loss of rhetorical terseness is the price paid, I am translating Calvin's words *filii* and *homines* inclusively since he had no intention at all to be exclusive in speaking of humans and Christians (see n. 3 above). I am of course aware that masculine titles and pronouns applied to God or the Mediator are also problematic to some. But the Mediator was in fact male, and Calvin's favorite title for God was "father" even though he did not exclude "mother." His words for the Deity (*deus, Dieu*) are masculine and require masculine pronouns without implying that God is male. Dogmatic theology perhaps can and should go further than historical theology in dealing with the problem.

[10]   Comm. 2 Cor. 1.20, CO 50:23. But *all* the promises are testimonies of fatherly goodwill (CO 50:22).

[11]   *Inst.* 1536, OS 1:105; *Institution*, 103. Cf. *Inst.* 1559, 3.20.36 (2:899).

[12]   Following Rom. 8:15 and Gal. 4:7, Calvin associates adoption with deliverance from servitude and fear (*Inst.* 1559, 2.7.15 [1:363–64], 11.9 [458–59]), and from Rom. 8:17 he takes the thought that adoption makes us fellow heirs with Christ (12.2 [465–66]). Further, he holds John 1:12 to mean that the right of adoption is contingent on being engrafted into Christ (Comm. John 1.12 [CO 47:11]). It is, of course, the experience of Christians that he has chiefly in mind. However, all humans—angels, too—were created to have God as their father, and from the beginning all other sonship was grounded in the eternal sonship of Christ the Word, though with the crucial difference that whereas he alone is born God's Son (*unigenitus*), others can only be born-again sons and daughters (*regeniti*). Believers have by free adoption (*gratuita adoptione*), or by a gift (*dono*), what Christ has by nature (*natura*). See *Inst.* 1559, 2.14.5–6 (1:488–89). Moreover, "believers" includes the saints under the Old Testament: by becoming flesh, Christ made more clearly known the heavenly fatherhood of which the patriarchs were already aware (ibid.; cf. Comm. Gal 4.7 [CO 50:229]). Naturally, Calvin also emphasizes the Pauline "Spirit of adoption"; indeed, that is the very first of the titles of the Spirit listed in *Inst.* 1559, 3.1.3 (1:540). Perhaps even more revealing than Calvin's explicit discussions of adoption are the ways in which his entire theological vocabulary, as I endeavor to show, is colored by father-son language.

The theme of adoption, the new birth, the transition from "children of wrath" to "children of grace," takes us to the heart of the reformers' protest against the prevailing gospel of the day; and for different reasons it inevitably touches also on the defense of their baptismal practice against reformers more radical than themselves. Calvin entered the fray with a passion and sometimes a rancor that embarrasses his friends but, happily, amuses good-natured Catholics and Baptists in our more generous times. I have often wished for an expurgated edition of the *Institutes,* like the pale blue "Shorter Bible" I read as a schoolboy, from which the less obviously edifying parts of the Old Testament were left out. But some of his keenest theological insights shine out in the midst of Calvin's meanest polemical sallies. (And perhaps even the Old Testament passages that were concealed from me as a boy can provide instructive texts of terror, as Phyllis Trible has shown.)[13] Today, in any case, the battle lines have changed. There are believer baptists in Calvin's church, and you will find at least as much Pelagianizing there as in Rome. Remember Father Louis Bouyer: brought up a Protestant, he converted to Roman Catholicism because only there, he decided, can Luther's *sola gratia* find a secure home.[14] How amazed Calvin would be, and perhaps a little incredulous!

ROME AND THE GOSPEL OF
FREE ADOPTION

It must be said at once that the Protestant reformers always believed their own view of the new birth to be more radical than Rome's. In the teaching of the medieval church they exposed what seemed to them to be a pernicious compromise between divine grace and human achievement. The design of the penitential system, no doubt, was to encourage moral seriousness both before and after the reception of grace. But it failed, in the eyes of the reformers, to display either the severity of God's judgment on sin or the wholly unconditioned character of God's grace. For the old self, which can contribute nothing to the offer of grace, must die; but the new self, precisely because it has

[13]   Phyllis Trible, *Texts of Terror: Literary-Feminist Readings of Biblical Narratives* (Philadelphia: Fortress Press, 1984).

[14]   Louis Bouyer, *Du Protestantisme à l'église,* Unam Sanctam, vol. 27, 2d ed. (Paris: Editions du Cerf, 1955); see especially xi, 44–45. Translated by A.V. Littledale as *The Spirit and Forms of Protestantism* (Westminster, MD: Newman Press, 1956); see xiii, 43–44.

cast itself entirely on God's grace, is entitled to a freedom and an assurance that the old church considered dangerous and presumptuous.

Death and New Birth

Disagreement on the first issue—the death of the old self—came to a focus in the Reformation critique of Penance,[15] and it concerns what Calvin expressly singles out as the two points in which the whole sum of the gospel is contained: forgiveness and repentance.[16] Calvin could see nothing in the Roman Sacrament of Penance but the false assumption that sinners can atone for their own unworthiness.[17] The point at issue with "the sophists" (that is, the medieval Schoolmen) is crucial, he says, because there is nothing in the whole of religion that we more urgently need to know than the conditions under which forgiveness is obtained. Without this knowledge, the conscience can have no peace with God but flees trembling from God's presence. By their insistence that full contrition and confession must precede absolution, and satisfaction must follow, the Schoolmen have subjected forgiveness to intolerable conditions. The requirement of full contrition can only subject the sinner to torment and drive her to despair. If they say, "Well, you have to do your best," when will anyone venture to assure himself that he has done his best? We (the Evangelicals) have done away with all this tormenting of souls and teach the sinner not to dwell on her own compunction or tears, but to fasten both eyes on the Lord's mercy alone.[18] Not even King David could list all his sins: he asked to be cleansed from secret faults (Ps. 19:12). And so, these cruel butchers, to soothe the wounds they have themselves inflicted, come up with

[15] The penetrating critique of Penance, the second false sacrament, in the 1536 *Institutes* (OS 1:169–202; *Institution*, 177–216) was later dismembered, and in 1559 portions appeared in five chapters. Most of it, somewhat enlarged, became book three, chapter four, on the scholastic doctrine of repentance. Some fragments went into the preceding chapter (chapter 3), on the true doctrine of repentance, and the following chapter (chapter 5), on purgatory and indulgences. The rest provided the sections in 4.11 on the power of the keys (secs. 1–2) and in 4.19 on the false sacrament of Penance (secs. 14–17). In what follows I have given references mostly to the 1559 edition.

[16] *Inst.* 1559, 3.3.19 (1:613). He mentions forgiveness and repentance in the reverse order, but I have taken forgiveness first in the exposition that follows. Sacramental "Penance" and "repentance" are of course the same word in Latin (*poenitentia*). The identification of forgiveness and repentance as the two main points of the *tota evangelii summa* appeared already in *Inst.* 1536, OS 1:171; *Institution*, 179.

[17] *Inst.* 1559, 4.17.41 (2:1418–19).

[18] Ibid., 3.4.2–3 (1:625–26).

this remedy: Each must do what he can! Then new anxieties creep in: I did not take enough time; I have not persevered in the duties prescribed; I have missed out many things through negligence, and my forgetfulness is inexcusable.[19] Anyway, how can we be so sure that even those who have done their best *have* met their obligation to God?[20]

Not even the priestly word of absolution brought a final word of assurance for the anxious medieval conscience because, as the Protestants saw it, the imposition of "satisfactions" to follow absolution left the penitent still bent down under a burden of anxiety. Forgiveness is a gift of sheer liberality: the creditor who gives a receipt for money paid does not forgive, but only the one who, without payment, cancels the debt out of kindness. Why, then, all the talk about satisfactions?[21] Remission of sins calls for nothing at all but love and gratitude from the freely pardoned sinner, who is a sinner no more. And the sinner who is forgiven much will love much. Jesus said of the woman who had washed his feet with her tears and dried them on her hair: "From this we know that this woman's sins are forgiven, for she loved much."[22] Calvin comments:

> By these words, as you see, he does not make her love the cause of forgiveness, but its proof. For they are taken from the comparable case of the debtor who was forgiven five hundred denarii: it was not said of him that they were forgiven because he loved much, but that he loved much because they were forgiven. The comparison should be applied in this way: "You think this woman is a sinner, but you should have recognized that she is not, because her sins have been forgiven her. Her love, by which she shows her gratitude for the benefit received, should have been your proof of her forgiveness." This is an argument *a posteriori*, by which something is proved from the evidences (*signis*) that follow. The Lord plainly attests the grounds on which she obtained forgiveness: "Your faith," he says, "has saved you" [Luke 7:50]. By faith, then, we obtain forgiveness; by love we give thanks and bear witness to the kindness of the Lord.[23]

In these searching reflections on the troubled conscience and free, unmerited forgiveness one reads the common spiritual experience and the deep pastoral concern out of which the Reformation was born.

---

19   Ibid., 3.4.16–17 (1:641–42).
20   Ibid., 4.17.41 (2:1419).
21   Ibid., 3.4.25 (1:651).
22   Cf. Luke 7:47. Calvin paraphrases the text rather than quoting it exactly.
23   *Inst.* 1559, 3.4.37 (1:667). The phrase *peccatricem non esse* apparently contradicts Luther's *simul iustus et peccator*.

Similar reflections had appeared earlier in the writings of Luther and Melanchthon,[24] and elsewhere Calvin offers another analysis of the troubled conscience that some have assumed to be autobiographical:

> But when, somehow, I had performed all that was required, I was still a long way from sure peace of conscience, though I did have some interludes of quiet. For whenever I went down into myself, or raised my mind to thee, extreme dread attacked me, and no expiations, no satisfactions, could relieve it. The more closely I examined myself, the sharper the stings that pricked my conscience. The only solace that remained was to lose myself in oblivion.[25]

Composed ostensibly as the shared testimony of every Protestant, these words do, no doubt, draw on Calvin's own taste of spiritual disquiet. He found the remedy (not a false solace) where Luther did: in the Pauline gospel of justification without works (Rom. 4:6) and in learning to repose all his hope in "the mere goodness of God."[26] The Roman church's compromise between divine grace and human works had given rise to anxieties of conscience that only a gospel of totally free forgiveness could cure. But, of course, this did not mean that the Protestants had no doctrine of repentance, only that they came to understand *poenitentia* differently than the Roman church.

The radicalness of Reformation theology appears precisely in its preaching of repentance, which is simply the recognition that our thoughts, feelings, and pursuits are all so marred and defective that, if we wish to enter the kingdom of God, we must be born again.[27] The old self does not need help to do more than its own honest best: it has to die. We do not learn the first principles of piety unless we are violently slain by the sword of the Spirit and reduced to nothing.[28] Behind the scholastic and the Reformation standpoints Calvin perceived two very different diagnoses of the plight of humanity, and two correspondingly different views of divine grace. The old self is not weak, but strong and perverse ("depraved"), energetically pursuing all the wrong goals. It still possesses the faculties of approving, reflecting, willing, striving, resisting. Its problem is that it approves vanity, rejects good, wills evil, strives after wickedness, and resists

---

[24]   For a comparison of Luther and Calvin on conscience see Randall C. Zachman, "The Testimony of the Conscience in the Theology of Martin Luther and John Calvin: A Comparative Study" (1990).

[25]   *Responsio ad Sadoleti epistolam* (1539), OS 1:485; TT 1:62.

[26]   Ibid., OS 1:469–70; TT 1:42.

[27]   *Inst.* 1559, 3.3.19 (1:614).

[28]   Ibid., 3.3.8 (1:600).

righteousness.[29] The remedy of divine grace, therefore, is not to
strengthen the old but to create the new, and this means that the old
must be destroyed to make room for the new birth. Just as
Nebuchadnezzar, if he had really believed, would have cursed the idols
of misunderstanding, so there cannot be a new will unless the old is
done away with—not, of course, insofar as it is will, but insofar as it is
a bad will.[30] "If God were said to *help* a weak will, something would be
left to us. But when he is said to *make* the will, whatever is good in it is
now placed outside of us."[31] And if grace is not assistance but a new act
of creation, then it is not so much offered as given to us. [32]

It is characteristic that, having made the death of the old self and the
resurrection of the new wholly a creative act of God's Spirit, Calvin
still retains a psychological interest in how regeneration works. To say
that the beginning of regeneration is the destruction of what is ours,[33]
certainly does not sound like an intelligible transformation of the
person, open to empirical description. It sounds like a miracle, and so
it is. Nevertheless, Calvin did in fact see regeneration, as he saw faith,
largely in cognitive terms. Repentance or regeneration (he uses the
terms synonymously) is not a transient crisis-experience, but the
entire life of the Christian—an assertion for which Calvin could have
appealed to the first of Martin Luther's Ninety-five Theses.[34] "In a
word, I interpret repentance as regeneration, which has no other aim
than to form again in us the image of God that had been marred and
almost wiped out through Adam's transgression . . . . This renewal
is not completed in one moment, or day, or year." It is a warfare that
ends only at actual physical death.[35] Remarkably, Calvin perceives the
entire process as a readily intelligible consequence of faith.

It is, of course, only through union with the crucified and risen
Christ that the death of the old self and the birth of the new takes

[29]   Ibid., 2.5.14 (1:334).
[30]   Ibid., 2.3.6 (1:296–98). On Nebuchadnezzar's idols, see pp. 80-81 above.
[31]   *Inst.* 1559, 2.3.9 (1:302). My emphasis. For another statement of the contrast
between *infirmitas* and *pravitas*, see Calvin's *Supplex exhortatio ad invictiss. Caesarem
Carolum Quintum*, etc. (1543), CO 6:483; TT 1:159. Calvin believed that the Council of
Trent fell into the same error of identifying sin with weakness in its sixth session: *Acta
Synodi Tridentini, cum antidoto* (1547), CO 7:443; TT 3:109. See further Gerrish, "The Chief
Article—Then and Now," *Journal of Relgion* 63 (1983):355– 75, especially 358–60.
[32]   *Inst.* 1559, 2.3.13–14 (1:308).
[33]   Ibid., 2.5.15 (1:335): "Dicimus principium regenerationis esse, ut quod nostrum
est aboleatur."
[34]   Luther, *Disputatio pro declaratione virtutis indulgentiarum* (1517), WA 1.233.10–
11; LW 31:25.
[35]   *Inst.* 1559, 3.3.9 (1:601). On the restoration of the image as the aim of regeneration, cf. Comm. Eph. 4.24, CO 51:208.

place,[36] and this union, as we have seen, is the effect of faith. But there is another reason why repentance cannot stand apart from faith, though they are not the same thing:[37] because only those who see God with the eyes of faith will devote themselves earnestly to the warfare of the Spirit.

> When we locate the source of repentance in faith . . . we want to indicate that none apply themselves seriously to repentance unless they know themselves to belong to God. But none are truly persuaded that they belong to God but those who have first grasped the grace of God . . . . Perhaps some have been led astray by the fact that terrors of conscience break or bend many people to compliance even before they have been imbued with a knowledge of grace or have even tasted it. And this is the "preparatory fear" (*initialis timor*) that some count among the virtues because they perceive it to be close to true and proper obedience. But I am not concerned here with the various ways in which Christ attracts us to himself or prepares us for the pursuit of piety . . . . I am only saying that none will ever revere God but those who are confident that he is well-disposed to them. None will willingly gird themselves to keep the law but those who have been persuaded that he is pleased with their obedience. This indulgence in bearing with us and putting up with our failings is a sign of fatherly favor.[38]

It is nothing less than the entire life of the Christian that is here made to turn around the right way of perceiving God, which is: to perceive him as a kindly father. And with this quotation we have already begun to make the transition to a second quarrel Calvin had with Rome. Not only did the penitential system sow religious disquiet by offering a boost instead of rebirth; it also, Calvin believed, opened up a pattern of Christian existence that never quite replaced servitude with the freedom of God's children.

The Freedom of God's Children

Disagreement on the second issue—the freedom and assurance of the new self—is focussed largely on the concept of "merit": the right to be

---

[36]   "Utrunque [sc. *mortificatio* and *vivificatio*] ex Christi participatione nobis contingit" (*Inst.* 1559, 3.3.9 [1:600]).

[37]   Ibid., 3.3.5 (1:597). Calvin finds here, in effect, yet another use for the principle "distinction without separation."

[38]   Ibid., 3.3.2 (1:594). This is much the same argument Calvin made earlier about the source of *pietas* (1.2.1 [1:41]). The relationship between faith, repentance, and regeneration in Calvin's theology is complex, as it is in Scripture. In 3.3.19 (1:613), he puts Christ's demand for trust in God's promises *after* the demand for repentance. The three-stage proclamation is: mercy, repentance, trust. In Comm. John 1.13 (CO 47:12-13) he notes the difficulty of determining whether faith or regeneration comes first.

rewarded by God for work done. The term is not itself found in Scripture, but the Schoolmen assumed that it said no more than the biblical word "reward."[39] Merit had played a cardinal role in Western theology since Tertullian (ca. 160–ca. 225), and Augustine (354–430) had found a place for it by arguing that the only merits we can acquire are gifts of grace, so that when he rewards us for work done God crowns his own gifts.[40] The Augustinian system of grace and merit became regulative in medieval scholasticism, but in different versions. Calvin was more inclined than Luther had been to make some careful distinctions. There are, first, "the more recent sophists," or "the sophists of the Sorbonne," who are "the Pelagians of our time." But then, second, there are "the sounder Schoolmen."[41] By "the sophists" Calvin evidently means the theologians of the *via moderna*, the Nominalists, who held that by doing one's best one could merit the grace of justification.[42] The "sounder Schoolmen (*saniores Scholastici*)" is a vaguer description, and it is difficult to determine who would find a place on the list. Questions would have to be answered, not only about Calvin's specific quotations from the Schoolmen, but also about the extent of his knowledge of the scholastic tradition in general.[43] But the most important issue that requires the division between sophists and sounder Schoolmen is clear.

Calvin addresses it directly in a chapter on the beginning of justification and its continual progress. In a passage that dates from 1543, he locates the controversy with Rome not in the question, "How must one be justified?" but rather, "How does the justified person live?" The situation has changed since Luther agonized in the monastery over the Nominalist formula, "God does not deny grace to those who do their best." By the time of his *Lectures on Romans* (1515–16), Luther had come to scorn the purveyors of "doing one's best" as fools

[39]   "Respondeo dicendum quod meritum et merces ad idem referuntur. Id enim merces dicitur, quod alicui recompensatur pro retributione operis vel laboris, quasi quoddam pretium ipsius." Thomas, ST IaIIae, Q. 114, a. 1.

[40]   On merit in Tertullian and Augustine, see J. Rivière, "Mérite," DTC 10,1: 619–22, 643–51.

[41]   *Inst.* 1559, 2.2.6 (1:263), 3.13 (307). Cf. 3.15.6–7 (1:794).

[42]   On the Nominalist doctrine that *facere quod in se est* acquires *merita de congruo*, not *de condigno*, see the selections from Holcot and Biel in Heiko Augustinus Oberman, *Forerunners of the Reformation* (1966; reprint ed., Philadelphia: Fortress Press, 1981), 142–50, 165–74. Contact was retained with the Augustinian scheme by the insistence that works before grace are meritorious only by the divine *pactio* that accepts them.

[43]   His affection for Bernard of Clairvaux has been studied particularly closely in recent years. See A.N.S. Lane (1976), Jill Raitt (1981), and Dennis E. Tamburello (1990).

and pig–theologians, crypto-Pelagians who had subverted nearly the whole church with their obnoxious formula.[44] To the end of his days, Luther never missed an opportunity to attack the Nominalists for their views on grace and merit, and he took it for granted that they spoke for Rome.[45] Perhaps it was his participation in conferences with the Roman Catholics that led Calvin to see things differently.[46] At any rate, in 1543 he could write: "On the beginning of justification there is no quarrel between us and the sounder Schoolmen."[47] The later French version of the *Institutes* (1560) inserted an explanation at this point:

> It is quite true that the poor world has been seduced hitherto (*jusque là*) into thinking that people prepare themselves to be justified of God by their own resources, and that this blasphemy has commonly reigned both in sermons and in the schools—as it is still upheld today by those who want to maintain all the abominations of the papacy. But those who have had any sense have always agreed with us.[48]

Perhaps this charmingly complacent assertion makes it sound as if Calvin still identified Rome with the Nominalists, whereas he saw himself in the tradition of the sounder Schoolmen. But he certainly recognized that there were representatives of this tradition on the other side, so to say: he had just explicitly stated that the controverted issue with Rome was *not* preparation for being justified.

What, then, is it that Calvin singles out as "the principal point of the dispute we have with the papists and, so to say, the nub of the matter"?[49] Actually, he has just laid down not one, but two points: first, that there has never been any work of a pious person that, if subjected to God's severe judgment, would not deserve condemnation; second, that even if there had been, it would have been spoiled and tainted by the sins under which its author otherwise labored.[50] The one point, in short, is this: the best that even the pious can do—the justified, the

[44]   *Vorlesung über den Römerbrief* (1515–16), WA 56.274.14, 502.14–503.12; LW 25:261, 496–97.

[45]   See, e.g., *In epistolam S. Pauli ad Galatas commentarius* (1535), WA 40[1]. 220.4–221.22, 364.29 ff. (LW 26:124–25, 230); 40[2] .15.15 ff; (LW 27:13). It is interesting that the formula that drove Luther to despair struck Zwingli as too easy: everyone always does their best, however trifling. See his *De vera et falsa religione commentarius* (1525), SW 3:679; LWZ 3:103. Cf. Calvin, *Inst.* 1559, 2.3.10 (1:304).

[46]   Especially the Regensburg (Ratisbon) Colloquy (1541). See Phillip Edward Pedersen, "The Religious Colloquy of Regensburg (Ratisbon), 1541" (Ph.D. diss., University of Chicago, 1978).

[47]   *Inst.* 1559, 3.14.11 (1:778); cf. *Inst.* 1539–54, CO 1:762.

[48]   VG 3:255.

[49]   Ibid.

[50]   *Inst.* 1559, 3.14.11 (1:778).

regenerate, the sanctified—is always spotted and corrupted, so that they must continue to live by the forgiveness of sins. God does not, as many people stupidly suppose, justify us once and for all, so that we may thereafter seek righteousness in the law. That would be to mock us with false hopes; for the law will always find something to accuse in us—unless the mercy of God counters it and absolves us again and again by a continual forgiveness of sins.[51] And this is the cardinal point that even the sounder Schoolmen do not quite grasp. They understand that "the sinner is delivered from condemnation by the free goodness of God and justified by receiving the forgiveness of sins."[52] (In other words, they do not, like the Nominalists, talk about preparing for justification by doing your best.) To be sure, even the sounder Schoolmen mistakenly include in the word "justification" the renewal by which the Spirit of God reforms us to obey the law. In Calvin's theological vocabulary, "justification" and "renewal" (or "regeneration") denote two distinct graces received through union with Christ: they are inseparable, but not to be confused.[53] This, however, is not his most serious objection to the sounder Schoolmen. The problem is that having ruled out merits before grace, they bring them back again afterwards. For this is the way they describe the righteousness of the regenerate: "Once reconciled to God through faith in Christ, a person is counted righteous before God by good works and accepted by the merit of works."[54]

Merit! That, in one word, is where Calvin refuses to follow even the sounder Schoolmen, who find room for merit only after a person has been justified by grace.[55] Whoever first introduced the word did a disservice to sincere faith. "For my part," Calvin assures us, "I like to avoid battles over words. But I do wish that Christian writers had always exercised restraint and had not taken it into their heads to adopt terms foreign to scripture where they are not needed and would produce much offense and very little fruit. . . . It is a word filled with

[51]   Ibid., 3.14.9–10 (1:776–77).
[52]   Ibid., 3.14.11 (1:778). French: " . . . que le pécheur, estant délivré de damnation par la bonté gratuite de Dieu, est iustifié d'autant qu'il obtient pardon de ses fautes" (VG 3:255). Latin: " . . . quin peccator gratuito a damnatione liberatus . . . "
[53]   *Inst.* 1559, 3.11.1 (1:725), 11.6 (732), 11.15 (745–46), 16.1 (798). Note from 11.15 that even Augustine's language is not entirely acceptable to Calvin.
[54]   Ibid., 3.14.11 (1:778). Cf. 3.4.27 (1:653), 15.6 (794).
[55]   The delusion of merit is *praecipuus causae cardo* (ibid., 3.15.1 [1:788]). Cf. the description of justification as the *praecipuus sustinendae religionis cardo* (11.1 [726]) and *pietatis totius summa* (15.7 [794]).

presumption and can only obscure the grace of God and imbue us with perverse pride."[56]

Calvin knows, of course, the warrants and qualifications by which the Schoolmen defended the concept of merit: good works obtain righteousness not by their own intrinsic worth, but by God's acceptance of them;[57] "merit" is implied in all of the many biblical passages about rewards;[58] and so on. In dealing with these "subterfuges," as he calls them, Calvin tends to overlook his own distinction between the sophists and the sounder Schoolmen.[59] But what often strikes the reader most is how close Calvin's own position comes to the scholastic arguments in all but the use of the word "merit."[60] Is it, after all, one may ask, a battle over words—especially if Calvin is willing, as he puts it, to "excuse" the appearance of the word "merit" in his favorite Schoolman, Bernard of Clairvaux?[61] The answer, I think, is no: the difference is more than verbal. It is a question of the dominant image through which the entire life of the new self is perceived. For Calvin, that means "sonship": perceiving ourselves in every department of our life, not as mere servants, but as children of an indulgent father. For "the moment you are engrafted into Christ by faith, you are made a child of God, an heir of heaven, a partaker in righteousness, a possessor of life." The only merits to speak of then are Christ's: "You acquire not the opportunity to gain merit for yourself, but all the merits of Christ, since they are communicated to you."[62]

---

[56]   Ibid., 3.15.2 (1:789). It is interesting to note that Calvin perceives the quest for merit after grace as a problem of pride more than anxiety. But he returns to the problem of the anxious conscience in chapter 19 (see p. 101 below).

[57]   Ibid., 3.14.12 (1:779).

[58]   Ibid., 3.18.4 (1:825): "Tantum ne correlationem meriti ac mercedis imaginemur, in qua importune haerent Sophistae."

[59]   The editorial notes in the editions by Barth and Niesel (OS), Benoit (VG), and McNeill and Battles (LCC) are invaluable aids for identifying the unnamed authors of opinions Calvin introduces by such vague expressions as "they say." I am not aware of any careful discussion in Calvin of the distinction between congruous and condign merit, or of the different applications given it by Thomas and the Nominalists. See Gerrish, *Grace and Reason* (Oxford: Clarendon Press, 1962), 120–35.

[60]   This is true, for instance, in his response to the idea of *gratia acceptans*, which admittedly implies the need for continuous forgiveness: "Acceptantem enim quam vocant gratiam, non aliam esse respondeo quam gratuitam eius bonitatem, qua nos in Christo complectitur Pater" (*Inst.* 1559, 3.14.12 [1:779]). Of course, Calvin sees the grounds for acceptance in the work of Christ. But no Schoolman ever thought of the works of the graced individual—or even the saints' works of supererogation—apart from Christ (see 14.13 [780]). Calvin's reference to a justice of God that has more to do with God's faithfulness to his promise than with rendering what is due (18.7 [829]) is close to the fundamental principle of Holcot and Biel.

[61]   Ibid., 3.12.3 (1:758); cf. 15.2 (789–90).

[62]   Ibid., 3.15.6 (1:794). On Christ's merits see 2.17.3 (1:530–31).

Now, of course the Bible talks about rewards. But they are rewards given to children, not to hired servants.

> The use of the word "reward" is no reason to infer that our works are the cause of salvation. First, let this be a fixed principle in our hearts, that the kingdom of heaven is not a servant's pay but a child's inheritance. They alone shall take possession of it who have been adopted by God as his children, and for no other reason than because of their adoption . . . . Thus Paul bids servants faithfully doing their duty to hope for a reward from the Lord but adds: "[the reward] of the inheritance [Col. 3:24]." We see how, in prescribed terms, so to say, we are carefully warned not to attribute eternal blessedness to works but to our adoption by God.[63]

As Calvin reads the parable of the laborers in the vineyard (Matt. 20:1–16), it puts the last nail in the coffin of merit: when evening comes, the Lord pays everyone the same, lest they imagine that the reward promised is a matter of merit.[64]

Everything seems to fall into place for Calvin once he has set the God of piety clearly before him: the father who has adopted us into the family. The whole of Christian existence—the life of the new self—is then perceived as nothing but the life of God's adopted sons and daughters, and it is in its very essence a life of confidence and freedom. Calvin can illustrate this theme in all its ramifications with sometimes astonishing beauty and human insight. One recalls that he had no children of his own; his only son died in infancy. But there were children in his household: Calvin's adopted children, so to say. He must have watched them keenly; he must even have liked them. And again and again something more than biblical prooftexting shines through his reflections on the life of God's children. Prayer becomes confiding in father, as children will unburden their worries in an intimate talk with their parents.[65] Suffering becomes bearable insofar as Christians recognize in it not an inflexible divine will that no one can resist, but the hand of the best of fathers, who is providing for their salvation in the very act of laying a cross upon them. This is the difference between philosophical and Christian patience. It makes it possible for afflictions to be borne with a quiet, thankful mind, even a cheerful heart.[66] And sometimes, when the suffering is chastisement for sin, God takes on the character (*personam*) of a father who regrets the severity, however deserved, that

---

[63]   Ibid., 3.18.2 (1:822).

[64]   Ibid., 3.18.3 (1:823)

[65]   Ibid., 3.20.12 (2:865): "Quemadmodum filii apud parentes familiariter querelas suas deponunt." This is not all that prayer means: it has two parts, petition and thanksgiving (20.28 [888]).

[66]   Ibid., 3.8.11 (1:711–12); cf. 2.12 (557), 8.1 (702).

he was compelled to mete out to his child.[67] What would the children do
if they imagined that the severity was vindictive, or that God is a judge
who punishes and not a father who chastises?[68]

It is the crucial importance of seeing God in the right *persona* that
underlies Calvin's thoughts on justification, works, and merit. He
brings this out with particular effect in his chapter on Christian
freedom, a theme that he takes to be an appendix to justification and
of no small value for understanding what justification means (its *vis*).
If we dare so put it, the chapter on freedom is where Calvin presents the
cash value of justification for being a Christian. The freedom intended
is the freedom of God's children, whose works are justified as well as
their persons. If their works are weighed by the standard of the law,
Calvin explains, how would unhappy souls gird themselves eagerly for
tasks for which they might earn no more than a reprimand? But if, freed
from all the inflexibility of the law, they hear God calling them with
fatherly gentleness, they will respond eagerly and cheerfully.

> In short, those who are bound by the yoke of the law are like servants
> on whom their masters impose certain tasks each day. Unless the exact
> measure of their tasks is met, they think they have achieved nothing and
> dare not face their masters. But children, who are dealt with more
> generously and more liberally by their fathers, do not hesitate to show
> them unfinished projects that they have only begun, or even spoiled a
> little. Even if they have not succeeded in doing quite what they wanted,
> they are confident that their obedience and readiness of mind will be
> accepted. Such children we ought to be, trusting confidently that our
> most lenient father will approve of them, however small, rough, or
> imperfect they may be . . . . And we need this assurance in no small
> measure: without it, everything we attempt is in vain, because God does
> not consider himself honored by any work of ours that is not done out
> of reverence for him. But who can manage it amid those terrors of
> uncertainty whether God is offended or honored by our work?[69]

In this way, Calvin lays the category of merit to rest and moves the
new self out of any lingering servitude into the freedom and confidence of the children of God. The life of the Christian rests securely on
the goodness of the heavenly father, which includes his willingness to
receive imperfect assignments from his children simply because they
are his children. Rightly or wrongly, Calvin believed that even the
sounder Schoolmen had failed to grasp the full meaning of the gospel
of adoption. And over the years, as he reflected on the Sacrament of

---

[67] Ibid., 3.4.33 (1:663).
[68] Ibid., 3.4.34 (1:663).
[69] Ibid., 3.19.5 (1:837); cf. 17.5 (807).

Baptism, he became convinced that the Anabaptists, too, did not grasp the full measure of the heavenly father's goodness in adopting sons and daughters to enjoy the privileges of his household.

ANABAPTISM AND THE SACRAMENT
OF FREE ADOPTION

The evidence of God's fatherly goodness is the word of promise in Jesus Christ: the word or gospel is the "spiritual seed (*semen*)" by which new sons and daughters of God are begotten every day in the church.[70] Where, then, do the sacraments come in? Calvin makes the transition from the spoken word to visible signs by comparing a sacrament to the official seal attached to documents of state: the word is the pledge of favor, and the sacrament is the seal appended to the word for the sake of ratification. Calvin did not invent the comparison, he says, but takes as his warrant the Pauline description of circumcision as a seal (*sigillum*) of the covenant (Rom. 4:11).[71] Sacraments in general are "seals by which the promises of God are imprinted on our hearts and certainty of grace is confirmed"; as such, although they are of no use in themselves, God wills them to become instruments of his grace. "This, then, should be taken as settled: sacred symbols are testimonies by which God seals his grace on our hearts." There is some ambiguity about what it is that bears the imprint of the seal—the document or the hearts of those for whom it is intended. Perhaps Calvin would reply: "Both." And in any case, he makes his customary point (to which I must return in the final chapter) that only the secret working of the Spirit makes the symbol effective.[72]

Visible Words of God

Calvin develops his notion of a sacrament in book four, chapter fourteen, of the 1559 *Institutes*.[73] It is a fascinating and important

---

[70]   Comm. 1 Cor. 4.15, CO 49:372–73 (alluding to 1 Pet. 1:23). Since the text makes the apostle Paul the "father," Calvin adds that although it is God alone who regenerates our souls, he does not exclude the *ministrorum operam*.
[71]   *Inst.* 1559, 4.14.5 (2:1280), 14.7 (1282). Actually, of course, Rom 4:11 speaks of circumcision as "seal of the righteousness of faith."
[72]   Comm. Rom. 4.11, CO 49:74.
[73]   On Calvin's doctrine of the sacraments in general see W.F. Dankbaar (1941). Despite additions over the years, the basic shape of Calvin's presentation on the sacraments was carried over from 1536. See *Inst.* 1536, OS 1:118–27; *Institution*, 118–27.

chapter, but it raises more dogmatic and exegetical problems than I can possibly hope to explore here. Dogmatically, the arrangement of the material is less convincing than the sequence followed in the *Geneva Catechism*, which moves directly from the word to the sacraments.[74] If, as both the Catechism and the *Institutes* assert, the sacraments are added to the word, then the order of the Catechism is plainly correct. The parallel discussion in the *Institutes*, though it opens by saying that "in the sacraments there is another aid to our faith connected with the preaching of the gospel," severs the connection. There is no chapter at all on the preaching of the gospel, and the most pertinent material lies a long way back, in the chapter on faith (chapter 2), at the beginning of book three. Perhaps Calvin felt that the word of the gospel, as the theme of his entire work, could not be reduced to a single chapter, any more than grace could be, a theme to which Thomas Aquinas (ca. 1225–74) devoted an entire "treatise" in his *Summa Theologiae*. But the problem remains. And if the systematic theologians are likely to wish for a chapter on the preaching of the word before the chapter on the sacraments, the New Testament scholars are even more likely these days to ask why theologians talk about "the sacraments" at all. There is no general concept of a sacrament in the Bible, they will say, and the attempt to create one before discussing Baptism and the Lord's Supper individually makes honest exegesis that much harder. For their part, the historical theologians can only concede the difficulties, and then take the post-canonical sources as they find them.

For his definition of a sacrament, Calvin appeals expressly to Augustine, "whom," he says, "we quote rather frequently as the best and most trustworthy witness of all antiquity."[75] It is true that not

---

[74]   *Catechismus*, OS 2:130; TT 2:83. Cf. *Petit traicté de la saincte Cene* (1541), OS 1:505; TT 2:166: "Or, ce qui est dict de la parolle il appartient aussi bien au Sacrement de la Cene."

[75]   *Inst.* 1559, 4.14.26 (2:1303). The most important study to date of Calvin's relation to Augustine in matters of sacramental theology is Joachim Beckmann (1926). But it is a tendentious study that asserts Calvin's independence of any of his fellow Reformers (p. 4) and views him as the culmination of an Augustinian tradition that needed to be purged of its Catholic leaven (p. 164). The crucial point, of course, is to determine *in what respects* Calvin's notion of a sacrament resembles Augustine's; and while I certainly see him following Augustine on the relation of *signum* to *res*, the thought that a sacrament is a sign added to the divine promise seems to me clearly Lutheran. (See also n. 94 below.) The still unfinished task of establishing Calvin's debts to Augustine in general has been greatly furthered by the work of Luchesius Smits (1957–58). Also pertinent is the question: What became of the Augustinian heritage in the sacramental controversies

Calvin only but Western theology in general owes to Augustine the fundamental contrast between a visible form and invisible grace, so that in a sacrament one thing is seen and another understood.[76] But Calvin's appeal to Augustine is misleading because it was Luther, not Augustine, whom he followed in defining a sacrament as a sign added by God to his promise; and, like Luther himself, he used the Lutheran formula, not only to interpret Baptism and the Lord's Supper, but also to define out of bounds the five extra sacraments of the church of Rome. Calvin must have read Luther's *Prelude on the Babylonian Captivity of the Church* (1520) with care and conviction.[77] Like Luther, he held that a sacrament is never without a preceding promise but is attached to it, as a kind of appendage, to confirm and seal it, or, more exactly, to confirm our faith in it.[78] Calvin's first attempt to define a sacrament in his *Institutes* was accordingly this: a sacrament is "an outward sign by which the Lord represents and attests his goodwill to us, to sustain the weakness of our faith."[79] But this is exactly the idea of a sacrament that

of the Middle Ages? The interesting study of Ratramnus by John F. Fahey argued that the ninth-century Benedictine's eucharistic thought, widely considered heretical in the Roman church, in fact rested on an authentically Augustinian theory of signification (of "figure" and "truth"). (See John F. Fahey, *The Eucharistic Teaching of Ratramn of Corbie*, Pontificia Facultas Theologica Seminarii Mariae ad Lacum, Dissertationes ad Lauream, no. 22 [Mundelein, IL, 1951]). A similar rehabilitation of Calvin might be possible, but even less welcome.

[76]   According to Augustine, Calvin points out, a sacrament is *rei sacrae visibile signum*, or *invisibilis gratiae visibilis forma* (*Inst.* 1559, 4.14.1 [2:1277]). The other Augustinian formula, *aliud videtur, aliud intelligitur*, is quoted in Calvin's chapter on the five "spurious" sacraments of Rome (4.19.15 [2:1463]).

[77]   The parallels are clear in the definition of a sacrament, the list of biblical sacraments (*Inst.* 1559 4.14.18–26), and the rejection of the five spurious sacraments (chap. 19). Interestingly, both Luther and Calvin wondered about the possibility of a third sacrament besides Baptism and the Lord's Supper; only it was Penance for Luther, and for Calvin, like Melanchthon, it was Ordination. Luther actually began his *Babylonian Captivity* by maintaining "for the present" (*pro tempore*) that there are three sacraments: Baptism, Penance, and the Bread (*De captivitate Babylonica ecclesiae praeludium* [1520], WA 6.501.33). But as the LW editor remarks, "the 'present' did not last very long as far as penance was concerned" (LW 36:18, n. 26): by the end of the treatise, only Baptism and the Bread met the double criterion of a divinely instituted sign added to the promise of forgiveness (WA 6.572.10–22; LW 36:124). On the status of Ordination among the first generation of Lutherans, see Hellmut Lieberg, *Amt und Ordination bei Luther und Melanchthon* (Göttingen: Vandenhoeck and Ruprecht, 1962). For Calvin's view of Ordination we have the interesting study of Léopold Schümmer (1965). Calvin does not follow Luther's peculiar argument for his notion of a sacrament, that a testament is a promise of one about to die. See pp. 146–48 below.

[78]   *Inst.* 1559, 4.14.3 (2:1278). Cf. Luther, *De captivitate Babylonica*, WA 6.517.38–518.9; LW 36:43–44.

[79]   *Inst.* 1536, OS 1:118; *Institution*, 118. This definition remained unchanged in the 1539 edition (CO 1:937–38, n. 4).

Zwingli had opposed in his controversy with the Lutherans! Must Calvin, then, simply reject the Zwinglian case out of hand?

Zwingli was deeply suspicious of Luther's sacramental doctrine because, he thought, it transferred to created objects a power that only the Spirit possesses: the power to awaken and sustain faith. He argued instead that a sacrament is a confession, not a confirmation, of faith, resting his case in part on the ancient use of the word *sacramentum* for a soldier's oath of allegiance.[80] Calvin held this to be incorrect philology: in the New Testament, at least, the word *sacramentum* ("sacrament") simply translates the Greek μυστήριον ("mystery").[81] Nevertheless, he came to acknowledge at least a secondary use for Zwingli's sacramental profession of faith or faithfulness, if only the false linguistic argument could be set aside.[82] In his formal definition of a sacrament in the 1543 edition of the *Institutes* he therefore combined the Lutheran and Zwinglian conceptions into one: a sacrament is "an outward symbol by which the Lord seals on our consciences the promises of his goodwill toward us, to sustain the weakness of our faith, and we in turn attest before other people (*apud homines*) our piety toward him."[83] And in the final edition of 1559 he added that the attestation of piety is made "in the presence of God and the angels as well as before other people."[84]

Even before he decided to add the Zwinglian component to his definition, Calvin claimed that his was a mediating concept of a

[80] See pp. 6-7 above and the citations from Zwingli's *Commentarius* and *Von der Taufe* on pp. 8-9, n. 28. In later writings, Zwingli did concede that the sacraments awaken, increase, and assist faith, though they cannot give it. See *Ad illustrissimos Germaniae principes Augustae congregatos, de convitiis Eccii epistola* (1530), SW 6,3:265, 269–70 (LWZ 2:113, 116–17); *Fidei expositio* (1536 [written in 1531]), CERP, 49, 51–52 (LCC 24:260, 263). I have taken account of this other strand in Zwingli's sacramental theology elsewhere, and I do not need to enlarge on it here, where it is Calvin's position that is under discussion. See Gerrish, "The Lord's Supper in the Reformed Confessions" (1966), reprinted as "Sign and Reality: The Lord's Supper in the Reformed Confessions" in *The Old Protestantism and the New* (1982), chap. 7, and "Discerning the Body: Sign and Reality in Luther's Controversy with the Swiss" (1988). Zwingli's views, though they lent themselves to the polemical oversimplifications of his adversaries, were complex, and they changed over the course of his career. There is an extensive secondary literature on the subject. A recent guide is W. P[eter] Stephens, *The Theology of Huldrych Zwingli* (Oxford: Clarendon Press, 1986), chap. 9.
[81] *Inst.* 1559, 4.14.2 (2:1277), 14.13 (1288–89).
[82] Ibid., 4.14.13 (2:1288–89).
[83] CO 1:937–38. It is interesting that Calvin changes the cardinal substantive from *signum* to *symbolum*. *Pietas* here probably is intended to incorporate the Zwinglian notion of "duty."
[84] *Inst.* 1559, 4.14.1 (2:1277).

sacrament.[85] Indeed, from the very first edition of the *Institutes* he presented his own position as a kind of via media between those who emptied the sacraments of their true significance (the Zwinglians) and those who wrongly ascribed a greater significance to the sacraments than to the word (the Romanists). Against the purely Zwinglian position, he always insisted that the attestation of our piety before others is only secondary in the sacraments,[86] and that no dishonor is done to the Spirit if we recognize that the Spirit uses the instrumentality of created things to nurture our faith. "Instead of the one blessing of God that they proclaim [i.e., the work of the Spirit], we take account of three. First the Lord teaches and instructs us by his word; then he confirms it by the sacraments; finally he illumines our minds with the light of his holy Spirit and opens our hearts for word and sacraments to enter."[87] Through the instrumentality of the symbols God truly fulfills (*praestat*) what he promises, but without resigning to them the primary operation, which remains his.[88]

Against the Romanists, on the other hand, Calvin denies that the sacraments are endowed with "I know not what secret powers," so as to confer grace on anyone who does not put the barrier of mortal sin in the way. For what is a sacrament received without faith but the most certain ruin of the church? Apart from the promise, a sacrament is nothing; and they are in error who think that something more is conferred on them by the sacraments than is offered by the word and received by faith. Justification rests in Christ alone, and is communicated to us no less by the preaching of the gospel than by the seal of the sacrament.[89] The difference between word and sacrament is simply

---

[85]   *Inst.* 1539: " Modus in iis omnibus optimus retinetur; ut neque deferatur illis quidquam quod non oportet, neque rursum quod illis convenit detrahatur" (CO 1:950). Cf. Comm. 1 Cor. 10:3 (CO 49:454); *Defensio sanae et orthodoxae doctrinae de sacramentis* (1555), OS 2:270 (TT 2:223); *Inst.* 1559, 4.14.17 (2:1293).

[86]   *Inst.* 1559, 4.14.13 (2:1288–89).

[87]   Ibid., 4.14.8 (2:1284). To the sacraments belongs only the *ministerium* (14.9 [1284]). God uses *mediis ac instrumentis* without resigning to them his power (14.12 [1287]). Cf. *Catechismus*, Q.312, OS 2:130–31; TT 2:84.

[88]   *Inst.* 1559, 4.14.17 (2:1293). The assertion that God fulfills what he promises was added in 1559. On this entire section, which contains the description of sacraments as heralds that only announce grace, see pp. 11-12 above. Cf. also *Catechismus*, Q. 312, OS 2:130-131; TT 2:84. The *opus* is the Spirit's, but that does not prevent God from using sacraments *tanquam secundis organis*.

[89]   *Inst.* 1559, 4.14.14 (2:1289–90). When the Council of Trent described Baptism as the instrumental cause of justification, Calvin's question was: "What then becomes of the gospel?" Baptism is an "appendage of the gospel." *Acta Synodi Tridentinae cum antidoto* (1547), CO 7:449; TT 3:116–17. If Baptism is placed first, the priorities are wrong,

that the sacraments picture what the word declares: namely, the content of the promises in Jesus Christ, or simply Christ himself, who is the matter or substance of the sacraments.[90] "Let it therefore stand as settled that the function of the sacraments is no different than the function of the word of God: to offer and present Christ to us and the treasures of heavenly grace in him. But they confer nothing and are of no use unless received by faith."[91]

Calvin is now equipped with the principles for explaining to us the Sacraments of Baptism and the Lord's Supper, the only two he retains of the medieval seven. The sacraments are "visible words," as Augustine said, which represent God's promises as if painted in a picture. They do not distract faith from the word but, quite the contrary, make faith rest on the foundation of the word even more firmly.[92] To be sure, they are not absolutely necessary additions to the proclaimed word. But they are gracious concessions to our physical nature and therefore not to be neglected.[93] Word and sacrament, correctly understood, fit naturally together. On the one hand, the sacraments make the promises clearer to us; on the other hand, they stand in constant need of the word to make us understand their meaning. It is the addition of the word to the element that brings about a sacrament, as Augustine said; and not simply because it is said, but because it is believed.[94] It follows

and the actual function of Baptism can only be misunderstood. A further risk, which Calvin overlooked, has appeared in later Calvinism: that less than he intended may be ascribed to preaching. This, I think, is what happened on both sides of the debate between Nevin and Hodge, neither of whom did justice to Calvin's persuasion that by faith in the proclaimed word Christ becomes "flesh of our flesh." See Gerrish, *Tradition and the Modern World* (1978), 61–63.

[90]   *Inst.* 1559, 4.14.5 (2:1280), 14.16 (1291), 14.22 (1298). Note that preaching, too, "depicts" Christ: Comm. Gal. 3.1, CO 50:202–3.

[91]   *Inst.* 1559 4.14.17 (2:1292).

[92]   Ibid., 4.14.6 (2:1281). On the concept of a *visibile verbum* see also *Defensio doctrinae de sacramentis*, OS 2:272–73 (TT 2:225– 27); *Ultima admonitio ad Ioachimum Westphalum* (1557), CO 9:181– 82, 217 (TT 2:399–400, 448–49).

[93]   Ibid., 4.14.3 (2:1278). Cf. *Catechismus*, Qq. 314–15, OS 2:131–32; TT 2:84. (This is the source of the first part of my epigraph for this chapter; the second part is from Q. 323 [OS 2:133; TT 2:86]). The *signorum virtus* lies in the promises (*Inst.* 1559, 4.16.4 [2:1327]), so that the addition of the sign or sacrament to the word or promise is not absolutely necessary (4.14.14 [2:1289–90], 16.26 [1349]). But, then, just as the word can exist without the sign, so, in extraordinary circumstances, can illumination be imparted by the Spirit without the medium of preaching (4.16.19 [2:1342]; cf. 16.31 [1357]).

[94]   *Inst.* 1559, 4.14.4 (2:1279). In their sacramental theology, both Luther and Calvin can be said to be working with this Augustinian dictum, but it does not coincide with their definition of a sacrament as a sign added to the promise—a definition that, taken alone, would reduce sacramental grace to the promise itself. Calvin's thesis that what

that a sacrament, like the word, is of no use where it does not give rise to understanding and does not awaken faith. In this sense, Calvin can even say that the essence of a sacrament lies in "the doctrine"; if this is taken away, all that is left is a cold, useless ceremony.[95] Indeed, what remains without the word is nothing but superstition and crass idolatry. And "word" means "promise," not some unintelligible incantation muttered in Latin over the elements: it is the promise that explains the force and use of the signs.[96] "Both word and sacraments, then, confirm our faith by setting before our eyes the good will of the heavenly father toward us, in knowledge of whom the firmness of our faith wholly stands and its strength increases."[97]

The key to a Calvinistic interpretation of the sacraments is, in short, to construe them as essentially word, promise, or proclamation. It is the efficacy of the word that is brought to light in a sacrament,[98] for a sacrament is a proclamation of the gospel— different in form, but not in function, from the preaching of the word. It would therefore be a mistake to suppose that Calvin simply replaced the sacraments with the word, though he did hold that one could be saved without them. Rather, his sacramental theology not only called for reconstruing the word as the primary means of grace and, in this sense, as charged with sacramental efficacy; it called also for reconstruing the sacraments as operative, like words, through the communication of meaning, even if, again like the word, they effect nothing less than the mysterious union with Christ.[99]

the promises do the sacraments do more clearly—"sacramenta . . . promissiones afferunt clarissimas" (14.5 [1280])—is later reaffirmed of the Eucharist in particular: "Id fit cum per Evangelium, tum illustrius per sacram Coenam" (17.5 [1364]). Cf. Gerrish, "The Reformers' Theology of Worship" (1961), especially 28.

    95   " Le principal que le Seigneur nous a recommandé, est de celebrer ce mystere avec vraye intelligence. Il s'ensuit doncq que la substance gist en la doctrine. Icelle ostée, ce n'est plus qu'une ceremonie froide et sans efficace" (De la Cene, OS 1:524; TT 2:190). Though the point is initially made with reference to the Lord's Supper, Calvin goes on to generalize it and to appeal to Augustine's dictum non quia dicitur, sed quia creditur, which originally referred to Baptism. "Sed observent lectores, externo et visibili symbolo simul verbum coniungi. Nam et hinc sacramenta vim suam mutuantur" (Comm. John 20.22, CO 47:439). "Itaque certum est nobis a Domino misericordiam, ac gratiae suae pignus cum sacro suo verbo, tum sacramentis offerri; verum non apprehenditur nisi ab his qui verbum et sacramenta certa fide accipiunt" (Inst. 1559, 4.14.7 [2:1282], with a reference to Augustine once more).

    96   Comm. Eph. 5:26, CO 51:224. Cf. Inst. 1559, 4.14.4 (2:1279– 80).

    97   Inst. 1559, 4.14.10 (2:1286).

    98   Ibid., 4.14.7 (2:1282).

    99   The same two-sidedness we have found in Calvin's understanding of faith and the word appears also in this statement on the sacraments: "Quantum igitur tum ad veram Christi notitiam in nobis fovendam, confirmandam, augendam, tum ad eum

Unamuno once suggested that for the Catholic Eucharist, which has a realistic, material, *dinglich* character, so that it works *ex opere operato*, Protestants substitute the "idealistic sacrament of the word."[100] The truth in this suggestion is that the Protestants at the time of the Reformation really did transfer to the proclamation of the gospel the salvific efficacy medieval scholasticism ascribed to a sacrament. But they did not substitute the one for the other. They kept both and interpreted each in the light of the other. And Luther, at least, never did lose the medieval sense of the *Dinglichkeit*, the sheer materiality ("thingness"), of a sacrament.[101] Calvin, it seems to me, went much further than Luther in rethinking the sacraments in cognitive ("idealistic") terms: that is, as vehicles in the first instance of meaning, although the communication of meaning leads to or "effects" a communion with Christ that eludes understanding. Our next task is to see how this works out in Calvin's teaching on Baptism, which he came to cherish in the conflict with Anabaptism as the ceremonial symbol of adoption.

The Grace of Baptism

The chapter on Baptism in the final edition of the *Institutes* is something of a patchwork, pieced together cumulatively from earlier editions. The discussion is further complicated by Calvin's attempt to fit a variety of baptismal motifs into the conception of a sacrament that

---

plenius possidendum, fruendasque eius divitias, illorum ministerio adiuvamur, tantum apud nos efficaciae habent; id autem fit ubi quod illic offertur, vera fide suscipimus" (*Inst.* 1559 4.14.16 [2:1291]).

[100] Miguel de Unamuno, *Tragic Sense of Life*, trans. J. E. Crawford Flitch (1921; reprint ed., New York: Dover, 1954), 66.

[101] Cf. Ernst Bizer, *Fides ex auditu: Eine Untersuchung über die Entdeckung der Gerechtigkeit Gottes durch Martin Luther* (Neukirchen: Erziehungsverein, 1958), 178: "Dieses Doppelte ist bezeichnend für die lutherische Lehre vom Sakrament: das Sakrament wird vom Wort aus verstanden, und das Wort selbst bekommt sakramentalen Charakter." Bizer is also among those who have stressed the *dinglich* character of the Lutheran Eucharist. Commenting on the opening question and answer on the Sacrament of the Altar in Luther's *Small Catechism* (see *Der kleiner Katechismus* [1529], BELK, 519–20; BC, 351), he writes: "Diese Definition bezeichnet nicht eine 'Handlung,' sondern eine 'Sache': Leib und Blut Christi 'unter' den Elementen, eben damit aber auch nicht eine Person, sondern zunächst jedenfalls Dinge" ("Die Abendmahlslehre in den lutherischen Bekenntnisschriften" [1955], 3). Albrecht Peters, among others, rejects the contrast between "body" and "person": "Die Gabe des Sakramentes [for Luther] ist die eine des Wortes, der totus vivus Christus mit seinem Fleisch und Blut" (*Realpräsenz: Luthers Zeugnis von Christi Gegenwart im Abendmahl*, Arbeiten zur Geschichte und Theologie des Luthertums, vol. 5 [Berlin: Lutherisches Verlagshaus, 1960], 109–10). But this interpretation, too, says more than Unamuno allowed for in his generalization about the Protestants.

he borrowed from Luther. The original section on Baptism, in the first edition of the *Institutes*, lacked any definition of the rite at all.[102] It began by simply asserting that God gave Baptism for two purposes: to serve our faith before him, and to serve our confession before other people. Calvin says very little about the second purpose, which, though included, is immediately downplayed as secondary.[103] This, of course, is to correct Zwingli. Under the first, more Lutheran heading, Calvin tries to distinguish three things that Baptism brings to our faith. First, as a symbol of *cleansing*, it assures us of forgiveness through Christ's blood our whole life long.[104] Second, as a symbol of *rebirth*, it shows us our mortification and renewal in Christ, which is a matter not of imitating him but of participation in him. Baptism is not only a lifelong token of forgiveness; it also initiates a lifelong struggle with original sin, a struggle in which progress is made until we pass from this life to the Lord.[105] Third, Baptism means *union* with Christ: it testifies that we are not only engrafted into Christ's death and life but so united and joined to him as to share in all the good things that are

---

[102]   The closest Calvin comes to a definition is in his summary contrast between Baptism and the Lord's Supper (OS 1:159; *Institution*, 164): Baptism is meant to be "like an entrance into the church and an initiation into faith."

[103]   *Inst.* 1536, OS 1:127; *Institution*, 128. For Calvin's brief reflection on the second purpose of Baptism, see OS 1:132; *Institution*, 133–34. "Siquidem nota est, qua palam profitemur nos populo Dei accenseri velle, qua testamur nos in unius Dei cultum, in unam religionem cum Christianis omnibus consentire, qua denique fidem nostram publice affirmamus." The fact that he mentions a second purpose of Baptism at all indicates a curious disharmony between the simple definition of a sacrament and the two-sided (albeit deliberately unbalanced) exposition of Baptism. The same disharmony appears in Calvin's *Instruction et confession de foy* (1537), where a sacrament is defined as *un tesmoignage de la grace de Dieu declare par signe exterieur* but Baptism is said to be given for *two* reasons: "Le baptesme nous a este donne de Dieu premierement a ce quil servist a nostre foy envers luy, secondement a nostre confession envers les hommes" (OS 1:411; *Instruction in Faith*, 68.).

[104]   *Inst.* 1536, OS 1.127–28; *Institution*, 128–29. Cf. OS 1:202 (*Institution*, 216): Baptism is the true sacrament of penance. Calvin's biblical warrants are Eph. 5:26, Titus 3:5, 1 Pet. 3:21, to which he could have added Acts 22:16.

[105]   Ibid., OS 1:128–32; *Institution*, 129–33. Here Calvin relies on Rom 6:1–11 and Col. 2:11–12, filled out with references to John the Baptist and the "baptism" of the people of Israel in the cloud and sea (1 Cor. 10:2). The struggle with sin is documented from Rom. 7 and Gal. 5:19–21. In Calvin's translation, as this passage indicates, *regeneratio* and *poenitentia* are the same thing. The *Geneva Catechism* draws out the pedagogical useful-ness of the twofold symbolism more explicitly: forgiveness is like washing, and the new birth is represented by immersion in, and emergence from, water (OS 2:133–34; TT 2:86). Forgiveness (or reconciliation) and rebirth (or repentance) are the two gifts (*duplex gratia*) received from union with Christ (*Inst.* 1559, 3.11.1 [1:725]).

his. Hence, for example, from the fact that we have put on Christ in Baptism Paul demonstrates that we are God's sons and daughters.[106]

Evidently Calvin's first look at Christian Baptism (in the 1536 *Institutes*) already takes it to exemplify his later, two-part definition of a sacrament, with the Lutheran component given precedence over the Zwinglian. The first two things that Baptism brings to faith are graphic representations of what Calvin identified in the conflict with Rome as the two main points of the gospel: forgiveness and repentence. Only the slightest—and somewhat indirect—connection is made between Baptism and becoming children of God. The result is a complex, perhaps even cumbersome doctrine of Baptism, in which the pieces fit together very loosely. To be sure, all three of the Sacrament's benefits to faith (the Lutheran component) rest on express scriptural warrants, but they resist the theologian's systematic impulse quite apart from the need to combine them with the other (Zwinglian) purpose of Baptism. The two symbols of washing and drowning are scarcely compatible, and there is very little symbolic foundation at all for the idea of adoption as distinct from rebirth.[107] Calvin the systematic theologian had a difficult task before him.

As his discussion moves on from the Lord's purpose in ordaining Baptism to our proper use and reception of it,[108] it becomes apparent, further, that the relation between sign and reality in the Sacrament was already a problem to him.[109] The problem grew as the Anabaptists gained strength, despite the brutal means taken against them by Roman Catholics, Lutherans, and Reformed alike. For the Anabaptists, the practice of baptizing infants was "the highest and chief abomination of the pope,"[110] and the Protestant Reformation had failed to do

[106] *Inst.* 1536, OS 1:132; *Institution*, 133. The reference is to Gal. 3:26–27. Sometimes Calvin quotes 1 Cor. 12.13 to support his notion of "engrafting" into Christ's body (e.g. *Inst.* 1559, 4.16.22 [2:1345]).

[107] The rite itself favors the image of a new birth rather than adoption (see, e.g., *Inst.* 1559, 4.16.2 [2:1325]). But Calvin did not perceive the two metaphors as exclusive.

[108] In the 1536 edition, the transition is made at OS 1:132; *Institution*, 134.

[109] The observation (which goes back to 1536) that those who administer Baptism are only *exterioris signi ministri*, whereas Christ is the *interioris gratiae author*, is not explained further in any edition (see *Inst.* 1559, 4.15.8 [2:1310]). How are the outer and the inner events related?

[110] The phrase appears in the Schleitheim Confession (1527), art. 1. See John Christian Wenger, *The Doctrines of the Mennonites* (Scottdale, PA: Mennonite Publishing House, 1950), 69–74. As the so-called Schleitheim Confession (originally composed in German, 1527) came to enjoy a widening circulation in French, Calvin was prevailed upon to publish a treatise against its distinctive teachings: *Brieve instruction pour armer tous bons fideles contre les erreurs de la secte commune des Anabaptistes* (1544). The first part refutes the seven articles of the Schleitheim Confession; for the article on Baptism see CO 7:56–64. There is a recent translation, with a historical introduction, by Benjamin Wirt Farley (1982); see 44–55.

away with it. A consistent program for reform of the church had to include the denial of Baptism to any but believers, who could give a credible testimony of their new birth. For their part, the three main churches closed their ranks in a rare show of solidarity against the unprecedented new "heresy." And yet, Calvin's ordering of the two functions of baptism did not exclude the Zwinglian view of a sacrament, from which the Anabaptist "heresy" logically arises: that is, the view that a sacrament is not a means of grace but a public testimony that grace has been received. He refers to the cleansing and renewal that comes from Christ as already having happened. To be sure, Calvin relegates "confession before others" to a secondary rank. But he speaks as if even the primary end of Baptism, the "confirmation of faith," itself remains tied to the past tense: the purpose of the Sacrament is to assure us that we really have received the things promised in the gospel, such as the forgiveness of our sins. To this extent, his interpretation of Baptism coincides with Zwingli's characteristic teaching that a sacrament is a sign of past grace (*factae gratiae signum*).[111]

To begin with, it is true, Calvin seems to follow a different path. Unlike Zwingli, he affirms unambiguously that God is the agent of Baptism, addressing us through the sign. What the Lord attests, and what the sign signifies, is an event or series of events that Calvin describes initially as inward and spiritual: God purifies us of our sins, weakens the power of our desire (*concupiscentiae*), and so on. These are things that God does to our soul within as truly and surely as we see our body outwardly washed and plunged under water. "For this analogy or similitude is the surest rule of sacraments, that in bodily things we should see and think about spiritual things." Not that the sacrament has itself the power to confer such graces; rather, the Lord

---

[111]   ". . . duntaxat talium donorum cognitionem et certitudinem in hoc sacramento percipi" (*Inst.* 1559, 4.15.2 [2.1304]). Zwingli describes a sacrament as *factae gratiae signum* in his "Augsburg Confession," the *Fidei ratio* (1530: SW 6,2:805; LWZ 2:48), where he expressly rejects the notion of a means of grace: sacraments do not confer grace, which comes from the Spirit alone, and the Spirit needs no means (no *dux* or *vehiculum*: SW 6,2:803; LWZ 2:46). Once again, as with the notion of a sacrament as an aid to faith (see n. 80 above), Zwingli's thoughts on sacramental grace are complex, if not downright inconsistent. In his *Fidei expositio*, written (though not published) just one year later (1531), he suggests that in the Eucharist the outward eating of the bread is a sign of a simultaneous feeding on Christ inwardly by faith (i.e., of a present experience), though he does not say that the inner event is effected by the outer: ". . . proprie sacramentaliter edis, cum scilicet intus idem agis quod foris operaris" (*Fidei expositio*, CERP, 48; LCC 24:259). Hence one finds in Zwingli early hints of the "symbolic parallelism" that became common in Reformed teaching on the sacraments (see pp. 166-69 below).

attests by this token that he *wants* to lavish them on us.[112] Now this, indeed, sounds as if the gifts have not yet been bestowed at all but lie still in the future. However, Calvin goes on to illustrate his argument from the story of Cornelius the centurion, who had already received the forgiveness of sins and visible graces of the Spirit and was baptized simply to exercise his faith, not to obtain more ample forgiveness in Baptism itself (Acts 10:47).[113] The baptism of Paul, recorded later in Acts, presents an obvious difficulty to this line of thought, because Ananias says: "Rise and be baptized, and wash away your sins" (Acts 22:16). But Calvin now assures us, with very little help from his text, that all Ananias meant was this: "Be baptized, Paul, to be certain that your sins *have been* forgiven."[114]

Calvin later had second thoughts about this argument, which plainly sees the virtue of the sacrament in its ability to assure us of what we already possess. The first function of a sacrament certainly goes beyond the Zwingli of the 1520s, who had deep misgivings about any suggestion that a created object might be a means of confirming faith, because only the Spirit can do that. But "confirming (or strengthening) faith" is an operation that remains, so it appears, in the domain of the memory and therefore hardly raises the sacraments above the level of *nuda signa*, "bare (or naked) signs" that provide no more than a reminder of a deed done, or an event past, the reality itself being absent. All Calvin seems to add to Zwingli's characteristic view in the 1536 edition of the *Institutes* is that to remember helps our faith, and by 1530 Zwingli himself was ready to concede as much. Oddly enough, it was apparently Luther's view of a sacrament as a pledge of a divine promise that pushed Calvin in this direction. But by 1541, at least, he correctly understood that it was precisely the notion of an "empty sign" that offended Luther most in Zwingli's sacramental theology.[115] And in the 1559 edition of the *Institutes* Calvin made two additions in the passage under consideration. First, in section 14 of

---

[112]   *Inst.* 1536, OS 1:132–33; *Institution*, 134. This is the passage, cited above (p. 12), in which Calvin appears to deny the instrumentality of a sacrament.

[113]   Ibid., OS 1:133; *Institution*, 134.

[114]   Ibid., OS 1:133; *Institution*, 134–35 (my emphasis). "Respondeo: dicimur accipere, obtinere, impetrare, quod nobis a Deo datum credimus, sive id tum primum agnoscimus, sive prius agnitum certius persuasum habemus." The heavily cognitive character of this language is striking.

[115]   "Tellement que Luther pensoit qu'ilz [sc. Zwingli and Oecolampadius] ne vousissent [1566: voulussent] laisser autre chose que les signes nudz, sans leur substance spirituelle" (*De la Cene*, OS 1:528; TT 2:195). On Zwingli's apparent change of mind about the ability of the sacraments to help faith, see n. 80 above.

what is now book four, chapter fifteen, he inserted the sentence: "Nor does he feed our eyes with only a bare show but leads us to the reality present (*rem praesentem*), and what he depicts (*figurat*) he effectively accomplishes at the same time." Second, in the following section (section 15), he added: "However, it is not my intention to weaken the force of baptism by not adding the reality and truth to the sign, insofar as God works through external means."[116]

These interesting changes may just possibly be construed as explanations of what Calvin meant all along. But the appearance, at least, is that he is moving, or has moved, to a somewhat different variety of sacramental theory than we find in the 1536 *Institutes:* the additions imply the actual giving of a present gift, not verification of a gift already given. And this is fully in line with the strong statement on Baptism in the *Geneva Catechism* (1545). Question 328 asks: "But is this all you attribute to the water, that it is only a picture (*figura*) of washing?" The answer expected of the pupil is this : "I think it is a picture in such a way that the truth is joined with it at the same time. For God does not deceive us when he promises us his gifts. It is therefore certain that pardon of sins and newness of life are both offered to us and received by us in baptism."[117] Here the grace itself, not just the reassurance that it has been won for us or already given to us, is the sacramental gift, and the focus of the divine activity moves from the past into the present.

It is may well be objected that Calvin has thereby opened himself to a worse problem than Zwinglian attenuation of sacramental grace. Baptism, after all, was administered in the Reformed churches mostly to infants, who appear to be incapable of an act of believing. It is one thing to argue that the Sacrament imparts something more to the recipient than reassurance of faith, quite another to say that what is imparted does not require faith at all. Is this what Calvin intended? Is the via media on the verge of collapsing back into medievalism?

Calvin notes the problem already in a section that goes all the way back to the first edition of the *Institutes*, to the time before he strengthened his language on sacramental efficacy. He stands firmly by the

---

[116]   *Inst.* 1559, 4.15.14,15 (2:1314, 1315).
[117]   *Catechismus*, OS 2:134; TT 2:87. In the sense intended, the English word "figure" and its verbal cognate "to figure" have a slightly archaic sound that is particularly out of place in a children's catechism. For this reason I have preferred "picture" and "depict" for Calvin's *figura* and *figurare*, even though he insists that a sacrament is not like a common portrait (*imago*) of the emperor (Calvin to Bullinger, 25 February 1547, CO 12:482).

principle that Baptism is nothing without the promise but admits that, since faith (if it comes) normally comes many years afterwards, the Sacrament is not one bit of use to us as long as the promise lies neglected. That, however, he insists, does not invalidate the promise: God remains trustworthy and will undoubtedly fulfill his promise for believers sometime in the future.[118] The admission that at the time our baptism was "not one bit of use to us (*non profuisse nobis hilum*)" was allowed to stand in later revisions of the *Institutes*. Alongside of it, however, Calvin introduced a somewhat different argument: that God adopts our babies even before they are born, so that there is no need to be anxious about the possibility of their falling ill and dying unbaptized. Their salvation is contained in the word: that is, in the promise that God will be not our God only but the God of our offspring. The Sacrament was added to the word like the seal on a document. "It follows that the baby children of believers are not baptized to make them sons and daughters of God for the first time, as though they were strangers to the church before. Rather, because they already belonged to the body of Christ by the privilege of the promise, they are received into the church by a solemn sign."[119] The problem of infant baptism, we may add by way of comment, now appears to put Calvin back in the Zwinglian camp again! The actual grace given lies in the past.

Calvin leaves us, then, with three tenses for construing the rite of Christian initiation: he can speak of the benefit as past, present, or future. Christian children are baptized in recognition that they were already adopted by God before they were even born, in the assurance that the reality is present with the sign, and in the expectation that the promise sealed in the Sacrament will eventually lead to their faith. I do not wish to argue that these three strands in Calvin's sacramental theology necessarily fall apart. But it does seem clear to me that, although he tries to weave them together in the final edition of his great systematic work, he first spun them separately to deal with distinct questions. The question that forced itself upon him with increasing importunity was, of course, what to do about the Anabaptists, who insisted on the baptism of believers

---

[118]   *Inst.* 1559, 4.15.17 (2:1317).
[119]   CO 1:1038, printed as an insertion to chapter 18, on the Lord's Supper. The editors of CO give this passage *minoribus typis*, by which they usually indicate an addition made in 1550 (see CO 1:xlvii). The LCC editors treat it as stemming partly from 1543, partly from 1545. In 1559 it was located in 4.15.20, 22 (2:1321, 1323).

alone. In 1539 Calvin added a long appendix to his treatment of Baptism; in the 1559 edition of the *Institutes* it became an entire chapter on infant baptism. [120]

The Symbol of Adoption

Calvin's defense of infant baptism in this chapter turns largely around his belief that Christian baptism is equivalent to Jewish circumcision, and that any objection to infant baptism would therefore be an objection as well to the unquestioned divine institution of circumcision.[121] I cannot go into the details of his case, which is argued not only with passion but also perhaps (or so it has been said) with the peevishness of a man in trouble. Much less can I take my own stand in the fray, which is all the more agitated these days because the defense is no longer against the "raving" of "certain fanatic spirits" outside the Reformed church;[122] there are powerful voices of dissent within.[123] But at the beginning of the chapter Calvin pledges to compose a disputation that will serve to explain the mystery of Baptism more clearly.[124]

---

[120]   For the 1539 "appendix" see CO 1:968–90 (chap. 11, secs. 19–51). It was incorporated almost intact into the 1559 *Institutes* (book four, chap. 16), in which only section 31 (against Servetus) was wholly new. Sections 17–23 have been identified as a direct response to Balthasar Hubmaier (1485–1528), *Von dem Christlichen Tauff der gläubigen* (1526).

[121]   The two stand in an anagogical relationship that makes circumcision the equivalent of Baptism by anticipation (*Inst.* 1559, 4.16.3–4 [2:1325–27]). The *promissio*, the *res figurata*, and the *fundamentum* are identical in both. The argument from the analogy with circumcision had already been advanced by Zwingli, *In catabaptistarum strophas elenchus* (1527), SW 6,1:48, 171; SWZ, 139, 236. Luther, too, appealed to the analogy in his *Von der Wiedertaufe an zwei Pfarrherrn* (1528), WA 26.158.17, 164.30, 169.20–35; LW 40:244, 252, 257–58.

[122]   *Inst.* 1559, 4.16.1 (2:1324).

[123]   Much of the dissent goes back to Karl Barth's *Die kirchliche Lehre von der Taufe*, Theologische Studien, no. 14 (Zollikon-Zurich: Evangelischer Verlag, 1943), trans. by Ernest A. Payne as *The Teaching of the Church Regarding Baptism* (London: SCM Press, 1948). The wider debate within the Reformed church does not concern us here. The outstanding study of Calvin's doctrine of Baptism is L. G. M. Alting von Geusau (1963). See also the articles by Egil Grislis (1962) and Jill Raitt (1980). Alting von Geusau argues that Calvin's defense of infant baptism as a sign of the covenant empties the rite of its sacramental nature: "Die Taufe ist für Calvin, wo es sich um Kinder handelt, eben kein Sakrament der Wiedergeburt und ebensowenig ein Heilmittel gegen die Erbsünde" (*Die Lehre von der Kindertaufe bei Calvin*, 264). This, of course, is to view Calvin's controversy with the Anabaptists from the other (Roman Catholic) side, and it goes too far to say that when Calvin views infant baptism as a sign of the covenant, he has to infer the impossibility of an efficacy of the sign for the child itself (261). That Calvin found it difficult to say what the efficacy of the rite was for the infant, however, is only too clear.

[124]   *Inst.* 1559, 4.16.1 (2:1324).

It is not simply a question of whether or not to administer the Sacrament to infants. Of particular importance to ourselves is to see what light the controversy with the Anabaptists can shed on the systematic place of Calvin's thoughts on Baptism.

The defense is given in all three tenses: past, present, and future. It is not difficult for Calvin to relate infant baptism to the past and the future; all he has to do is to hold firmly to the principle that a sacrament is a form of the word or promise. The baptism of a child proclaims, first, that the children of believing parents have been born into the covenant people: they have the *word* of Baptism, or the thing signified, so why deny them the *sign*, which is only an appendage to the word? Infants are to be baptized so as not to be torn away from the body of Christ, to which they already belong; since they are received by God as heirs of the covenant as soon as they are born, they should be admitted to Baptism.[125] Secondly, the sacrament—exactly as word, promise, or proclamation—does of course call for faith. It does so throughout the entire life of the one who has been baptized. Infants are baptized for future repentance and faith. Taught the truth of Baptism at a later age, they will be all the more fired with eagerness for renewal as they learn that they were given the token of renewal in earliest infancy so that they might reflect upon it throughout the entire course of their life.[126]

The difficulties arise chiefly when Calvin turns from the past and the future and tries to explain what happens in the present, at the actual moment of administration. Perhaps he is handicapped at this point by the admission, made in the previous chapter, that Baptism is "not one bit of use" as long as the promise is neglected. But now he refuses to rule out the possibility of infant regeneration. Indeed, he speaks with surprising extravagance of "the dogma we have now established concerning the regeneration of infants."[127] "What is the risk," he asks, "if infants are said to receive now some part of the grace that in a little while they will wholly enjoy in its bountiful fullness?"[128] Well, Calvin, I should think the risk is that any such admission threatens to undermine the categories of sacramental thinking that

---

[125] Ibid., 4.16.5 (2:1328), 16.22 (1345), 16.24 (1347). For Calvin's supporting use of 1 Cor. 7:14 ("Your children . . . are holy"), see ibid., 4.16.6 (2:1329), 16.15 (1337). Cf. Comm. 1 Cor 7.14, CO 49:413.

[126] *Inst.* 1559, 4.16.20 (2:1343), 16.21 (1344).

[127] " . . . quod iam constitutum est a nobis dogma de infantium regeneratione" (ibid., 4.16.26 [2:1349]).

[128] Ibid., 4.16.19 (2:1342).

you have so far relied on: goodwill, promise, knowledge, assurance. This may not be a bad risk to take. But Calvin is clearly on thin ice when he reminds us, as evidence for infant regeneration, that John the Baptist was sanctified in his mother's womb (Luke 1:15), and that Christ himself was sanctified from earliest infancy.[129] For what does "sanctified" mean here? And can it mean the same thing for the infant Christ and the unborn John, if the one was, and the other was not, preserved from the taint of original sin?

Even if we set aside these unhelpful proofs, the question remains whether Calvin's basic sacramental concept of a visible word can survive the notion of infant regeneration. He struggles to keep within a cognitive framework, but he ends up with language that has gone on holiday. The "grace" of the Sacrament, he assumes, must be knowledge of God, so perhaps the Lord shines with a tiny spark on those he will illuminate fully in the future. But what could even a tiny spark of "knowledge" be in the mind of an infant? Calvin says: "I would not wish to make the rash claim that infants are endowed with the same faith that we experience in ourselves, or have a faith-knowledge quite like ours. I prefer to leave that in suspense."[130]

[129]   Ibid., 4.16.17–18 (2:1340–41). Calvin's argument in 16.17 is addressed to the objection that young children should be excluded from Baptism because they cannot understand the mystery that it signifies. His reply, in summary form, is (1) that no one is saved except by union with Christ, which carries with it life or rebirth and justification or forgiveness; (2) that some infants must certainly be saved; (3) that if they can be saved, they may also be baptized. Cf. 16.22 (1345): "Parvuli peccatorum remissione donantur: ergo signo privandi non sunt." To the question how there *can* be regeneration without "knowledge of good and evil," the answer (again in summary) is (1) that the possibility of infant regeneration is demonstrated in the case of John the Baptist; (2) that we dare not deny God the power to do it again whenever he chooses. Calvin's "dogma" of *infant* regeneration is not quite a dogma of *baptismal* regeneration since the Sacrament is not in itself an infallible guarantee that the particular infant being baptized has been, is being, or later will be, regenerated. He admits elsewhere that many children of believers renounce their birthright through their own unfaithfulness (Comm. Acts. 3.25, CO 48:76; cf. Comm. Eph. 5.26, CO 51:223). This however, is not the point he wants to emphasize. See further pp. 169-73 below.

[130]   Inst. 1559, 4.16.19 (2:1342). Cf. the expression *regenerandi gradus* in 16.31 (1357): there are "degrees of regeneration." On the possibility of *fides infantilis*, cf. Luther, *Von der Wiedertaufe*, WA 26.156.3–157.6; LW 40:241–43. Luther's argument is only that there *may* be such a thing as infant faith; even if, in fact, there is not, the word remains firm and subsequent faith completes the sacrament (WA 26.159.25, 162.9; LW 40:246, 249). Earlier, Luther had spoken of the faith of others (*fides aliena*) as requisite to the sacrament (*De captivitate Babylonica*, WA 6.538.6; LW 36:73). Naturally, he came to believe that behind the *Schwärmer* (the Anabaptists), as behind the papists, a *Werkteufel* was busily engaged in transforming a work of God into a human work (*Von der Wiedertaufe*, WA 26.161.35; LW 40:248). Calvin used the notion of infant faith explicitly in *Inst.* 1536 (OS 1:136; *Institution*, 138), but it is not so much replaced as modified by the later passages on infant regeneration (*pace* Beckmann, *Vom Sakrament bei Calvin*, 99).

Perhaps that is where I should leave it, too. It will not be expected of me to solve the problem of infant baptism. But it is surely pertinent to ask whether Calvin's conclusion has left him where his strong ecclesial instinct might have led him. It would no doubt be a defect in his doctrine of Baptism if he had gone no further than his early admission that the profit of the Sacrament lies wholly in the future. In Calvin's own metaphor, a "seed" is planted at baptism. But why, given his strong sense of the covenant community, does he look for the seed in the child and not rather in the church or in the child's situation? He asserts that the seed of faith and repentance lies hidden within the infants by the secret working of the Spirit.[131] That, it seems to me, is to abstract the child from the church—which runs exactly counter to Calvin's defense of infant baptism as a sign and seal of the covenant. Suppose, then, he had brought this assertion more fully into harmony with another, which he made earlier. After speaking of the benefit of infant baptism to the pious parent, he continued:

> The children, too, receive some benefit from their baptism: by being engrafted into the body of the church, they are commended more to the care of the other members. Then, when they have grown up, they are spurred thereby in no small measure to an earnest zeal for worshipping God, who took them to be his children by the ceremonial symbol of adoption before ever they were old enough to recognize him as father.[132]

If we venture to discover in these words what Calvin calls the "force" of the Sacrament, which infants are too young to grasp,[133] then it is a force that can at no time be reduced to a matter of bare cognition. The influence of "mother church" on a child is never wholly a matter of instruction; it operates at subconscious levels that leave ample room for Calvin's profound sense of the mystery of the Sacrament and the secret working of the Spirit. "For," as he has told us earlier, "there is no other entrance into life unless [the church visible] conceives us in her womb, gives birth to us, feeds us at her breasts, and, finally, protects us with her care and guidance until, putting off this mortal flesh, we become like the angels."[134] The church is mother to those for whom God is father. The force of Baptism must have something to do with this good Calvinistic

---

[131]   *Inst.* 1559, 4.16.20 (2:1343).

[132]   Ibid., 4.16.9 (2:1332).

[133]   "Nobis vero pluris Dei authoritas, cui visum est infantes sibi consecrare, ac initiare sacro symbolo cuius nondum per aetatem vim tenebant" (ibid., 4.16.31 [2:1358]).

[134]   Ibid., 4.1.4 (2:1016).

principle (borrowed from Cyprian).[135] But, be that as it may, the more important point for our present quest is this: Calvin's defense of infant baptism has brought us back full circle to his favorite theme, the paternal goodness that adopts sons and daughters in Christ. Baptism has become the "symbol of adoption." In this respect, at least, Calvin brought his doctrine of Baptism into line with his leading dogmatic themes.

Surprisingly enough, the first edition of the *Institutes*, though it contains some of Calvin's most eloquent affirmations of God's fatherhood and our adoption in Christ, scarcely related Baptism to adoption at all.[136] It was apparently the quarrel with the Anabaptists that led Calvin to integrate his thoughts on Baptism more closely with the metaphor of adoption into the family of God.[137] That to enter the church is to become a child in the household of God is not expressly conveyed by the visual symbolism of the baptismal rite itself (the sprinkling or pouring of water). But it suggests itself naturally enough when the candidate for Baptism is a newborn child. On the other hand—with how much justice we need not ask—Calvin was convinced that the logical consequence of believer baptism is the abandonment of infants wholesale to damnation. His horror at this supposed implication runs through the chapter on infant baptism. Against it stands his own passionate belief that God's care for the children of the covenant is a most remarkable testimony to the overflowing generosity of the father and fountain of good. Seen in its systematic connection, his case for infant baptism is in fact a kind of a fortiori argument from the divine goodness.

First, Calvin discovers sufficient evidence of God's goodness already in the story of God's covenant with Abraham and his "seed." When the Lord commanded Abraham to practice circumcision, he stated first that he would be God to Abraham and his seed, and God

---

[135]   Ibid., 4.1.1 (2:1012).

[136]   The idea of adoption is alluded to, by way of illustration, as one of the benefits of union with Christ (OS 1:132; *Institution*, 133). It is not linked, as one would have expected, with the image of entrance into the church (OS 1:159; *Institution*, 164).

[137]   This can be traced in the additions that appear in the 1539, 1543, and 1545 editions. They are readily identified in *Inst.* 1559, 4.15.1 (2:1303, the opening definition of the Sacrament), 15.20 (1321), 15.22 (1323); 4.16.4 (2:1327), 16.7 (1330), 16.30 (1352). Cf. 4.16.31 (2:1356), where, in a passage new to the 1559 edition, Christ's embrace of the children is called the *tessera adoptionis*. The shift to Baptism as the Sacrament of adoption in the 1539 edition of the *Institutes* is also carried a minute step further by the addition in 1559 of the words *paterni Dei favoris* to the characterization of the promise (4.16.4 [2:1327]); from 1539 to 1554 the promise was *misericordiae Domini*.

added, so Calvin says, that "to him belonged the abundance and sufficiency of all things."[138] There is not much in the text (Genesis 17) to support this alleged divine addition. Possibly Calvin is interpreting the name by which the Lord identified himself on this occasion: "El Shaddai," which Calvin took, in his commentary, to be a double indication of power, since power is what each word separately suggests. It is as if God wanted to declare that he had sufficient power for Abraham's protection, so that "I am El Shaddai" was a tacit promise, reassuring Abraham and giving him confidence.[139] Characteristically, Calvin interprets God's power as God's ability to do good for his people: Abraham was to consider that the hand of God would be to him the wellspring of every good (*omnis boni scaturiginem*).[140] The very fact that God's promise was made to Abraham's descendants as well as to Abraham is, in Calvin's eyes, the most remarkable testimony to the Lord's amazing goodness. He interprets Exodus 20:6 to say that the Lord shows his covenant mercy to a thousand generations, and comments: "The immense liberality of God extended here not only supplies the most ample material for proclaiming his glory but floods devout hearts (*pia pectora*) with no ordinary joy, which rouses them to love such a devoted father (*pium patrem*) more intensely in return when they see that for their sake he cares for their posterity."[141]

The second step in the argument is to ask whether the promise of the gospel can possibly be any less gracious than the promise made to Abraham. Obviously not. The gospel is the clearer publication of the goodness of God. Christians are Abraham's posthumous children, and as such have a share in the covenant.[142] Although they come later, they cannot receive less—unless we suppose that Christ by his coming curtailed the father's grace. And this could not be said without insult to Christ, through whom the father's infinite goodness was poured out more liberally than ever before.[143] It was because he came to enlarge, not to limit, the father's mercy that he embraced the infants and rebuked the disciples for trying to keep them away. Therefore, it is unthinkable to refuse them Baptism.[144]

---

[138]   *Inst.* 1559, 4.16.3 (2:1326).
[139]   Comm. Gen. 17.1, CO 23:234.
[140]   *Inst.* 1559, 4.16.3 (2:1326).
[141]   Ibid., 4.16.9 (2:1332). Cf. 2.8.21 (1:387).
[142]   Ibid., 4.16.14 (2:1336).
[143]   Ibid., 4.16.6 (2:1328–29).
[144]   Ibid., 4.16.7 (2:1329). The argument from the covenant (and the virtual identity of Baptism and circumcision) forms the core of Calvin's defense of infant baptism also in the treatise against the Anabaptists (see n. 110 above). When children are baptized,

Whether or not this is a sound proof for the practice of infant baptism, I do not have to decide. It is at least an excellent proof of what stood at the heart of Calvin's theology. The baptism of infants becomes, in his defense of it, an astonishing testimony to the goodness of God that constantly surrounds us and takes us into his adopted family. The goodness is there before we were born; it will still be there to bless our children when we ourselves have passed on. Baptism for Calvin is the sacrament not only of prevenient grace, but also of posthumous grace. "Let it then be beyond controversy," he concludes, "that God is so good and generous to his own that he is pleased for their sake to count among his people also the children they have produced."[145] What Satan must be trying to do through the assault on infant baptism is to diminish the glory of the divine goodness.

> For how sweet is it to pious minds to be reassured, not only by the word but even by a display they can see, that they obtain so much grace with the heavenly father that their posterity are in his care? Here we can see how he assumes the role (*personam*) of a most provident father toward us (*providentissimi erga nos patrisfamilias personam*), not laying aside his concern for us even after our death but caring and providing for our children. Then should we not follow David's example and with all our heart revel in thanksgiving, that his name may be blessed for such an illustration of goodness?[146]

The alternative, which the devil is busy fostering, can only be impious ingratitude and indolence in teaching piety to our children.[147]

Calvin's gospel of the heavenly father announces that God takes sinners into his household to be his adopted children, for no other reason than because he wishes to be their father: he seeks in himself the reason to be kind, not in them,[148] and in Jesus Christ he provides the space in which his fatherly love is free to operate.[149] This is what Calvin believed himself to be fighting for in his relentless campaigns against those who (he thought) diluted free grace with talk of merit and,

---

the "doctrine" is addressed not to them but to their parents and the whole church, and it is, quite specifically, the doctrine that the covenant is extended to the children of believers. Infant regeneration and the possibility of infant faith are not invoked to buttress the case.

   [145]   *Inst.* 1559, 4.16.15 (2:1338).
   [146]   Ibid., 4.16.32 (2:1359).
   [147]   Ibid.
   [148]   ". . . a se ipso causam petens cur illi [sc. peccatori] benefaciat" (ibid., 3.11.16 [1:746]).
   [149]   Ibid., 2.16.2–4 (1:504–7).

equally, those who (he thought) turned Baptism into a human decision. How fair he was to his opponents on the right and on the left is
a question I have had to set aside, important though it has become to
present-day ecumenical theology. For now, the task is to understand
Calvin through the stand he took in the debates of the time, not to
praise him as a just or generous opponent.

One cannot say, of course, that gratuitous adoption is Calvin's
central dogma, as though everything else in his system were deduced
from it.[150] Rather, it is part of a complex of ideas, or (better) of images,
that shape the system from beginning to end. Neither is Calvin's
identification of Baptism as the symbol of adoption to be taken in a
reductive sense: the "mystery" of Baptism, as he properly calls it,
defies reduction to a single formula. Nevertheless, the Sacrament,
precisely as the symbol of adoption, does reflect that same complex of
ideas and images that shapes his entire theology: the immense goodness of the heavenly father (the wellspring of every good), the duty of
God's children to give him unceasing thanks (which is the duty of
piety), union with Christ as the only access to the father's goodness,
and the word of promise as the effective means by which Christ
becomes the bread of life. And the same complex of ideas will meet us
yet again in his thoughts on the Lord's Supper. For once God, by
Baptism, has received wayward children of Adam into his household
to be his own children, it remains for him to carry out the duty of a
good father, which is to feed his sons and daughters and to provide
them with all the necessities of life.[151]

---

[150]   "Free" or "gratuitous" is his frequent characterization of adoption (*gratuita
adoptio*). See, e.g., *Inst.* 1559, 2.14.5 (1:488). Sometimes, as in the very next section, he
speaks of sonship as a gift (*donum*) for all except Christ, as we have seen.
[151]   *De la Cene*, OS 1:504; TT 2:165.

FIVE

THE EUCHARISTIC OFFERING

*Once God has received us into his family, to treat us not
merely as servants but as children, he undertakes to feed us,
too, throughout the entire course of our life, so that he may
fulfill the role of the best of fathers, concerned for his children.
And even that was not enough for him: he wanted to assure us
of his unfailing generosity by giving us a pledge.*

The definition with which Calvin began his discussion of Baptism,
from the 1543 *Institutes* on, placed the first of two sacraments immediately under the image of the divine family. "Baptism is the sign of the
initiation by which we are received into the fellowship of the church,
so that, engrafted into Christ, we may be counted among God's
children."[1] The discussion of the second sacrament preserves the
familial imagery. The chapter on the Lord's Supper in the final edition
of the *Institutes* (book four, chapter 17) begins by declaring that the
heavenly father, having received them into his family, provides his
children with food.[2] Calvin liked to sum up the relationship between
the two sacraments by describing Baptism as the sign of adoption or
of entrance into the family, the Supper as the sign of the father's
constant provision of sustenance. The Catechism asks: "In what ways
are [the two sacraments] alike and different?" The answer is: "Baptism
is like an entrance for us into the church: it gives the testimony that we,

---

[1]   *Inst.* 1559, 4.15.1 (2:1303); cf. 4.15.12 (2:1313).
[2]   Ibid., 4.17.1 (2:1359–60); quoted as the epigraph to this chapter.

who otherwise are strangers and aliens, are received into the family of God and included in his household. The Supper, on the other hand, attests that God shows himself a father to us by feeding our souls."[3]

Pedagogically the contrast may well be effective. But in theology nothing is quite so simple, and the image of divine parenthood is not going to see us through all the intricacies. An editorial comment in the standard translation of the *Institutes* points out that most sections of the chapter on the Lord's Supper are composed of materials that originated in earlier editions, "skillfully woven into a continuous argument."[4] But this, I think, is kinder to Calvin than he deserves. The chapter is in fact even more of a patchwork than the chapter on Baptism, and the additions to the final revision by no means achieve a smooth argument; sometimes they add to an unevenness that was already present.

It appears to have been Calvin's first intention, in the 1536 edition, to order his main thoughts on the Lord's Supper by distinguishing three "uses" for which the Sacrament was instituted: to confirm faith, to awaken thankfulness, and to encourage mutual love.[5] To the three uses Calvin then added some reflections on worthy and unworthy participation, frequency of communion, Rome's withholding of the cup from the laity, and the Roman mass.[6] A little later, he commented also on the proper administration of the Supper.[7] But this arrangement was unevenly executed from the first, and by the final edition of the *Institutes* the appearance of the word "thirdly" at the beginning of section 38 probably mystifies most readers: it is a relic of an order almost lost. Or perhaps their puzzlement will already have been occasioned by the last sentence of the previous section: "This," Calvin concludes, "is the sacrament's second use, which pertains to outward confession." What happened to the first use? Calvin seems to acknowledge the problem by a slight change of adverbs: instead of the *hactenus* ("thus far") with which he once wound up the first use, he now says *antea* ("previously") to indicate that he has left the first use a long way back.

---

3   *Catechismus ecclesiae Genevensis* (1545), Q. 323, OS 2:133 (cf. pp. 142–43); TT 2:86 (cf. pp. 92–93). See also *Inst.* 1559, 4.17.1 (2:1360), and the passage from *De la Cene* quoted above (p. 123).

4   LCC 21:1359, n. 1.

5   *Inst.* 1536, OS 1:136–45, 145, 145–46, respectively; *Institution*, 139–48, 148, 148–49. Cf. *Petit traicté de la saincte Cene* (1541), OS 1:505–6; TT 2:167.

6   *Inst.* 1536, OS 1:146–49, 149–50, 150–52, 152–59; *Institution*, 149–53, 153–54, 154–56, 156–64.

7   Ibid., OS 1:161–62; *Institution*, 166–68.

Calvin's treatment of the Lord's Supper became increasingly burdened over the years with polemical digressions against Zwinglians, Roman Catholics, and Lutherans. This is not surprising. After all, as the Philosopher says: "We are all accustomed to address our inquiry not to the subject matter itself, but to those who disagree with us."[8] Aristotle thought this no bad habit, since it is objections that keep our inquiry going. The risk, however, is that someone else's questions may bury our own. This is what happened to Calvin, and to be faithful to my inquiry I must continue to look amid the polemics for Calvin's own eucharistic thought and its coherence with his total theological vision. I propose to take his own threefold scheme, but to combine the second and third uses into one. This, it seems to me, is where he himself leads us.

It was the first use of the Lord's Supper—to confirm faith in God's promise—that seduced him into ever-expanding controversies over the Real Presence, since the confirmation of faith is nothing less than Christ's offering of his body and blood in the Sacrament. If, by contrast, the second use of the Sacrament—to awaken gratitude—receives less attention, this may be partly because Calvin in effect goes over it again in his critique of the Roman mass. In the 1559 *Institutes* the critique becomes a separate chapter (book four, chapter 18). There Calvin replaces the sacrifice of the mass with an evangelical sacrifice of praise, which coincides with the second use of the Supper—and with the Zwinglian notion of a sacrament. Further, in his doctrine of a genuine, "eucharistic" sacrifice Calvin not only takes up the second use of the Supper but combines it with the third: to encourage mutual love. The spiritual gift of the holy banquet moves the communicants, on their side, both to gratitude and to love: indeed, obedience to the commandment of love *is* thanksgiving, which for Calvin is not only a liturgical but also an ethical concept. Hence in 1539 he actually added to his first thoughts on the sacrifice of praise the assertion that it includes "all the duties of love—duties by which, in embracing our brothers and sisters, we honor the Lord himself in his members."[9]

The Lord's Supper, as Calvin presents it, is thus the occasion of a twofold self-offering: in it Christ gives his crucified body to his people, and they in turn present their bodies as a living sacrifice to God, which

---

[8]   Aristotle, *De caelo*, 294B. This, I think, accounts for at least some of the lack of balance that Jean Cadier finds in Calvin (*La Doctrine calviniste de la sainte cène* [1951], 83).
[9]   *Inst.* 1539, CO 1:1032; cf. *Inst.* 1559, 4.18.16 (2:1443–44).

is their spiritual worship.[10] But, of course, neither self-giving—Christ's or his people's—takes place only in the Sacrament. We must therefore ask, first of all, what it means to call the Supper a "sacrament" if, as it appears, the Supper effects nothing that is not already happening. Then we can show how for Calvin the two-sidedness of the Lord's Supper—as pledge and public confession—exhibits both the twofold structure of a sacrament and the fundamental theme of grace and gratitude.

THE SUPPER AS SACRAMENT

The first use of the Lord's Supper is to confirm the promise that the Lord's body, once given up for us (*pro nobis semel traditum*), is now and always will be ours. He has been so engrafted into us, and we into him, that an actual exchange (*commutatio*) has occurred: his riches for our poverty, his strength for our weakness. The point of the Sacrament is that it promises these things by picturing them. As bread nourishes the body, so Christ's body is the food of our spiritual life. Similarly, the strength, refreshment, and good cheer that wine brings to the body Christ's blood imparts to us spiritually.[11]

These are the kinds of expression Calvin employs to describe how the Sacrament fulfills its first use. I have simply summarized his opening paragraphs on the Lord's Supper in the first edition of the *Institutes*. The language is intended to be edifying rather than exact, and it remains ambiguous, as far as I can see, whether the Sacrament actually offers us something or only confirms that we possess it already. I have drawn attention to this ambiguity in chapter one, and I will need to return to it again later and resolve it by some plainer statements. But two conclusions can safely be drawn at this stage. First, the Sacrament serves as a kind of instruction, an "object lesson," we might say: it confirms, attests, shows, signifies, teaches; and the communicants, on their side, recognize, learn, grasp, reflect, and consider. Second, what they are to grasp is not only that Christ died for them, but also that in some sense they have a continuing connection with his bodily existence. The Sacrament signifies, or points to, this mysterious connection.

---

[10]   This is how Calvin construes Rom. 12:1: "Intellexit enim [Paulus] spiritualem colendi Deum ritum . . . " (*Inst.* 1559, 4.18.16 [2:1444]).

[11]   *Inst.* 1536, OS 1:136–38; *Institution*, 139–40. Cf. *Inst.* 1559, 4.17.1–3 (2:1359–63).

To be sure, the fact that Christ's body is, as Calvin puts it, "ours" benefits us only because it was once given for our salvation. But when he asserts that Christ's body and blood are our food and drink, he evidently means the body and blood not only as broken or shed, but also as somehow "received." Christ says: "Take, eat." Calvin comments: "By bidding us take, he indicates that [the body] is ours. By bidding us eat, he indicates that it becomes one substance with us."[12] What Calvin does *not* say, however, is that this mysterious union with Christ is given exclusively in the Eucharist. On the contrary, we have seen already (in chapter three) that it is in fact the function of the gospel, according to Calvin, to make Christ ours, so that we might be engrafted into his body.[13] The mysterious communion that results was a matter on which Calvin wrote an important letter to his fellow reformer Peter Martyr Vermigli (1500–1562).

Calvin admitted the extraordinary difficulty of putting the subject into words, but he still managed to make some interesting observations about it. The communion in question is something subsequent to the union with Christ that was already effected by the incarnation, but antecedent to the communication of his benefits.

> As for my promise to write concerning the secret communication we have with Christ, I shall fulfill it less substantially than you have expected; for although it is a subject of great importance, I think that between ourselves it can be suitably defined in a few words. I forego speaking of the communication we have with God's Son by reason of his putting on our flesh, to become our brother by sharing the same nature. The discussion concerns only the communication that flows from his heavenly virtue and breathes life into us and causes us to grow together into one body with him. What I say is that the moment we receive Christ by faith as he offers himself in the gospel, we become truly members of his body, and life flows into us from him as from the head. For in no other way does he reconcile us to God by the sacrifice of his death than because he is ours and we are one with him. That is how I interpret the passage in which Paul says that believers are called into the κοινωνία [*koinonia*] of Christ (1 Cor. 1:9). The words "company" or "fellowship" do not seem adequate to convey his thought: it suggests to me the sacred unity by which the Son of God engrafts us into his body, so as to communicate to us all that is his. Thus we draw life from his flesh and blood, so that they are not undeservedly called our "food." How it happens, I confess, is far above the measure of my intelligence. Hence I adore the mystery rather than labor to understand it.[14]

---

12   *Inst.* 1536, OS 1:137; *Institution*, 140.
13   See pp. 82–86 above.
14   Calvin to Peter Martyr, 8 August 1555, CO 15:722–23.

Calvin is content to acknowledge that it is the divine power of the Spirit that pours this life from heaven to earth. But he does try an analogy to represent the Spirit's mysterious operation: while the body of Christ remains in heavenly glory, life flows from it to us as a root transmits the sap to the branches. Calvin then adds that there is also a second communication, which is the fruit or effect of the first: namely, our enrichment with Christ's gifts, which is likewise to be ascribed to the power of his Spirit. For Christ does not dwell idly in us but makes the power of his Spirit known in palpable gifts—patience, self-control, zeal for righteousness and piety, devotion to prayer, meditation on the future life.[15]

Calvin ends with a summing-up that reminds us that he has not, up till now, said anything at all to Peter Martyr about the Lord's Supper; he has been speaking of a mystical union effected rather by the gospel through faith. "Believers," he says, "come into this communion on the very first day of their calling. But insofar as Christ's life grows in them, he offers himself every day to be enjoyed by them." Calvin then adds: "This is the communication that they receive in the Holy Supper."[16] He cannot mean "only in the Supper." Like the initial gift of union with Christ himself, the gifts of the Spirit, too, are surely received by the preaching of the word. But Calvin does seem to intend at least a relative difference of function between preaching and the Eucharist: the first communication is associated chiefly with the gospel, the second chiefly with the Sacrament. And this, of course, is suggested by the eucharistic symbolism itself, which has to do with the growth and nurture of a life that is already there. In any case, it becomes very clear in the letter to Peter Martyr that there is a mystical communion with Christ, according to Calvin, even apart from what Christians some-times call "the Holy Communion," and he describes it expressly as a communion with Christ's flesh and blood. Union with Christ is not exclusively, or even primarily, a "sacramental" idea in the narrow sense. Neither is the image of Christ as the bread of life. This Calvin states categorically in his important exposition of John 6.

Jesus' great discourse on the bread of life, Calvin assures us, cannot have been about the Lord's Supper: it would have been absurd and untimely for him to discourse on the Supper before he had instituted

---

[15] Ibid., cols. 723–24.
[16] Ibid., col. 724. The switch from *communicatio* to *communio* and (in the very next sentence) back again is apparently without any change of meaning.

it. Besides, if to eat Christ's flesh meant to receive the Sacrament, then unbelieving communicants would receive life, and infants, who are barred from the Sacrament, would not. What, then, was in fact the subject of Christ's discourse? Calvin says it was about "the uninterrupted communication that we have *apart from* the use of the Supper," or "uninterrupted eating by faith." For "faith alone is the mouth and, so to say, the stomach of the soul."[17]

Now it may sound as if Calvin intended no more by "feeding on Christ" than simply "believing in him," and this would certainly obviate difficult questions about the meaning of Christ's flesh in the Johannine discourse. "Unless you eat the flesh of the Son of man and drink his blood, you have no life in you . . . . My flesh is food indeed, and my blood is drink indeed" (John 6:53, 55). This is a "hard saying," as even Jesus' own followers said (v. 60). But if "eating" were simply a metaphor for "believing," then to eat the flesh of the Son of Man and to drink his blood would be no more problematic than having faith in his words or in the deeds of his human existence. This is a conclusion that Calvin resolutely declines to draw. Instead, he invokes his distinction between "faith" and "the effect of faith,"[18] and makes it clear that the communion with Christ that faith effects is somehow a communion with his flesh and blood. Hence, although the discourse on the bread of life is not about the Lord's Supper, neither is it about a purely spiritual or cognitive relationship with Christ such as one might have with any other sage of antiquity.

But, of course, once it is established that "eating Christ's flesh" is not believing, the question must be asked: What, then, is it? What exactly can the strange expression "My flesh is food" possibly mean? Indeed, the question has become more intractable than ever precisely because the reduction of "eating" to "believing" had seemed to dissipate some of the strangeness. The text says: "The bread which I shall give... is my flesh" (v. 51). Calvin refuses what to many will seem the most natural interpretation: that Jesus is speaking only of the crucifixion that awaits him, and that to have life is to believe in the saving efficacy of his death. In Calvin's eyes, this cannot be a sufficient interpretation because the sacrifice once offered would be of no avail if we did not now "feast on the sacred banquet." He explains that there

---

[17]   Comm. John 6.53–56, CO 47:154–56 (my emphasis). For the phrase *de perpetua fidei manducatione* the French version (published the same year: 1553) has *de la maniere perpetuelle et ordinaire de manger la chair de Christ, qui se fait par la foy seulement.*" Cf. on John 6:63: *spirituale fidei os* (CO 47:159).
[18]   Comm. John 6.35, CO 47:145, translated on p. 74 above.

are two senses of the word "giving": first, there is the giving that takes place every day whenever Christ offers himself to us, and, secondly, there was the one and only giving that took place on the cross. The order in which Calvin mentions them is not intended to rank them in importance but follows the order in which they appear in Jesus' discourse. The two givings are inseparable and mutually dependent. The flesh of Christ is life-giving because in it everything requisite to salvation was accomplished. But it does not actually save us unless we draw life from it. And no redemption could have been wrought in Christ's flesh if it were not the "channel" of his own divine life.[19] Once again, an inadequate reading of the text has been disqualified—but not replaced with a clear alternative.

Calvin returns to the problem in his commentary on verse 63, Zwingli's favorite text: "It is the spirit that gives life, the flesh is of no avail" ("profiteth nothing," as the old King James Version reads). Calvin rejects the view of those who argue that Christ's flesh profits us as crucified, not as eaten. Quite the contrary, the crucified flesh must be eaten if it is to be of profit. The meaning of the text is that the flesh has its life-giving power not from its own earthly nature but from the Spirit: apart from the Spirit, the flesh is indeed of no avail. Christ is referring, then, simply to the *way* in which his flesh must be eaten. Anyone who stops at the earthly nature of flesh will find in it nothing but mortality. "But those who lift up their eyes to the virtue of the Spirit diffused throughout the flesh will feel (*sentient*) from the effect itself and the experience of faith that it is not for nothing called `life-giving.'" Where Christ adds: "The words that I have spoken to you are spirit and life," Calvin observes: "The word (*sermo*) is called `spiritual' because it summons us upward to seek Christ in his heavenly glory, under the leading of the Spirit, by faith, not by carnal perception."[20]

The appeal to experience in this passage is crucial. Calvin has still not achieved much clarity about "eating Christ's flesh"; he has again simply ruled out an inadequate reduction of the idea. But he does take the further step of inviting the reader, in effect, to examine her own experience. Whatever more there is in eating than there is in believing, it is something that the believer can sense and experience for herself as the result of raising her mind heavenward.

---

[19]   Comm. John 6.51, CO 47:152–53.
[20]   Comm. John 6.63, CO 47:159–60.

It is Calvin's favorite image of the fountain that seems to come closest to expressing his thoughts. Christ's discourse is about the life-giving power with which his flesh is endowed. But in verse 57 he turns to the principal cause or prime source of life, which is the Father. To forestall an objection, Christ says, "The living Father sent me, and I live because of the Father." For it might seem that by making himself the cause or author of life Christ takes from God what is his alone. He therefore grants that he only supplies to others what is given to himself from elsewhere. This, of course, is said with respect to Christ's flesh: for although the Father is the beginning of life, the eternal Word himself also is properly life. That he lives because of the Father does not apply to his "unclothed divinity": it is a description of the Son of God made manifest in flesh.

Calvin infers that there are accordingly three stages of life: "It should be noted that three stages of life (*vitae gradus*) are counted here. The living Father occupies the first place: he is the wellspring (*scaturigo*), but distant and concealed. The Son is next: in him we have, as it were, a fountain that is open to us (*fontem nobis expositum*), and through which life is poured to us. Third is the life we draw from him."[21] As Calvin has already asserted, life at this third stage is placed in Christ's flesh, so that it may be drawn from there.[22] The image is of a continuous stream of life gushing from its hidden source in the Father to the eternal Word, his Son, and then "channelled" to the believer through the flesh of the Word incarnate. "For as the eternal Word of God is the fountain of life (*fons vitae*), so his flesh, like a channel, pours out to us the life that resides intrinsically (as they say) in his deity."[23] This, to be sure, is an image, not an exact description, much less an explanation, and it does not harmonize perfectly with the image of eating. But it is a striking image and perhaps conveys some sense of Calvin's own "experience of faith" that required such language.

Where, then, does the Lord's Supper come in? Calvin tells us repeatedly that Christ is not here speaking of the Supper, and this is all the more remarkable because he does not hesitate to use the image of a "sacred banquet" to interpret Christ's meaning; and he has freely used what to many was eucharistic language when he spoke of

[21]   Comm. John 6.57, CO 47:156.
[22]   Comm. John 6.51, CO 47:152: "Quia vis illa arcana conferendae vitae, de qua loquutus est, ad divinam eius essentiam referri poterat, nunc descendit ad secundum gradum, ac vitam illam in sua carne positam esse docet ut inde hauriatur." This is the *secundus gradus* because here Calvin does not refer to the hidden source in the Father.
[23]   Ibid.

Christ's daily offering of himself.[24] The explicit connection with the Supper is made almost casually when Calvin remarks: "But at the same time I admit that nothing is said here that is not pictured (*figuretur*) and truly offered (*praestetur*) to believers in the Supper: indeed, Christ wanted the sacred Supper to be like a seal (*sigillum*) of this discourse."[25]

This, in short, is what makes the Supper a sacrament: not that it brings about a communion with Christ, or a reception of his body, that is not available anywhere else, but rather that it graphically represents and presents to believers a communion they enjoy, or can enjoy, all the time. Whatever changes there may have been over the years in Calvin's sacramental theology, he does not seem to have wavered on this cardinal point: the holy banquet is a sign and pledge of union with Christ.[26] The reason why it was instituted was not because something happens there that happens nowhere else, but because daily communion with the body and blood of the Lord is too mysterious to comprehend: it can only be attested and represented.[27] And it is always possible to have and to enjoy it more abundantly.

[24]   Ibid., CO 47:153.

[25]   Comm. John 6:54, CO 47:155. Calvin recalls this remark later in his comments on 6.56: "Nam sicuti ad externum signum inscite restringitur haec doctrina, sic tenendum est quod prius dixi, illic obsignari doctrinam quae hic habetur" (CO 47:156). The two words *figura* and *sigillum* are closely associated because a sigillum is a "little image" or, by transference, a seal bearing such an image.

[26]   See, e.g., Comm. Eph. 5.29: "Denique eam nostri cum Christo unionem hic Paulus describit, cuius in sacra coena symbolum et pignus nobis datur . . . . Ita ostendimus nullam nos in coena repraesentationem docere, nisi cuius effectus et veritas hic a Paulo praedicatur" (CO 51:225–26). Cf. *Inst.* 1559, 4.17.1 (2:1359–60). The bread is a *symbolum et pignus* of communion with Christ, not the *res ipsa* (*Consensus Tigurinus* [1551], OS 2:253; TT 2:220), but it is a *pignus* by which Christ actually communicates himself to us (*Secunda defensio piae et orthodoxae de sacramentis fidei, contra Ioachimi Westphali calumnias* [1556], CO 9:68; TT 2:274).

[27]   *De la Cene*, OS 1:505, TT 2:166–67. Four years earlier (1537) the Geneva Confession, of which Calvin and Farel were coauthors, stated: "La cene de nostre Seigneur est ung signe par lequel soubz le pain et le vin il nous respresente la vraye communication spirituelle que nous avons en son corps et son sang" (*Confession de la foy*, OS 1:423; LCC 22:30). Cf. the more detailed catechism published the same year: "Les signes sont le pain et le vin, soubz lesquelz le Seigneur nous presente la vraye communication de son corps et de son sang, mais spirituelle . . ." (*Instruction et confession de foy*, OS 1:412; *Instruction in Faith*, 70). The raison d'être of sacramental representation was set out in a passage added to the *Institutes* in 1543: because the mystery of union with Christ is incomprehensible, he sets it before us in a *figura et imago* (CO 1:991; cf. Inst. 1559, 4.17.1 [2:1361]).

THE GIFT OF GRACE: THE OFFERING OF
CHRIST

Once the idea of communion with Christ's life-giving flesh, effected through the word, has been presented as the heart of Calvin's gospel, his doctrine of the Eucharist is already half stated. The role he assigns to the Lord's Supper in the life of the church presupposes that communion with Christ is not whole and perfect from the very first, but subject to growth, vicissitudes, and impediments. He does not think of "receiving Christ" as a crisis decision, achieved once and for all, but rather as a magnitude subject to variation. In fact he is willing to say of receiving Christ what he refuses to admit concerning justification: it is partial (*ex parte*).[28] An infinitesimal faith in Christ is enough for receiving justification, but a fuller possession and enjoyment of Christ is always open to the believer. It is with this fuller possession that the Eucharist has to do.[29]

The very nature of the symbolism suggests to Calvin that the Supper is a matter of nourishing, sustaining, and increasing a communion with Christ to which the word and Baptism have initiated the children of God. To be sure, he makes no rigid, doctrinaire distinction between Baptism and the Lord's Supper: he recognizes the possibility that engrafting into Christ, normally the function of Baptism, may be effected in the second Sacrament.[30] Still, the eucharistic symbolism points, as a rule, to the deepening of a communion already begun; it is an aid by which the Christian, being already engrafted into Christ, may be united with him more and more, until the union is made perfect in heaven.[31]

The special reverence Calvin felt for the Sacrament of the Lord's Supper is too plain to be overlooked. Nowhere is the man's piety more clearly disclosed. The person of the living Christ dominates his reflections on the Sacrament, and yet the presence of the Lord remains

---

[28]   *Catechismus*, Q. 346, OS 2:139; TT 2:90. Cf. Calvin to Bullinger, 25 February 1547, CO 12:486–88.

[29]   On faith and justification: *Inst.* 1559, 3.11.7 (1:733); cf. 2.19 (565). On the fuller possession and enjoyment of Christ: *De la Cene*, OS 1:507, 517 (TT 2:169, 182); *Dilucida explicatio sanae doctrinae de vera participatione carnis et sanguinis Christi in sacra coena ad discutiendas Heshusii nebulas* (1561), CO 9:490 (TT 2:534–35).

[30]   The Supper is "adminiculum . . . quo inseramur in corpus Christi, vel insiti magis et magis coalescamus" (*Inst.* 1559, 4.17.33 [2:1407–8]). Normally, the ministers are to make sure that those to whom they give the Lord's Supper have already been incorporated into Christ by Baptism (*La forme des prieres et chantz ecclesiastiques* [1542, 1545], OS 2:39; *Calvin's Ecclesiastical Advice*, 165).

[31]   *Inst.* 1559, 4.17.33 (2:1407–8).

in the end a mystery to be adored, not captured in theological explanations. What Calvin wrote to Peter Martyr about ineffable communion with Christ in general is echoed in his language about the Eucharist, in which the communion is nurtured: he is content to marvel at what he cannot comprehend. Nevertheless the main features of his interpretation of the Sacrament can now be summarized. I put them in the form of six propositions with brief elucidations. And at this stage it should not be misleading to note how he defines his own standpoint in opposition to the views he finds defective in others, since it can now be shown how his positive intent determines the polemic and not vice versa.[32]

Six Calvinistic Propositions

1. *The Lord's Supper is a gift.* This is fundamental to the whole orientation of Calvin's thinking on the Sacrament. Nor is it by any means something obvious; it is precisely at this point that he parts company with Zwingli and stands in uncompromising opposition to Rome. I shall return to his estimate of the Roman mass later. Calvin found the Zwinglian position scarely less defective than the Roman Catholic. To Zwingli, the Supper was an occasion for thankful recollection of Christ's death, and so for taking one's stand with the Christian community: the celebration moved at the level of the imagination and the understanding, and talk about "partaking of Christ's body" could only be a metaphor for believing in his once-for-all sacrifice. Calvin certainly emphasized the place of thanksgiving in the Supper; it was the point from which he criticized the Roman mass. But the Zwinglian view made primary in the Sacrament what was strictly secondary,[33] and Calvin wanted to assert, first of all, that the body of Christ was once sacrificed so that believers might partake of it now. Christ gave his body on the cross; he gives it daily.[34] True partaking of

[32]   The propositions and elucidations (originally seven in number) were first drafted for an ecumenical meeeting of Lutherans and Presbyterians and published in 1968; reprinted in *The Old Protestantism and the New* (1982), chap. six, 112–15. Calvin avoids express mention of Zwingli and his followers by name, but the targets of his criticisms can usually be identified. On his sense of the mystery of the Sacrament, see *Inst.* 1559, 4.17.7, 10, 32 (2:1367, 1370, 1403); *Ultima admonitio ad Ioachimum Westphalum* (1557), CO 9:248; TT 2:490.

[33]   See pp. 105-6 above.

[34]   *Inst.* 1559, 4.17.1, 5 (2:1361, 1364). Of course, it is also true that partaking of Christ's body would have no saving significance had it not once been sacrificed (4.17.3, 5 [2:1362, 1364]). See also *Ultima admonitio ad Westphalum,* CO 9:241–42 (TT 2:482); *De vera participatione Christi in coena,* CO 9:486 (TT 2:529); *Optima ineundae concordiae ratio*

him as the bread of life is more than believing, as eating is more than seeing; the mysterious communion of believers with Christ's life-giving flesh is not faith, but a consequence of faith.[35] Indeed, the very concept of faith is itself at issue here: faith does not see Christ in the distance but embraces him.[36] The Supper is a gift; it does not merely remind us of a gift.[37]

2. *The gift is Jesus Christ himself.* This Calvin never tires of saying. The gift is not to be identified with the benefits (*bona*) of Christ; first and foremost the gift is Jesus Christ himself, who is their source (*fons*).[38] Nor is communion solely with Christ's divinity. In the Eucharist the church has to do with the whole Christ—indeed, in a special sense with his body and blood. For it was in his humanity that he won redemption, in his flesh, the "channel" through which his divine life flows to us. "It is not merely a question of being made partakers of his spirit; we must also participate in his humanity, in which he rendered all obedience to God his father. . . . When he gives himself to us, it is in order that we may possess him entirely. . . . Our souls must feed on his body and blood as their proper food."[39]

(1561), OS 2:292 (TT 2:574:). Sometimes Calvin speaks of a daily (or present) "offering" of Christ's body: e.g., *Defensio sanae et orthodoxae doctrinae de sacramentis* (1555), OS 2:265; TT 2:207. In all of these passages, the present giving or offering of the body is to us, not to God, and the full formula is: "Idem ergo corpus quod semel Filius Dei Patri in sacrificium obtulit, quotidie nobis in Coena offert, ut sit in spirituale alimentum" *Ineundae concordiae ratio*, OS 2:293 [TT 2:576–77]; cf. *Secunda defensio contra Westphalum*, CO 9:48 [TT 2:249]). Nevertheless, the thought of a eucharistic offering of Christ to God is not foreign to Calvin (see below, pp. 153-54).

[35]   *Inst.* 1559, 4.17.5 (2:1365). Receiving life from Christ is not a matter of mere knowledge (ibid.) or imagination (17.11 [1372]). Cf. pp. 73-76 above.

[36]   *Inst.* 1559, 4.17.6 (2:1366). Cf. pp. 71-72 above.

[37]   "Eos vero qui Coenam volunt externae solum professionis notam esse, nunc praetereo . . . . Unde sequitur, nisi in Deum respicimus, et amplectimur quod offert, nos sacra Coena recte non uti" (*Inst.* 1559, 4.17.6 [2:1366]).

[38]   *De la Cene*, OS 1:507 (TT 2:169–70); Comm. 1 Cor. 11.24 (CO 49:487). Cf. *Consensus Tigurinus*, OS 2:249 (TT 2:215); *Defensio doctrinae de sacramentis*, OS 2:269 (TT 2:222–23); *Secunda defensio contra Westphalum*, CO 9:72–73 (TT 2:280–81); *Inst.* 1559, 3.1.1 (1:537); *Ineundae concordiae ratio*, OS 2:295 (TT 2:578).

[39]   *De la Cene*, OS 1:508; TT 2:170. Cf. *Confessio fidei de eucharistia* (1537), OS 1:435–36 (LCC 22:168–69); *Inst.* 1559, 4.17.7, 9 (the passage in which Calvin appeals to Cyril of Alexandria), 33 (2:1367, 1369, 1405); *De vera participatione Christi in coena*, CO 9:470 (TT 2:507). Sometimes Calvin describes Christ's flesh as itself the *fons vitae* (*Ultima admonitio ad Westphalum*, CO 9:194; TT 2:417); more often it is the means by which life from the *absconditus deitatis fons* flows to us (*Defensio doctrinae de sacramentis*, OS 2:282; TT 2:238). From the first, Calvin believed that one of the "benefits" of the Eucharist is that it assures us of the vivification of our own flesh by Christ's: *Inst.* 1536, OS 1:143 (*Institution*, 146); *Instruction et confession de foy* (1537), OS 1:413 (*Instruction in Faith*, 70–71).

3. *The gift is given with the signs.* Once again a criticism of both Zwingli and Rome is implied. Against both, though for different reasons, Calvin levels the same accusation, that they misrepresent the nature of a sign. In the Roman Catholic theory of transubstantiation the sign is in effect transformed into the thing signified: the substance of the bread becomes the substance of the body. The symbolic relationship is destroyed by a failure to maintain the distinction.[40] In the Zwinglian view, on the other hand, sign and reality are divorced, or at least their unity is not clearly affirmed, since the body of Christ is absent from the Supper. This, too, in its own way, destroys the symbolic relationship, in which the sign guarantees the presence of what is signified. "Distinction without separation," the ancient christological formula, applies equally well to the sacramental union of sign and thing signified. Hence, when the elements are offered to us, Christ is offered to us with his body and blood. The signs present what they represent. They are not bare or empty signs but are joined with the reality they signify.[41]

4. *The gift is given by the Holy Spirit.* This is all that can properly be meant if one ventures to talk of a "spiritual" presence (or "spiritual" eating) in the Calvinist Supper. It should not be taken to mean that Christ is present only in spirit, or only in the believer's imagination. (Both these views have been erroneously attributed to Calvin, although he takes pains to deny them in all his major writings on the Lord's Supper.) In Calvin's view, it is precisely the body and blood of Christ that are made present to the believer by the secret power of the Spirit; by assigning the presence of the body and blood to the work of

[40]   *De la Cene,* OS 1:520, 526 (TT 2:185–86, 193); Comm. 1 Cor. 11.24, CO 49:487; *Ultima admonitio ad Westphalum,* CO 9:231 (TT 2:467); *Inst.* 1559, 4.17.14 (2:1376); *Confession de foy au nom des Eglises reformees de France* (1562), CO 9:769 (TT 2:159). Calvin was not averse to the idea (which he found in the Fathers) of a "conversion" by which the elements, though unchanged in substance, are set apart for sacramental use and in this sense are no longer common food (*Inst.* 1559, 4.17.14–15 [2:1375–77]). In later Reformed theology (and service books) the idea of a changed use was developed into a kind of prototype of modern Roman Catholic theories of transfinalization or transignification, as I suggested in a review in the *Christian Century* (84 [1967]:274). The affinity has been explored in detail by Jill Raitt (1971, 1972).
[41]   *De la Cene,* OS 1:509–10, 527–28; TT 2:171–73, 195–96. Cf. Comm. 1 Cor. 10.3: "Confundunt papistae rem et signum: divellunt signa a rebus profani homines" (CO 49:454). See also *Consensus Tigurinus,* OS 2:249; TT 2:215. Occasionally, Calvin asserts that the Lutheran *est* (the literal interpretation of the eucharistic words of institution) also destroys the relation of *signum* to *res* (e.g., *Ultima admonitio ad Westphalum,* CO 9:203; TT 2:428–29). I return to this point in chapter six, pp. 164-65. On Calvin's fondness for the formula "distinction without separation," see Wilhelm Niesel, *The Theology of Calvin* (1956), 247–49.

the Spirit he believed he could avoid any suggestion that Christ, if
there is a true communion with him, must somehow be enclosed in the
elements of bread and wine.[42] He held that the Holy Spirit is the bond
of union between the worshipper and the true, life-giving flesh of
Christ, and he admitted that the mind could not be expected to
comprehend what he thus proposed as an item of faith.[43] It follows that
the sacraments are strictly the Spirit's means or instruments: where
the Spirit is absent, the sacraments achieve no more than the sun
shining on blind eyes or a voice sounding in deaf ears.[44]

5. *The gift is given to all who communicate*, pious and impious,
believers and unbelievers. This is not to say that it makes no difference
whether we believe or not: if we receive the elements without believing, we receive them to our condemnation, not discerning the Lord's
body.

> Christ holds out this spiritual food, and gives this spiritual drink, to all.
> Some feed upon them eagerly, others disdainfully refuse them. Do the
> food and drink lose their nature because some reject them? . . . Nothing
> is taken away from the Sacrament: on the contrary, its truth and efficacy
> remain unimpaired even if the wicked (*impii*) go away empty from
> outward participation in it. . . . The integrity of the Sacrament, which
> the whole world cannot violate, lies in this: that the flesh and blood of
> Christ are no less truly given to the unworthy than to God's elect
> believers.[45]

6. *The gift is to be received by faith.* The sixth proposition rests on the
intimate connection of the sacraments with the word of God, and it is
directed, above all, against the impersonalization of sacramental
efficacy in medieval scholasticism. The Schoolmen taught that the
sacraments of the "new law" confer grace provided only that no

---

[42]   *De la Cene*, OS 1:530 (TT 2:198); *Ultima admonitio ad Westphalum*, CO 9:162, 164,
215 (TT 2:374, 376, 445); *Inst.* 1559, 4.17.33 (2:1405). But "spiritual" in this sense does, of
course, imply "not carnal" (not, that is, as though the body were chewed, swallowed,
and digested): *Ineundae concordiae ratio*, OS 2:294 (TT 2:578). Hence Calvin can also say
that the adverb *spiritualiter* is used for *two* reasons: *Consilia*, CO 10¹:157 (*Ecclesiastical
Advice*, 21–22). But it is nonetheless an actual communion with the body that takes place:
believing is not imagining (*Defensio doctrinae de sacramentis*, OS 2:282; TT 2:238), neither
is eating merely believing (*Secunda defensio contra Westphalum*, CO 9:74–75; TT 2:283–84).
Calvin speaks of both a presence of the body and a communion with the body (or
partaking of it), sometimes in the same passage (e.g., *Inst.* 1559, 4.17.32 [2:1404]), and he
prefers to qualify the presence or communion as "true" rather than "real," though he is
unwilling to quibble over words: spiritual communion is feeding on Christ in fact
(*reipsa*), not in imagination (*Defensio doctrinae de sacramentis*, OS 2:283–84; TT 2:239–40).
[43]   *Inst.* 1559, 4.17.10 (2:1370).
[44]   Ibid., 4.14.9, 14.12 (2:1284, 1287).
[45]   Ibid., 4.17.33 (2:1406–7). Cf. Comm. Gal. 3:27, CO 50:222.

obstacle of mortal sin is in their way. Calvin detected in this "pestilential" notion a superstitious attachment to the sacramental sign as a mere physical thing—and, indeed, an implicit denial of the cardinal Reformation doctrine of justification by faith. A sacrament received without faith cannot be a sacrament correctly understood as an appendage to the divine word or promise. The word could in fact achieve its ends without the sacramental seal.[46] When the word accompanies the sacrament, it must retain its essential character as proclamation; it is not a magical formula empowered to consecrate the elements even if mumbled in Latin. The sacramental word is not an incantation, but a promise. The eucharistic gift therefore benefits those only who respond with the faith that the proclamation itself generates.[47]

Calvin and the Lutherans

My explanations of the six Calvinistic propositions say nothing directly about Calvin's disagreements with the Lutherans. This is intentional. Rightly or wrongly, he always saw himself as Luther's kin, even as Luther's disciple. When he first became acquainted with the inner-Protestant controversy on the sacraments, Calvin's instinctive sympathies were more with Wittenberg than with Zurich, and he tells us that he did not even trouble to read Oecolampadius or Zwingli for himself. Later, he more than once professed his adherence to the Lutheran Augsburg Confession (although, naturally, he preferred the Reformed French Confession of 1559, of which he was himself the principal author). He was kindly regarded by Luther's circle and by Luther himself, and while he resided in Strasbourg he was treated as one of the Lutheran delegates to the conferences, organized under imperial patronage (1540–41), between Protestants and Roman Catholics. As Ernst Bizer remarked, among the Lutherans Calvin "passed for one of themselves."[48]

---

[46]   *Inst.* 1559, 4.14.14 (2:1289–90). See also pp. 103–4 above.

[47]   *Inst.* 1559, 4.14.4, 17.15 (2:1279–80, 1377). The word is addressed, not to the elements, but to the communicants (17.39 [1416]).

[48]   For documentation, see my essays "John Calvin on Luther" (1968) and "Strasbourg Revisited: The Augsburg Confession in a Reformed Perspective" (1979), reprinted (the former with a changed title) in *The Old Protestantism*, chaps. 2 and 15. Bizer's remark is in his *Studien zur Geschichte des Abendmahlsstreits im 16. Jahrhundert* (1940), 244. A recent and detailed examination of Calvin's statements on the Augsburg Confession will be found in Danièle Fischer (1984).

None of which is to say that Calvin merely parroted Luther's opinions on the Lord's Supper, or closed his mind to what he believed was sound in the opinions of the Swiss. In his first *Institutes* (1536), although he took the decisive step of adopting Luther's definition of a sacrament, he distanced himself already from some of the specific Lutheran beliefs about Christ's bodily presence in the Eucharist,[49] and as the Reformation progressed he took up his self-consciously mediating stance between Wittenberg and Zurich. He was able to do so because, in his own judgment at least, he had grasped Luther's key sacramental principle and had discovered that the Swiss, after all, did not so much reject it as fail to assert it clearly: the principle that sign and reality in the sacraments belong together. To begin with, Calvin had refrained from reading Oecolampadius and Zwingli precisely because he read in Luther that they left nothing in the sacraments but naked, empty figures.[50] But this, Calvin later decided, was unjust, and he repeatedly argued that belief in the union of sign and reality was the actual—and sufficient—bond of agreement in sacramental theology between the Lutherans and the Swiss. In 1554, for instance, when the Reformed pastor of the French congregation in Strasbourg was under attack, Calvin wrote to one of his chief Lutheran accusers:

> If Luther, that distinguished servant of God and faithful doctor of the church were alive today, he would not be so harsh and unyielding as not willingly to allow this confession: that what the sacraments depict is truly offered to us (*vere praestari*), and that therefore in the sacred Supper we become partakers of the body and blood of Christ. For how often did he declare that he was contending for no other cause than to establish that the Lord does not mock us with empty signs but accomplishes inwardly what he sets before our eyes, and that the effect is therefore joined with the signs? This much, unless I am greatly mistaken, is agreed among you: that Christ's Supper is not a theatrical display of spiritual food but gives in reality what it depicts, since in it devout souls feed on the flesh and blood of Christ.[51]

[49] For details, see Alexandre Ganoczy, *The Young Calvin* (1987), 139–45.

[50] *Secunda defensio contra Westphalum*, CO 9:51; TT 2:252–53. Calvin does not have a favorite term to convey the opposite of an "empty" sign; but since he speaks of the "efficacy" of the sacraments (e.g., in his *Defensio doctrinae de sacramentis*, OS 2:271 [TT 2:225]), it seems appropriate to use the expression *efficacious* signs, provided that the efficacy is taken in a strictly instrumental sense. Christ alone gives the signs their efficacy (Comm. Acts 1.5, CO 48:7; cf. Comm. Tit. 3.5, CO 52:431). One might perhaps equally well appropriate a term from J. L. Austin and call the Calvinistic sacraments "performative" signs, because their efficacy resides wholly in the divine promise. See further the discussion in chapter six.

[51] Calvin to John Marbach, 25 August 1554, CO 15:212–13.

By 1554, as Calvin's letter itself betrays, it was becoming more and more difficult to defend his interpretation of the fundamental point of agreement. Nevertheless, in the two turbulent decades between 1541 and 1561 he never wavered in his conviction that the essential point in sacramental theology was the union of sign and reality, and that it was a point on which concord between the Lutherans and the Swiss could readily be obtained, if only combativeness and rancor could be laid aside.

During Calvin's Strasbourg years (1538–41), the most eloquent testimony to his attempt at a balanced estimate of the eucharistic debate was presented in his *Short Treatise on the Lord's Supper* (1541), written in Strasbourg but published in Geneva. There is reason to believe that Luther himself may have examined the pertinent section and given it his approval.[52] In it, Calvin takes care not to side unequivocally with either party: each is gently faulted, and promptly absolved. The cardinal issue, in Calvin's eyes, was plainly the efficaciousness of sacramental signs, which Luther had affirmed from the beginning and the Swiss came to affirm later. Luther is reproached for using somewhat crude metaphors in defense of Christ's bodily presence in the Sacrament. But it is difficult to explain so lofty a matter without some impropriety of language. Zwingli and Oecolampadius, on the other hand, applied all their wits to discrediting the medieval idolatry of a crude, carnal presence. But they, too, were at fault: so engrossed were they in the task of criticism that they quite forgot to show what presence of Jesus Christ one ought to believe in, and what communion of his body and blood is received in the Supper. Luther inferred that they intended to leave nothing but naked signs without the spiritual substance. In Calvin's irenic judgment, this was not in fact what they meant: they did not deny the truth, but they did not teach it as plainly as they should. In their anxiety to maintain that the bread and wine are called the body and blood of Christ simply because they are signs of them, they were not careful to add that they are signs in such wise that the reality is joined with them. And now, Calvin believes (too sanguinely, as it turned out), all passion and bitterness can be laid to rest.[53]

I am not at all convinced that Calvin's attempt to excuse Zwingli and his friends can be endorsed.[54] Zwingli's "fault" is not merely that

---

[52]   See *The Old Protestantism*, 286–87, n. 53.

[53]   *De la Cene*, OS 1:527–29; TT 2:195–97.

[54]   See also Calvin's remarks in his *Secunda defensio contra Westphalum*, CO 9:59, 83, 91–93; TT 2:262, 295, 306–9.

he forgot to mention something of importance that he could and should have said plainly. Rather, his mind was of a cast that made it exceedingly difficult, if not impossible, for him to say what Calvin and the Lutherans wanted to hear. The cornerstone of Zwingli's thinking on the sacraments was that the Spirit has no need of "vehicles" by which to impart grace: the sacraments do not give grace but testify that grace has been given.[55] If Calvin was able to negotiate a consensus with Zwingli's successor, Heinrich Bullinger, that was because they agreed that God, who needs no sacramental means, nevertheless makes use of them freely and effectively. Consequently, the two reformers could expressly assert: "Although we distinguish, as is proper, between the signs and the things signified, yet we do not sever the reality from the signs."[56]

Sadly, the Zurich Consensus, which brought about harmony between the French and the German branches of the Swiss Reformed church, did not satisfy all the Lutherans. It became the occasion for a new and bitter round of eucharistic debates, in which Calvin, by achieving agreement with the pastors of Zurich, lost credibility with some of Luther's followers.[57] The chapter on the Lord's Supper in the final edition of his *Institutes* is partly the result of the endless altercations in which he became embroiled. He was drawn (reluctantly, so he said) into ever-expanding argument over issues on which he had never concealed his disagreement with the Lutherans: he held it impossible to take the words "This is my body" literally; impossible to suppose that Christ's body is everywhere; impossible so to construe

---

[55]   "Dux autem vel vehiculum spiritui non est necessarium . . . [S]piritus sua benignitate adest ante sacramentum, et perinde gratia et facta et praesens est, antequam adferatur sacramentum. Ex quibus hoc colligitur . . . sacramenta dari in testimonium publicum eius gratiae, quae cuique privato prius adest" (Zwingli, *Fidei ratio* [1530], SW 6,2:803–4; LWZ 2:46–47).

[56]   *Consensus Tigurinus*, OS 2:249; TT 2:215. The sacraments are *organa* "quibus efficaciter, ubi visum est, agit Deus" (OS 2:250; TT 2:216). Cf. the Augsburg Confession (1530), art. 5: "Nam per verbum et sacramenta tamquam per instrumenta donatur spiritus sanctus, qui fidem efficit, ubi et quando visum est Deo" (BELK, 58; BC, 31).

[57]   *Secunda defensio contra Westphalum*, CO 9:45–46; TT 2:247. See Tylenda (1974). The Lutherans by no means spoke with one voice. Quite apart from Melanchthon's alleged crypto-Calvinism, there were Lutherans who simply acknowledged their differences with Calvin and did not let them become grounds for breaking off fellowship (ibid., CO 9:58; TT 2:261). Even his two most energetic opponents disagreed with each other. Westphal held that the body of Christ is chewed by the teeth (he endorsed the notorious first recantation of Berengarius). Heshusius denied it, though he insisted that the body is received by mouth, and he thought that the union of the bread with the body was such as to render the formulas *sub pane* and *cum pane* improper (Calvin, *De vera participatione Christi in coena*, CO 9:469–70, 473; TT 2:506, 510–11).

the nature of his eucharistic presence that even the wicked take the body, when it is given them, in their mouths.[58]

These are not, of course, trivial issues. If, however, we are to remain faithful to our policy of looking strictly for what was of primary importance to Calvin himself, we will not let them distract us too much. Our reading of the *Institutes* must be guided by what he continued to insist upon as the main thing, both in Luther's mind and in his own. In 1555 he wrote:

> I know how many overstatements [Luther] let slip in debate. But whenever he wanted to commend his cause to devout and upright judges, what was it that he professed himself to be contending for? That he could not allow the sacraments to be thought of simply as outward badges of profession and not also as tokens and symbols of God's grace toward us; and that he judged it degrading to compare them with empty, useless pictures, seeing that in them God truly attests what he depicts and at the same time performs and fulfils by his secret power what he attests.[59]

This being Luther's actual concern, Calvin saw no reason for the Lutherans and the Swiss to let disagreement over the *manner* of Christ's presence in the Eucharist become, or remain, divisive; that could only be to change the crucial issue.[60]

> Since there is perfect agreement on the matter, what could be more ridiculous than to split the churches and stir up frightful commotions on the grounds that some think the bread is called the body because the body is presented (*exhibetur*) under it and with it, and others because the bread is not a deceptive, empty symbol, but a symbol to which its reality is joined, so that all who receive the sign by mouth and the promise by faith become truly partakers of Christ?[61]

---

[58]   Calvin himself (with variations in wording) singles out these dividing issues in his *Secunda defensio contra Westphalum* (CO 9:47–49, 91; TT 2:248–50, 307) and *Ultima admonitio ad Westphalum* (CO 9:183, 244; TT 2:402, 486). They are all facets or corollaries of the one fundamental issue: the mode of communion. I return to them in the final chapter.

[59]   *Defensio doctrinae de sacramentis*, OS 2:270; TT 2:224. Cf. *Secunda defensio contra Westphalum*, CO 9:91; TT 2:306–7.

[60]   See the references in the previous note.

[61]   *Defensio doctrinae de sacramentis*, OS 2:287; TT 2:244. Cf. *Ultima admonitio ad Westphalum*, CO 9:248; TT 2:491. In his treatise on scandals, Calvin argued that Luther, Oecolampadius, and Zwingli were agreed on "the sum of *pietas*" as a whole and should have been able to agree on the Lord's Supper. There was nothing any more, in calmer times, to prevent unity in the affirmation that sacraments are not empty figures, since their use is efficacious through the power of the Spirit, though there was still diversity of opinion over the mode of communication (*De scandalis* [1550], OS 2:214–16; *Concerning Scandals*, 80–83). This, however, was on the eve of the new eucharistic controversy; by 1559 Calvin was complaining bitterly that for some people the be-all and end-all of *pietas* was to enclose Christ under the bread (*Inst.* 1559, 4.17.33, [2:1405]), and that the doctrine of the papists was more modest (17.30 [1402]). Cf. *De vera participatione Christi in coena*, CO 9:473; TT 2:510.

Only this confession of Calvin's faith, not the tedious and acrimonious polemic, can open up a sound interpretation of his doctrine of the Lord's Supper in the final edition of the *Institutes*. And the same priorities reappear still later, in a brief reaffirmation of sacramental faith written twenty years after the *Short Treatise on the Lord's Supper*.

In 1561 he tried once more to lift up the fundamental point of agreement, as he saw it, in a gem-like appendix to a more diffuse polemical work. Titled *The Best Method of Obtaining Concord, Provided the Truth be Sought Without Contention*, it is the calm voice after the storm. Again Calvin discovers the crucial point of agreement in the belief that sacraments are not only marks of outward profession before humans but also testimonies and tokens of the grace of God, so that God is said to perform by the secret power of his Spirit what he depicts by the outward signs. They are not empty signs; it follows that in the Lord's Supper communion with Christ's body and blood is truly offered us. The body was not only given once to expiate sin, but is given daily for nourishment.[62] The sole question in dispute is the mode of eating. Calvin gives his own opinion on the question forthrightly enough. But once the proper limits are set up, he has no difficulty in affirming with the Lutherans that the body is given under, or with, the bread, or that we are indeed fed substantially with the flesh of Christ. [63]

If we ask why, for Calvin, everything turned around the notion of efficacious signs, or signs through which God acts efficaciously, the answer is plain: because it alone can adequately safeguard the gift character of the Sacrament. Calvin's uneasiness with Zwingli's sacramental theology carried him, in effect, over ground already traversed by Luther in the controversy with his onetime colleague Andreas Bodenstein von Carlstadt (ca. 1480–1541). Luther was shocked at Carlstadt's view of the Lord's Supper, which, Luther supposed, turned the Blessed Sacrament into a religious exercise. Instead of receiving the crucified and risen Lord, who offered himself with the broken bread and the poured-out wine, Carlstadt strove to focus his thoughts on Jesus of Nazareth suffering on the cross. In Luther's eyes, nothing less than the gospel was at stake: a gift of God was being made into a human work. For Calvin, too, the Sacrament was a gift of grace, and the gift was Jesus Christ. The signs could not be mere reminders; they were efficacious means of grace. Through the bread of the Supper the Lord who once gave his body on the cross gives it again and says,

---

[62]   *Ineundae concordiae ratio*, OS 2:291–92; TT 2:573–74.
[63]   Ibid., OS 2:292–93; TT 2:574–76.

"Take, eat." To make the Sacrament a profession of faith, as Zwingli did, is to diminish the Lord's giving of himself.[44] And Luther and Calvin agreed that the Roman Catholics, in their own very different way, also compromised the eucharistic gift.

GRATITUDE: THE OFFERING
OF THE CHURCH

In the final version of the *Institutes*, Calvin's critique of the Roman mass becomes a chapter by itself (book four, chapter 18). Unlike the preceding chapter, on the Lord's Supper, it retains the integrity of its earliest form: the insertions made in later editions do not interrupt the flow of the argument, and changes in the order of presentation are few and minor. Here, it seems, was a topic on which Calvin found no reason to alter his earliest opinions. True, the later insertions indicate a growing awareness of how the "papists" were responding to criticisms of the mass. At one point, for instance, we find this new sentence added in 1539: "I admit that they have a ready answer, in which they even reprimand us for misrepresenting them: they say that they are being accused of thinking what they have never thought and never could." But Calvin retracted nothing, and it is still a serious question

---

[44] For Luther's critique of Carlstadt, see his *Wider die himmlischen Propheten, von den Bildern und Sakrament* (1525), especially WA 18.136–37, 195–98, 202–4; LW 40:146–47, 206–8, 212–15. Whether Luther's attack on Carlstadt lacks understanding as well as charity, I cannot pause to consider here. As for Zwingli, Locher argues that Zwingli's "remembrance" (*memoria*) did not mean looking back to the past, but bringing the past into the present (Gottfried W. Locher, *Zwingli's Thought: New Perspectives*, Studies in the History of Christian Thought, vol. 25 [Leiden: E.J. Brill, 1981], 222–23). Locher cites the passages in Zwingli that expressly affirm a spiritual presence (*fidei contemplatione*) and concludes that "the character of the Lord's Supper as a *gift* is clearly stated" (p. 224). These, of course, are not Zwingli's only affirmations. They do caution us against oversimplifying his stand; he was not the helpless instrument of a *Werkteufel*. But perhaps there was more to his evangelical piety—and more to his celebration of the Eucharist—than he was able to thematize consistently in his theology, which other reformers subjected to acute criticism. See also H. Wayne Pipkin, "The Positive Religious Values of Zwingli's Eucharistic Writings," in E. J. Furcha, ed., *Huldrych Zwingli, 1484–1531: A Legacy of Radical Reform*, Papers from the 1984 International Zwingli Symposium, McGill University, ARC Supplement, no. 2 (Montreal: Faculty of Religous Studies, McGill University, 1985), 107–43. Luther, it should be added, argued expressly against Carlstadt (in the passages cited) that the "remembrance" of Christ in the Eucharist must be interpreted as an outward "proclamation" (1 Cor. 11.26); it belongs to the word, in which the forgiveness won on the cross is distributed. According to Calvin, "remembrance" implies only that Christ is not *visibly* present; but he is present to us by his *virtus* (Comm. 1 Cor. 11.24, CO 49:489). "Dico memoriam rei praesentis in coena esse" (Calvin to Bullinger, 25 February 1547, CO 12:481).

just how fair the Protestant reformers were to Rome's teaching on the sacrifice of the mass.[65] Once again, my limited design is to understand Calvin's own position through the polemic, and to see how his thoughts on the mass cohere with other parts of his system. The opinions expressed are not necessarily, as they say, those of the editor.

The Sacrifice of the Mass

Calvin must have drawn inspiration for his assault on the mass from Luther's *Babylonian Captivity*. The resemblances are too close to be merely coincidental, and Luther's sacramental thinking was distinctive, not least on the Eucharist. Luther singled out the sacrifice of the mass as the worst of the three captivities to which Rome had subjected the Sacrament of the Altar. (The other two were the withholding of the cup from the laity and the opinion that the elements undergo a transubstantiation.) The view that the mass is a good work and a sacrifice is not only in itself the worst abuse of all; it also brings a host of other abuses in its train, which have turned the Sacrament, as Luther puts it, into a profitable business.

Luther rested his central argument on the words: "This cup is the New Testament in my blood" (1 Cor. 11:25).[66] He took the word "testament" ($\delta\iota\alpha\theta\eta\kappa\eta$) to mean "last will and testament" — a promise made by someone about to die, in which a bequest is designated and heirs are named. Christ's bequest is the forgiveness of sins, and his

[65]   The insertion reappears in *Inst.* 1559, 4.18.5 (2:1434). For the discussion of the mass in chapter four of the first edition, *De sacramentis*, see OS 1:152–59 (*Institution*, 156–64). In the 1539 edition (chap. 12) and the editions from 1543 through 1554 (chap. 18), the mass was discussed in the chapter *De coena Domini*, as can most conveniently be verified from the *synopsis editionum* in CO 1:li–lviii; see p. lvi. Cf. *De la Cene*, OS 1:517–20; TT 2:182–85. Whether the Eucharist has a sacrifical character is a major item of discussion in present-day ecumenical theology, and the views of the Protestant reformers on the question have naturally been brought into the conversation. Francis Clark, *Eucharistic Sacrifice and the Reformation* (Westminster, MD: Newman Press, 1960), who is mainly interested in the critique of the mass by the English reformers (and in later, Anglo-Catholic misapprehensions about medieval "abuses"), provides a wealth of material on late medieval interpretations of the mass. I am not aware of any study of Calvin's views that is as detailed as Carl F. Wisløff's study of Luther, *The Gift of Communion: Luther's Controversy with Rome on Eucharistic Sacrifice*, trans. Joseph M. Shaw (Minneapolis, MN: Augsburg Publishing House, 1964). A brief article by Joseph N. Tylenda (1976) argues in general for the compatibility of Calvin's thought with a sacrificial intepretation of the Eucharist. In what follows I have taken another look at Luther's and Calvin's actual language about "offering Christ," developing the thoughts in my earlier article, "Do We 'Offer Christ' in the Lord's Supper?" (1959).

[66]   Luther, of course, took the parallel passage in Luke (22:20) to be original. (Its authenticity is disputed.) I have given the English of 1 Cor. 11:25 in the KJV; the RSV has "covenant" for "testament."

heirs are those who believe his promise. All the promises of God from
the beginning of the world pointed toward this testament of Christ, so
that some day God had to become human and die. For, as the Letter
to the Hebrews says, "where a testament is, there must also of
necessity be the death of the testator" (Heb. 9:16 [KJV]). The promise
or testament is accordingly, in Luther's eyes, the heart of a true,
evangelical mass; and anyone can see that these two, promise and
faith, go together, because faith is simply believing the word of
promise. When you go to mass, you go prepared, not to do something,
but to believe and accept all that is promised. We are like a penniless
beggar who is given a huge bequest from a very rich lord: no one
imagines that the beggar does a good work when he comes to collect
his gift. But what is supposed to happen in the Roman mass? They say
it is a good work and a sacrifice. And so, Luther comments, "we come
in our arrogance to give what we ought to receive: with unheard-of
perversity we mock the mercy of the giver by giving as a work what
we receive as a gift." "Therefore, just as distributing a testament or
accepting a promise is the very opposite of offering a sacrifice, so it is
a contradiction in terms to call the mass a sacrifice, for we receive the
one and give the other."[67]

In general, though a little less colorfully, Calvin borrows this line of
argument, but without its linguistic support: he had his doubts about
taking "testament" in the account of the Last Supper to mean "last will
and testament." In his commentary on 1 Corinthians (1546), he suggests a different linguistic association, which is perhaps equally
implausible: sacraments are called by the name "testament" because
they are *testimonies* of God's will to us. Calvin pledges to return to the
word *testamentum* in his commentary on the Letter to the Hebrews, if
the Lord grants him enough time.[68] The time was granted, and the
reader who looks into the later commentary (1549) will discover that
Calvin found the word being used by his author in a way that required
some justification. Strictly the Hebrew word *berith* means "covenant,"
not "testament," whereas the Greek *diatheke* ($\delta\iota\alpha\theta\acute{\eta}\kappa\eta$) means both.

---

[67]   Luther, *De captivitate Babylonica ecclesiae praeludium* (1520), WA 6.512–26, quotations at 520.33, 523.38; LW 36:35–57, quotations on pp. 48, 52. According to Luther, the
priests all imagined that their good work was offering up Christ to God (WA 6.522.24;
LW 36:50). He presented his idea of the evangelical mass as a testament in *Eyn Sermon
von dem neuen Testament, das ist von der heyligen Messe* (1520), in which he even compared
the Sacrament to a "requiem" (*begengniß*) Christ has made to help us remember him
(WA 6.358.26; LW 35:85).
[68]   Comm. 1 Cor. 11.25, CO 49:489.

God never made a testament or will under the law; God made a covenant, which is an agreement between parties who are alive and well. The necessity for Christ's death, therefore, cannot be proved either from the word "testament" or from the matter itself: that is, presumably, from antecedents to the New Covenant that are recorded in the Old Testament. Hence the argument in Hebrews 9:16 admittedly seems weak. Calvin defends the author of the letter by insisting that, as far as the word "testament" is concerned, he is simply playing on the secondary meaning of the Greek; but as for the matter, there is a genuine resemblance of the ancient covenant to a testament precisely because it was ratified by blood.[69] Hebrews 9:16 is thus justified partly as a play on a word, partly as the expression of a sound enough point. But Calvin himself makes little use of the verse in question. In the *Institutes* he does not, like Luther, launch his case against the Roman mass with the definition of *testamentum* as "last will," although he does allude to Hebrews 9:16 in the course of his argument.[70] He is content, rather, to take Luther's fundamental thesis: the Sacrament of the Lord's Supper is a promise and a gift, and its essential nature is therefore perverted by the pestilential belief that the mass is an offering to obtain forgiveness.[71]

Once again, as in his critique of merit, Calvin acknowledges that there have been "sounder Schoolmen," but he does not delay over their subtleties. He turns straight to his target, the Roman "antichrist" and his prophets, who have infected the entire world with the error that the mass is a work by which the priest who offers Christ, and those who participate in the oblation, merit God's goodwill. This is not just a popular opinion; the action and the words that accompany it directly imply a kind of appeasement of God. Calvin begins by listing five overlapping objections to this error and then proceeds to develop them one by one in the following sections.[72] First, the Roman mass dishonors Christ, who was appointed priest forever and needs no priests to succeed him. Second, it buries the cross, as though the effectiveness of Christ's sacrifice were limited. The cross of Christ is thrown down as soon as an altar is raised up. Are we allowed to sew more patches every day onto such a sacrifice, as if it were incomplete? Third, the mass consigns Christ's death to oblivion by adding to it as

[69]   Comm. Heb. 9.16, CO 55:113–14.
[70]   *Inst.* 1559, 4.18.5 (2:1434).
[71]   Ibid., 4.18.1 (2:1429).
[72]   Listed in ibid., 4.18.1 (2:1430); developed respectively in 18.2 (1430–31), 18.3–4 (1431–33), 18.5 (1433–34), 18.6 (1434–35), and 18.7 (1435–36).

many testaments as there are masses. Must it not follow, then, that Christ is slain repeatedly? Fourth, the mass robs us of the benefit of Christ's death. For who will think themselves redeemed by the death of Christ when they have seen a new redemption in the mass? Finally, the mass weakens and destroys the Sacrament by the very notion of making satisfaction or paying a price to God.

The first four of Calvin's objections are variations on a single theme: the perfect sufficiency of Christ's atoning death. Nothing should be allowed to divert attention from the sacrifice made once and for all on Calvary, but the finished work is in fact gravely impaired by any suggestion that further oblations are required. Now Calvin was candid enough to state the various ways in which his adversaries sought to turn aside these criticisms, which had become standard features of Protestant polemics. The Roman church's priests, it was said, are not Christ's substitutes, as though he were dead, but only his assistants (*suffragani*) in his own eternal priesthood, which therefore does not cease to endure. They do not offer different sacrifices, but repeat the same one many times. Indeed, some argue that the mass is not a repetition, but an application, of Christ's sacrifice. In any case, it is a sacrifice without blood, not, as Calvin alleged, a cruel slaying of Christ in a thousand places at once.[73]

The argument of the more subtle adversaries (the *subtiliores*) that the mass is an application, not a repetition, of Christ's sacrifice brought them very close to the Protestants. But it is here, I think, that the fifth and most Lutheran of Calvin's objections comes in: he still sees in the mass, even with this congenial qualification, a distortion of the nature of a sacrament. He already hints at this line of attack in developing his second objection, in the course of which he mentions the distinction between "repeating" and "applying." Christ's passion is applied not when it is confirmed by new oblations, but when its "fruit" is communicated to us by the preaching of the gospel and the administration of the sacred Supper. "This, I say, is the way in which the sacrifice of the cross is duly applied to us: when it is communicated to us to be enjoyed and we receive it in true faith."[74]

Calvin understands a sacrament to be by definition a gift, and therefore not an oblation to appease God—indeed, not a "work" at all. This he has said earlier in his chapter on the sacraments in general. The notion of an *opus operatum* (literally, "a work done") was objectionable

---

[73]   Ibid., 4.18.2 (2:1430), 18.3 (1432), 18.5 (1434).
[74]   Ibid., 4.18.3 (2:1432).

to him not only because, in the formula *ex opere operato*, it seems to imply an impersonal causality that bypasses the need for faith, but also because, from the viewpoint of the recipients, a sacrament is not something to be done at all. Even their receiving is what Calvin terms, a little oddly perhaps, an *actio mere passiva* (a "purely passive action"). Hence he concluded the chapter on the sacraments in general with a solemn warning against the nonsense of the sophists about an *opus operatum:* it is not only wrong but contradicts the nature of sacraments, which God so designed that believers, poor and lacking all good things, would bring nothing to them but the hand of a beggar (*nihil praeter mendicitatem*).[75]

The point made of sacraments generally is now applied to the sacred Supper and the terrible parody of it in the Roman mass. Here Calvin's language echoes Luther's sharp contrast between giving and receiving, but with a very interesting difference: Calvin goes on to stress more than Luther that turning the Supper into a work done has robbed it not only of its character as a gift, but of its corporate character too. Here is the crucial passage, which I need to quote at length. In the midst of it Calvin makes a striking shift from divine gift to corporate act.

> The Supper itself is a gift of God, which should have been received with thanksgiving. The sacrifice of the mass is supposed to pay a price to God that he himself is to receive as satisfaction. Sacrifice differs from the Sacrament of the Supper as widely as giving differs from receiving. And this is surely the most wretched ingratitude of humans that where they ought to have acknowledged the bountiful goodness of God and given thanks, they make God a debtor to themselves. The Sacrament promised that by the death of Christ we are not restored to life once only but continually made alive, for our salvation was then completed in every part. The sacrifice of the mass sings quite a different old song: that Christ must be sacrificed every day to do us any good. [Now Calvin's point shifts.] The Supper was to be distributed in a public gathering of the church, to teach us of the communion by which we are all bound together (*cohaeremus*) in Christ Jesus. The sacrifice of the mass dissolves this community and pulls it apart. For after the error came to prevail that there had to be priests to sacrifice in the place of the people, as though the Supper had been turned over to them, it ceased to be communicated to the church of believers as the Lord commanded. The door was opened to private masses, which suggest a kind of excommunication rather than the community established by the Lord. For when the little sacrificer is about to devour his victim by himself, he segregates himself from the entire company of believers. And in case anyone misunder-

75   Ibid., 4.14.26 (2:1303).

stands me, I call it a "private mass" wherever there is no participation in the Lord's Supper among believers, even if a large crowd of people are otherwise present.[76]

The two thoughts that are interwoven in this trenchant protest are: first, that the Eucharist is a gift; second, that the gift is a genuine meal, or, at least, given in the external form of a genuine meal.

Hence Calvin diverges somewhat from Luther even when, like Luther, he sets giving and receiving, in sharp opposition. The outward form of the Sacrament, for Luther, was the making of a last will and testament; for Calvin, it is participation in a feast. And precisely as a feast, the New Testament Eucharist stands in a twofold opposition to the Roman mass: it precludes the language of work and sacrifice, and it cannot tolerate any impairment of the sense of community. As Calvin saw it, it was a matter of the Protestant ecclesial consciousness against Catholic individualism (which is not how Gregory Dix saw it). Once the authentic Sacrament of the Lord's Supper had been transformed into the Roman mass, it was seen but once a year in mutilated form, when the people did receive communion, but only in one kind.[77] The Lord's injunction was to take the cup and divide it among ourselves (Luke 22:17). Paul spoke of a "breaking of bread" that has to do with the communion of the body and blood (1 Cor. 10:16). There is no Lord's Supper where, instead, one person seizes for himself what should have been done among many. And where several masses are celebrated in side chapels, the people are scattered instead of gathering in one assembly to recognize the mystery of their oneness.[78] In short, the Lord has given us a table at which to feast, not an altar on which to offer a victim; and he has not consecrated priests to offer sacrifice, but ministers (servants) to distribute the holy banquet.[79]

---

[76]   Ibid., 4.18.7 (2:1435–36). The necessarily corporate nature of the Sacrament led Calvin's church to abandon the practice of giving communion to the sick in their homes, a step for which the Lutheran Westphal rebuked him (*Secunda defensio contra Westphalum*, CO 9:102; TT 2:320–21). Actually, Calvin himself favored sick communion, arguing that it is not a private act but a continuation of the public Eucharist (Calvin to Olevianus, 1 December 1563, CO 20:200–1; cf. to Venceslas Zeuleger, 29 August 1558, CO 17:311–12).

[77]   *Inst.* 1559, 4.18.20 (2:1448). The minimal requirement of annual communion was laid down by the Fourth Lateran Council (1215).

[78]   Ibid., 4.18.8 (2:1437).

[79]   Ibid., 4.18.12 (2:1440): "Mensam ergo nobis dedit, in qua epulemur; non altare super quod offeratur victima; non sacerdotes consecravit, qui immolent: sed ministros, qui sacrum epulum distribuant." In section 10 Calvin admits that some of the ancient fathers can be cited in support of a sacrificial mass, but he explains that they meant only a remembrance of the one sacrifice on the cross (1438).

The Sacrifice of Praise

And yet, for all the severity of his attack on the sacrifice of the mass, as the Roman church understood it, Calvin had no wish to exclude sacrificial language entirely from the evangelical Eucharist. Believers do sacrifice to the Lord and offer a pure oblation.[80] In a sense, they even offer Christ. Here, too, Calvin may have been picking up a hint from Luther. In his *Babylonian Captivity*, Luther found a modest place for sacrificial language in the Sacrament of the Altar and even for talk of good works, if a distinction is drawn between the mass itself and the prayers of the mass. The mass proper is the testament, which needs to be received, not offered. But we do, of course, offer prayers in the mass, and these may even be called "the works of the mass." The important thing is not to confuse mass and prayer, sacrament and work, testament and sacrifice: the one descends, the other ascends. That is to say, the one comes to us from God through the ministry of the priest and requires us to believe, while the other proceeds from our faith, through the priest, to God and requires him to listen.[81]

In his *Treatise on the New Testament*, published earlier the same year (1520), Luther had reflected much more fully and boldly on the sacrifice that has a place in the Eucharist. Since the treatise was in German, and Calvin knew no German, he cannot have been directly influenced by it in its original form. Still, it is natural enough to compare its statements on sacrifice with Calvin's, quite apart from questions of influence. Luther starts from the principle that in the Sacrament it is God who gives: we should be careful not to presume that we give something to God. But he goes on to insist that we are nevertheless to bring the spiritual sacrifice of prayer, praise, and thanksgiving, and of our very selves. Here is a sacrifice that every believer can and should make, since we are all spiritual priests. It can be made anywhere and at any time, even apart from the mass; it is made with special force and effect, however, in company with others. Now (Luther goes on) we do not offer this sacrifice before God by ourselves: we lay it upon Christ, insofar as we trust that he is our priest in heaven. Strictly, then, we do not offer Christ, but Christ offers us; or, we offer ourselves *with* Christ, and he offers himself *for* us in heaven.

---

[80]   Ibid., 4.18.4 (2:1433). The concluding words "de qua [sc. oblatione] mox dicetur" point forward to sections 13 and 16–17.
[81]   *De captivitate Babylonica*, WA 6.522.14, 526.10; LW 36:50, 56. Luther also thinks it appropriate to speak of "offering" the bread and wine for blessing; but once consecrated, they are no longer offered but received as a gift from God (525.1; 36:54).

In this sense, it is quite legitimate to call the mass a "sacrifice." But Luther's thoughts carry him a step further (he is thinking out loud, as we say): he finally ventures to assert that, if we move Christ by our prayers to offer himself for us, then we do, in a way, offer Christ to God. By this somewhat roundabout route, sacrificial language is retrieved—by connecting it not directly with Christ's propitiatory death but rather with his intercessory work on the grounds of his death. The key formula is this: "We offer Christ to God—that is, we give him cause and move him to offer himself for us and us with him." As usual, Luther comes up with a suitably graphic illustration for a complicated train of thought: I am simply moving the king's son to present my petition to his father.[82] That is what it means to say that believers "offer Christ" in the Sacrament of the Altar.

In his commentary on a passage in the Book of Numbers (Num. 19:1-10), Calvin too speaks of "offering Christ," and he means by the expression much the same as Luther. He is trying to uncover the obscure spiritual meaning of the Lord's commandment to slay a red heifer, which was then to be burned outside the camp together with its skin and dung. Calvin dismisses the fantasies of those who speculate on the details ("I would rather be ignorant than assert anything doubtful"), but he does not doubt that the ritual was a figure whose truth was fulfilled in Christ. What catches his attention in particular is that the whole people were instructed to bring the heifer for sacrifice. And this suggests to him the fact that each of us should offer Christ to the father (necesse est ut Christum quisque Patri offerat). "For although he alone offered himself, and indeed once for all, nevertheless a daily offering, effected by faith and prayers, is commanded of us." Calvin hastens to add that this is not the kind of offering that the papists have invented, who turn the Supper into a sacrifice, imagining that Christ must be daily slain if his death is to profit us. Rather, by the offering of faith and prayer we apply to ourselves the virtue and fruit of Christ's death. According to Calvin, there is, in fact, a clear distinction between two offerings in this passage. Though they bring it, the people are not permitted to slay the heifer; that is the peculiar office of the priest. The people made their offering indirectly (mediate), by the hand of the priest. And that is how it is today: "To propitiate God, we set Christ before

---

[82]   Von dem neuen Testament, WA 6.368–72; LW 35:98–103. See especially WA 6.371.24; LW 35:102: " ...und damit Christum fur gott opffern, das ist, yhm ursach geben und bewegen, das er sich fur uns und uns mit yhm opffert." Initially, Luther apparently takes the illustration (360.15; 35:99) to preclude any thought of offering Christ, but later the language of "moving" is used to explain and justify exactly this thought, as the quotation makes clear.

his face. But it is necessary for Christ himself to come between and to discharge the office of priest."[83]

Did Calvin never realize how amazingly close this language brought him to the thinking of the more subtle "papists"? Perhaps not. But his comments on Numbers 19:2–3 cannot be taken for his central thought on the eucharistic sacrifice, intriguing though they are. In the *Institutes*, he makes a somewhat different distinction between two kinds of sacrifice or offering. He begins from the limiting principle that not every sacred ceremony or religious action is a sacrifice, but only those in which something is offered to God. He then argues that in the Old Testament rituals two kinds of offering must be distinguished. An offering was either intended to make satisfaction for sin, or else served as a "symbol of divine worship and an attestation of religion." The second kind may take the form of supplication, or thanksgiving, or simply an exercise of piety in renewing the covenant, and includes burnt offerings, libations, oblations, first fruits, and peace offerings. How well this venture into Old Testament scholarship holds up may be open to question. What, for instance, does Calvin mean by "oblations," seeing that he has already called the first kind of sacrifice an "oblation"? Be that as it may, the general contrast between two types of offering suggests to him, by anagogical interpretation, a useful distinction in speaking of Christian sacrifices. He proposes to call the two types of Christian sacrifice propitiatory, or a sacrifice of expiation, and eucharistic, or a sacrifice of praise and reverence.

There has been but one propitiatory or expiatory sacrifice to appease God's wrath: it was prefigured under the law and accomplished once and for all by Christ alone. The eucharistic sacrifice, by contrast, is continual and takes place wherever God's name is known. In the words of Malachi's prophecy: "From the rising of the sun to its setting my name is great among the nations, and in every place incense shall be offered to my name, and a pure offering."[84] And so we come back

---

[83]   Comm. Num. 19.2–3 , CO 24:333–34.

[84]   *Inst.* 1559, 4.18.13 (2:1441–42), 18.16 (1444). Calvin actually inverts the order in which he had mentioned the Old Testament prototypes, and he gives the eucharistic sacrifice Greek epithets (λατρευτικόν, σεβαστικόν, εὐχαριστικόν). The two types of sacrifice were differentiated in the very first edition of the *Institutes*. My exposition follows the last edition, in which the material was amplified without substantive change. Section 14 repeats the accusation that the Roman mass is blasphemy against this one sacrifice; the sale of masses even recalls Judas's betrayal of Christ for money. Section 15 invokes Plato's support against the absurdity of human propitiatory offerings. Calvin takes the second verb in Mal. 1:11 to be in the future tense (Lat. *offeretur*), whereas in previous editions he had construed it as present (*offertur*), as does the RSV.

to a familiar theme: the sacrifice of thanksgiving is presented to God only by those who, loaded with his boundless favors, repay him with their whole self and everything they do.[85] Note that Calvin is not speaking of a merely liturgical sacrifice that occurs only in the course of public worship: he is speaking of the entire existence of the Christian, or of the church, an existence that public worship enacts and confirms. The eucharistic sacrifice means prayer and praise, but also whatever we do to worship God, including the duties of love; for when we embrace our brothers and sisters in love, we honor the Lord himself in his members. Kindness and sharing are offerings that please God; all the good works of believers are spiritual oblations (*hostiae*). "All these things finally depend on that larger sacrifice by which we are consecrated in body and soul as a holy temple to the Lord . . . , so that everything in us may serve his glory and be filled with zeal to increase it."[86]

The sacrifice of praise, so understood, belongs to the *esse* or essence of the church, defining its very being. "It is so necessary to the church," Calvin says, "that it cannot be absent from it."[87] But, equally, it belongs to the very essence of public worship: "The Lord's Supper cannot be without a sacrifice of this kind. . . . From this duty of sacrificing, all Christians are called a 'royal priesthood' (1 Pet. 2:9)."[88] In short, the eucharistic sacrifice defines the church as a royal priesthood, whose sacred office is represented but not exhausted in the words and actions of the holy banquet. The church is a priestly, eucharistic community. What makes it such is, of course, the expiatory sacrifice of Christ. Hence, while the eucharistic sacrifice in itself has nothing to do with appeasing God's wrath but is concerned solely with magnifying and exalting God,[89] it is certainly a proclamation of Christ's atoning death (1 Cor. 11:26), and we do not appear before God with our gifts apart from Christ's intercession. Calvin does not say here that by our prayers we offer Christ, but rather that he is our intercessor, our high priest who opens an access for us, and even the altar on which we lay our gifts. He it is who made us a kingdom of priests to the father (Rev. 1:6).[90] The eucharistic sacrifice thus arises out of the two parts of Christ's priestly office. For we have no access to God except by the

[85]   Ibid., 4.18.13 (2:1441).
[86]   Ibid., 4.18.16 (2:1444).
[87]   Ibid.
[88]   Ibid., 4.18.17 (2:1445).
[89]   Ibid., 4.18.16 (2:1444)
[90]   Ibid., 4.18.17 (2:1445).

sacrificial death of Christ in our place; in this sense, the dignity of the priesthood fits him alone. And yet he is also our eternal intercessor, who shares the dignity of the priesthood with us: we are priests in him, offering ourselves and all that is ours to God.[91]

Calvin's doctrine of the Lord's Supper is a complex mixture of several motifs. Even when one tries to focus on a single category, such as "sacrifice," it is difficult to achieve perfect clarity and consistency because words are being used equivocally. Suppose we accept Calvin's general definition of a sacrifice as "anything that is offered to God." The sacrifice Christ is said to have made on the cross is still an offering of a different sort than he makes daily, according to Calvin, in heaven. Again: it is one thing to offer a sacrificial victim, another thing to offer a sacrifice of praise. And language is being stretched to the breaking point if one says that we "offer Christ" simply in the sense of moving him by our petitions to present himself before God the Father.

The distinction between a propitiatory and a eucharistic sacrifice helps even if it runs counter to our own usage, in which the "eucharistic sacrifice" commonly means the propitiatory sacrifice of the mass. But, quite apart from this difficulty, the distinction perhaps obscures Calvin's own perception of the Sacrament as in fact the occasion for *two* acts of self-giving: Christ's giving of himself to the church and the church's giving of itself to God. It is this double self-giving that makes the Supper both embody and represent the perpetual exchange of grace and gratitude that shapes Calvin's entire theology. The sacred banquet prepared by the father's goodness is the actual giving, not merely the remembering, of a gift of grace, and precisely as such it demands and evokes the answering gratitude of God's children.

---

[91]   Ibid., 2.15.6 (1:501–3); cf. 16.16 (524–25). The bond between the two parts of Christ's priesthood lies in the fact that his intercession is founded on his sacrifice (Comm. 1 Tim. 2.6, CO 52:272). On the differences between Calvin's and Luther's interpretations of the royal priesthood, see my essay "Priesthood and Ministry in the Theology of Luther" (1965), reprinted with revisions in *The Old Protestantism*, chap. 5; see especially the concluding section.   There is an excellent discussion of the church's thankful self-offering in Ronald S. Wallace, *Calvin's Doctrine of the Christian Life* (1959), part 1.

SIX

THE MYSTICAL PRESENCE

*It is true that believers are joined together by the blood of
Christ, so that they become one body .... And I hear what Paul
immediately adds as a kind of explanation [1 Cor. 10:17]: that
we are all made one body because we partake together of the
same bread.*

In his *Humble Exhortation* to the Emperor Charles V and the princes
and other orders meeting at the Diet of Speyer (1544), Calvin tried to
make clear what exactly was distinctive about the reformation with
which he and his friends were identified. It was certain, he wrote, that
they differed only in this: they educated people more effectively in
true humility and gratitude, leading them to renounce all confidence
in themselves and to ascribe every good thing they possessed, as in
truth they should, to the kindness of God.[1] It would be hard to come
up with any other formula that better expressed Calvin's Calvinism
than this. Of course, it is always self-incriminating to claim that one
has more humility, or is more grateful, than others. But at least the
program and the priorities are clear. The practical end in view is
nothing but the true humility and thankfulness that constitute piety.
And the ground on which piety rests is the recognition that God alone
is the source of good. The Calvinistic motto, certainly, is that the chief
human end is to glorify God, but God, Calvin believed, is treated with

---

[1]   *Supplex exhortatio ad invictiss. Caesarem Carolum Quintum*, etc. (published 1543),
CO 6:484; TT 1:160.

the honor he deserves when he is recognized as the author of all good things. "It follows that our receiving them all from his hand should be attended with continual thanksgiving."[2] Sometimes Calvin even wondered if he insisted too much on the mercy of God—as though it were uncertain or obscure. But he decided that the point needed to be insisted on at greater length.[3] And that has been my own warrant in this book for returning repeatedly to the fatherly goodness of God.

A consistently "eucharistic theology," though the term was not his, was the goal from which Calvin never let himself be distracted. His fiercest polemic was reserved for those he perceived to be compromising the first principles of a eucharistic theology: that God alone is the fountain of good, and that the humanity of Jesus Christ is the only access to the fountain. His relentless campaign against the arrogance of human "works," which often strikes the outsider as demeaning to humanity, can be properly grasped only as the obverse of his confession of the divine goodness, in which alone the source of authentic human activity must be found. And even the believer's participation in the humanity of Christ is not an option that he or she could equally well have declined: it is a gift given by the Spirit through the efficacious power of the word proclaimed and made visible in the sacraments.

The Lord's Supper, then, although Calvin described it a little misleadingly as an "appendage" to the gospel, was for him a dramatic presentation of all that the gospel proclaims. In the Sacrament God does still more clearly what he always does, providing his children with the bread of life; and they in turn enact the meaning of authentic human existence as a continuous sacrifice of praise. The contrast sometimes alleged between an evangelical piety and a sacramental piety[4] finds no support in Calvin. In particular, the "uncongenial foreign element" that Hodge discovered in Calvin's doctrine of the

[2]   *Inst.* 1559, 3.20.28 (2:889).
[3]   Ibid., 3.14.6 (1:772). This and the preceding quotation provided me with two of my epigraphs for the book. Micah 7.18 ("Who is a God like thee, pardoning iniquity . . . ?") suggests to Calvin that the glory of God shines chiefly in God's prevenient good will to sinners, and he adds characteristically: "Nisi enim simus certo persuasi de eius misericordia, nulla vigebit in nobis pietas . . . . Reverentia igitur Dei et cultus eius pendent a sensu bonitatis et gratiae" (Comm. Mic. 7.18, CO 43:428–29).
[4]   For example, the contributors (E.S. Abbott et al.) to *Catholicity: A Study in the Conflict of Christian Traditions in the West* (Westminster: Dacre Press, 1947) assumed that those who are saved by faith alone are likely to maintain their relationship with God "outside the frame-work of the sacramental life" (p. 25). This is said from an Anglo-Catholic perspective, but the contrast expressed cuts across party lines and could equally well be documented from liberal, evangelical, or neoorthodox sources.

Lord's Supper is already present in Calvin's gospel.[5] To the question whether there is a true communion with the body and blood of Christ in the Lord's Supper, he answers in effect: yes, and apart from the Supper, too. Any who wish to set evangelical and sacramental religion in sharp opposition to each other must define both "gospel" and "sacrament" very differently than Calvin did, and it may remain a puzzle to them why he thought that Christians should gather to celebrate the Sacrament at least once a week.[6]

If I have now reached my goal of showing the eucharistic shape of Calvin's entire theology, there is no need to summarize the preceding chapters in detail. But I must admit that I have kept to my course only by leaving out a great deal.[7] My main purpose, moreover, has been to let Calvin speak—as far as possible, in his own words—not to criticize or to defend him, and I do not wish to change the mode of discourse too much in this concluding chapter. I recognize that the present-day systematic theologian will have misgivings about Calvin's favorite image of the Divine Father. I have not tried to uncover any dark Freudian secrets beneath his obsession with father language. I have not addressed the question whether "father," along with "king" or "sovereign," is a worn-out religious symbol, or the older theology's more radical question whether personal language, masculine or feminine, is fittingly applied to the mysterious ultimate Ground of Being. Much less have I paused to inquire whether, in general, the human encounter with the cosmos is plausibly symbolized as an encounter with paternal love. Some may think that, when measured by the test of human experience, the better symbol might be the implacable despot of vulgar Calvinism, whom we all too complacently deplore. These are all questions for the discipline of dogmatic, systematic, or constructive theology, which these days must view every Christian formula in a much wider experiential context than Calvin dreamed of, and must candidly ask whether our symbolic preferences have more

---

[5]   See p. 5 above.

[6]   It would of course be unhistorical to assert that infrequency in celebrating the Lord's Supper is necessarily symptomatic of undervaluing the Sacrament. Leigh Eric Schmidt has shown an interesting correlation of sacramentalism with revivalism in the communion seasons of the Scottish tradition, in which sacramental festivity was in part a product of infrequent celebration: Leigh Eric Schmidt, *Holy Fairs: Scottish Communions and American Revivals in the Early Modern Period* (Princeton, NJ: Princeton University Press, 1989).

[7]   Some of the themes passed over in the lectures I have now, in the published version, tried to explore in substantive notes that need not distract the reader from the main argument.

to do with our limited situation, or even our own deep wishes, than with an absolute revelation from God.

I shall not even presume in this closing chapter to make a detailed case for the importance of Calvin's eucharistic thought to his own church, or to argue for its pertinence to ecumenical dialogue (though I do in fact believe his voice needs to be heard in both of these two theological forums). Rather, I return at last to the two main internal problems that I mentioned in the first chapter and then quietly set aside—or at least kept at arm's length, though never quite out of view. The questions addressed to him by his critics in his own day, and still mooted among scholars today, have to do with the efficacy of sacramental signs and the sacramental presence of Christ's body and blood. After all that has now been said, particularly in chapter five, can these questions be considered finally answered? Much, it seems to me, turns around the precise way in which the questions are formulated. No one who identifies sacramental mediation with the Roman Catholic doctrine of *ex opere operato* efficacy, or who accepts the Lutheran doctrine that there is no Real Presence without a *manducatio oralis* (orally consuming the body), will expect to find either doctrine in Calvin, who expressly rejected them both as mistaken. But it is still possible that he may finally have worked out coherent alternatives that affirm unequivocally the efficacy of the sacraments and the reality of Christ's bodily presence in the Eucharist, despite the admitted wavering of his earliest endeavor (in the 1536 *Institutes*). It is also possible, of course, that his stand remains problematic, and this is a possibility I shall glance at in conclusion. It would be manifestly wrongheaded to request a precise mechanical diagram from someone who held the Sacrament of the Lord's Supper to be a mystery. But it is reasonable to expect that any theologian worth his or her salt will be able to show the difference between a mystery and a muddle.

EFFICACIOUS SIGNS

Why would anyone continue to think that by 1539, say, Calvin still assigned no real efficacy to the sacraments? There are four main reasons. In the light of what we have shown of Calvin's sacramental theology, the first three reasons can perhaps be laid to rest. First, the Roman Catholic critics argued (and still do) that the Reformation's emphasis on faith robbed the sacraments of all objectivity. This, of course, is the Catholic riposte to Protestant rejection of the scholastic *ex opere operato:* the doctrine that sacraments are effective causes of grace simply by reason of their being duly performed, provided only that the recipient does not put the obstacle of mortal sin in the way.[8] Calvin agreed with the Lutheran principle, forcefully affirmed by Luther himself in his *Babylonian Captivity*, that there is no sacrament without faith (*nullum sacramentum sine fide*).[9] When Bullinger accused him of binding grace to the sacraments, just like the papists, Calvin replied that the grace of God is indeed tied to the sacraments, not temporally or spatially, but only "insofar as one brings the vessel of faith to obtain what is there depicted."[10] This, however, is not to be construed as though God, in Calvin's view, gives his grace only where he comes across someone who has faith. Nothing could be more totally foreign to Calvin's way of thinking than the notion that God, as he puts it, sits in a watchtower waiting to see how things will chance to turn out.[11] If the administration of a sacrament is met by faith, it can only be a faith that God has already given and intends to confirm—precisely by the sacrament itself. The issue, accordingly, concerns the finality, not the objectivity, of a sacrament: what it gives is not some mysterious power, but the increase of faith.[12] And as a matter of fact the grace is offered even to those who do not believe; therein lies the "integrity" of the sacrament.[13] This is, to be sure, a different understanding of sacramental efficacy from the Roman Catholic view, but it is not a collapse into subjectivity.

Secondly, in the Roman Catholic view, the entire notion of a sacrament was undermined by Calvin's repeated insistence that sal-

---

[8]   The subjective condition for the reception of sacramental grace in medieval theology is briefly discussed in Reinhold Seeberg, *Lehrbuch der Dogmengeschichte*, vol. 3, 2d and 3d rev. ed. (Leipzig: A. Deichert, 1913), 461–62.

[9]   Luther, *De captivitate Babylonica ecclesiae praeludium* (1520), WA 6.533.29–534.2; LW 36:67. Luther insisted on the *proverbium* that it is not the sacrament, but faith in the sacrament (*fides sacramenti*), that saves (WA 6.532.28; LW 36:66).

[10]   *Calvini responsio ad annotationes Bullingeri* (1549), CO 7:701. Cf. *Inst.* 1559, 4.17.33 (2:1407): with Augustine, Calvin holds that one carries away from the sacrament no more than one collects with the vessel of faith. Changing the image slightly, Calvin can also say that the empty bottle cannot be filled with liquid as long as it is corked and sealed (*Confession de foy au nom des Eglises reformees de France* [1562], CO 9:768; TT 2:158).

[11]   *Inst.* 1559, 1.18.1 (1:231).

[12]   "Nam virtutem illis [sc. sacramentis] affingere, quam externus tantum usus instar canalis in animas infundat, plane insipida superstitio est. Quod si fidem mediam intercedere oportet, nemo sanus negabit, eundem Deum, qui his subsidiis infirmitatem nostram levat, fidem etiam dare " (*Defensio sanae et orthodoxae docrinae de sacramentis* [1555], OS 2:277; TT 2:232). See also *Inst.* 1559, 4.14.7 (2:1281–83), 14.14 (1289–90). Those who receive the sacrament to their benefit are believers by God's choice (*electi Dei fideles*): ibid., 4.17.33 (2:1407).

[13]   *Inst.* 1559, 4.14.7 (2:1281–82), 17.33 (1407).

vation can be had even without Baptism or the Lord's Supper. For the Catholics, the justice requisite to salvation is begun, increased, and (when lost) restored, entirely by the Sacraments of Baptism, the Eucharist, and Penance. The sacraments are unconditionally necessary to salvation.[14] It will not do to reply with the later Reformed doctrine of a *necessitas praecepti*: that although God is not bound to use the sacraments, we are—because God has commanded them. No doubt there is a principle here that could be supported from Calvin himself, who asserted that any who do not use the sacraments are guilty of tacit denial of Christ and should not be considered Christians.[15] A tough assertion, it would dismay many of Calvin's spiritual offspring. But it rests on what he considered to be the secondary use of a sacrament, to identify ourselves with the church. Those who refuse the sacraments reject Christ by refusing to be counted among his people; the church does not excommunicate them as a punishment, but in effect they have already excommunicated themselves. The question of sacramental efficacy, on the other hand, pertains to the primary use of a sacrament, to confirm faith.

That the sacraments are not absolutely necessary for salvation does not devalue them as efficacious means of grace. Rather, it defines their efficacy as dependent on the sacramental word, and their effect as by no means limited to the moment of reception. The indispensable component in a sacramental action is not the sign but the word, which the sign confirms and seals; and we are not to imagine that a sacrament adds to the word an efficacy of a totally different order. The sacraments are efficacious precisely as a form, though not the only form, of the word. The need (not the necessity) for them lies in the fluctuation of the life of faith and the incompleteness with which the gift of communion with Christ is received. There *is* a sacramental "plus." But

---

[14]   See, e.g., the *Canons and Dogmatic Decrees of the Council of Trent* (1564), session 7, proem and canon 4. Contrast the citations from Calvin on p. 107, n. 93, above.

[15]   *Catechismus ecclesiae Genevensis* (1545), Q. 363, OS 2:142; TT 2:92. Cf. *Defensio doctrinae de sacramentis*, OS 2:281; TT 2:236. In Q. 315 of the Catechism the necessity for receiving the sacraments is derived from their first use, but here too it is the attitude of the one who neglects them that is the issue: to treat the sacraments as though one did not need them is to be guilty of an arrogance that despises Christ, refuses his grace, and extinguishes the Spirit (OS 2:131–32; TT 2:84–85). Although Calvin does here rebuke those who neglect the sacraments as "not necessary," the necessity of the sacraments, as he intends it, cannot be absolute—as though no one could be saved without them— since this is something he expressly denies (see, e.g., *Inst.* 1559, 4.14.14 [2:1290], 15.20 [1321], 15.22 [1323]). Q. 315 of the Catechism also speaks of *our* "necessity" (the sacraments are *subsidia necessitatis nostrae*), where the sense is clearly that of "need" (*opus*). Cf. *Confession de foy*, CO 9:764; TT 2:152.

there is not a different gift, only a different manner of giving insofar as a sacrament recruits all the five senses, not hearing only, and so presents the one and only gift still more effectively—that is, more clearly and forcefully.[16]

In his insistence that the word and not the sign as such determines a sacrament, Calvin was still in agreement with Luther.[17] The third reason why Calvin is commonly perceived as undermining sacramental efficacy was largely an inner-Protestant matter, which set Calvin at odds with the Lutherans. It was a matter of guilt by association: the Lutherans heard Calvin saying things that Zwingli had said about signs and symbols, and they assumed that he meant what Zwingli had meant.[18] In actual fact, Calvin held a totally different theory of signification from Zwingli's, even though it equally clearly separates him from Luther.[19]

---

[16]   *Inst.* 1559, 4.14.5 (2:1280), 14.14 (1289), 17.5 (1364); *Catechismus*, Qq. 314, 346 (OS 2:131, 139; TT 2:84, 90). Cf. p. 107, n. 93, above. Calvin asserts that the flesh of Christ dwells *essentialiter* in believers even apart from the use of the Supper: the substance of the flesh is no more *sub pane* than *in sola virtute fidei*, and Christ was no less bodily present in Paul when he was writing his letters than when he received the bread of the Supper (*Dilucida explicatio sanae doctrinae de vera participatione carnis et sanguinis Christi in sacra coena, ad discutiendas Heshusii nebulas* [1561], CO 9:509, TT 2:560). If there is a "plus" in the Eucharist, then, as Hartvelt remarks, for Calvin it is only a "cognitive plus" (G. P. Hartvelt, *Verum Corpus* [1960], 115).

[17]   Luther, *De captivitate Babylonica*, WA 6.518.17 (LW 36:44): you can have the word apart from the sign. It is a debated question among Luther scholars whether Luther, unlike Calvin, believed in a distinctive eucharistic gift (an *Abendmahlsproprium*) over and above what is given in the word. E. Sommerlath undoubtedly gives the majority view when he identifies the *proprium* of the Lutheran sacrament precisely with the "Verbindung mit der Leiblichkeit Christi" ("Abendmahl, III. Dogmatisch," RGG³ 1:35). The contrary view, advocated by Albrecht Peters, is that there is no special eucharistic gift, since the whole Christ is present with his body and blood in the word also. The *proprium* is not the *Was*, but the *Wie*: in the Eucharist the Lord penetrates into our very mouths, not into our hearts only (Peters [p. 109, n. 101, above], 139′).

[18]   See pp. 5-6 above.

[19]   Inner-Protestant differences over the nature of sacramental signs constitute one of the most fascinating aspects of the sixteenth-century eucharistic debates. I have explored the matter in greater detail elsewhere and here am only summarizing. See further "The Lord's Supper in the Reformed Confessions" (1966), reprinted in *The Old Protestantism and the New* (1982), chap. 7, and "Discerning the Body: Sign and Reality in Luther's Controversy with the Swiss" (1988). It should be stressed that in his sacramental theology Calvin does not intend to provide a *general* theory of signification or representation: he grounds the sacramental union of sign and reality strictly in the divine institution, and the efficacy of the sacraments in the work of the Holy Spirit. See, e.g., Calvin to Bullinger, 25 February 1547, CO 12:482-83, 485; Comm. 1 Cor. 11.24, CO 49:486. The point of these two passages—that a sacrament is more than a portrait or a statue of some dignitary—is echoed in John W. Nevin's critique of Jonathan Edwards (*The Mystical Presence* [1846], 121–22). See also *Inst.* 1559, 4.14.3 (2:1278): the sacraments are not natural but divinely made signs. Cf. n. 24 below.

Zwingli was reluctant to acknowledge any other causality than that of God, the first cause. Hence, the very notion of *sacramental* causality was offensive to him. It seems to detract from the immediacy of the divine activity if one assigns even an instrumental function to the creaturely elements of water, bread, and wine. Signs, for Zwingli, are not instrumental, but indicative or declarative. They have a twofold use: they signal the fact that something has already been accomplished by the activity of God, and they declare the commitment of the redeemed to live in faithfulness to the God who has redeemed them. In their first use, the sacraments retain the notion of signification: the water of Baptism pictures the cleansing received from Christ, and the bread and wine of the Eucharist point to the body broken and the blood shed on the cross. But in their second use the sacraments are not so much signs as tokens or emblems, like an engagement ring or the white cross that identifies a Swiss Confederate.[20]

Luther read the sacramental teaching of the Zwinglians (the "fanatics," as he amiably calls them) with horror. He noted that in their support they appealed to Augustine, who called the Supper a "sign" of Christ's body. But, says Luther, they stupidly misinterpret him. For Augustine, a sacrament is not a sign of something absent, but of something invisibly present. Out of a sign the fanatics make a symbol—a badge or token of identification, like (Luther disturbingly reminds us) the yellow badge by which Jews are identified. In appealing to Augustine, they simply give us something else to clout them on the head with, as though we did not have enough weapons already.[21] Interestingly, however, Luther does not undertake to defend the Real Presence with a more authentically Augustinian understanding of signs. He in fact *could* not, because, for him, the Real Presence *was* the sign in the Sacrament of the Altar; the pledge God adds to his promise

---

[20]   See, e.g., *Fidei ratio* (1530), SW 6,2:804–5 (LWZ 2:47–48); *Von der Taufe, von der Wiedertaufe und von der Kindertaufe* (1525), SW 4:218 (LCC 24:131); *Fidei expositio* (1536), CERP, 51 (LCC 24:262–63). The simile of the ring perhaps conveys more when Zwingli says that it bears the image of the husband, who is absent in body but present in his wife's remembering (*Ad illustrissimos Germaniae principes Augustae congregatos, de convitiis Eccii epistola* (1530), SW 6,3:278–81; LWZ 2:122–23). But nothing is added to his understanding of the sacraments when he admits that created things, though not strictly causes, may be instruments of God's working, since he goes on to insist that all that the sacraments in fact do is to announce and represent what the Spirit has done already (*Sermonis de providentia dei anamnema* [1530], SW 6,3:111–13, 165–69, 172–76; LWZ 2:155–57, 189–92, 194– 96).

[21]   Luther, *Dass diese Wort Christi "Das ist mein Leib" noch fest stehen wider die Schwärmgeister* (1527), WA 23.209–15, 269; LW 37:104–7, 141.

is not the bread but the presence of Christ's body in the bread. Hence Luther's view, albeit for a quite different reason, is no more Augustinian than Zwingli's—and does not try to be. The bread of the Eucharist is not the sign of the body; the sign rather—the pledge of God's promise—is what Luther calls *Fleischbrot* ("fleshbread"), a single new substance formed out of the union of the bread and the body. The words "This is my body" are therefore not an instance of symbolism but of synecdoche, naming the part for the whole, since what Christ offered his disciples at the Last Supper was his body *with* the bread. The old Augustinian notion of a sacrament as a sign of a sacred thing has been left behind.[22] And, incidentally, Carlstadt has been left holding the field as the only honest-to-goodness literalist of the day. Carlstadt had assumed that when Jesus held out the bread with the invitation "Take, eat," he must have paused, pointed at himself, and said: "*This* is my body."[23]

It is not to be wondered at if many Lutherans greeted the appearance of John Calvin with deep suspicion. He, too, like Zwingli, based his doctrine of the Lord's Supper in part on a theory of signification borrowed from Augustine. The crucial difference is, however, that Calvin did not only *appeal* to Augustine but also, in this respect as in so many others, *was* essentially Augustianian. The bread and wine received in the Sacrament were for him signs and guarantees of a present reality: the believer's feeding on the body and blood of Christ.[24] Moreover, quite unlike Zwingli, he had no difficulty with the

[22] Luther, *De captivitate Babylonica*, WA 6.518.10 (LW 36:44); *Vom Abendmahl Christi, Bekenntnis* (1528), WA 26.442–45 (LW 37:300–3).

[23] Cf. Luther, *Wider die himmlischen Propheten, von den Bildern und Sakrament* (1525), WA 18.144–64; LW 40:154–75.

[24] But because the reality is not contained in the elements (in a strictly local sense), Calvin prefers to interpret the words "This is my body" as an instance not of synecdoche but of metonomy, in which one substitutes for a word ("bread") the name of the thing that it suggests or points to ("my body"). More exactly, in the case of the institution of the Supper: "Restat igitur ut propter affinitatem quam habent cum suis symbolis res signatae, nomen ipsum rei fateamur attributum fuisse symbolo" (*Inst.* 1559, 4.17.21 [2:1385–86]). Calvin does not mean that the words of institution merely exhibit a commonplace rhetorical device. His argument is a fortiori: "Quod si humanitus excogitata symbola, quae imagines sunt rerum absentium potius quam notae praesentium, quas etiam ipsas fallaciter saepissime adumbrant, earum tamen titulis interdum ornantur: quae a Deo sunt instituta, multo maiore ratione rerum nomina mutuanter, quarum et certam minimeque fallacem significationem semper gerunt, et adiunctam habent secum veritatem" (ibid.). As usual, the argument is clinched with citations from Augustine. Cf. *Secunda defensio piae et orthodoxae de sacramentis fidei, contra Ioachimi Westphali calumnias* (1556), CO 9:87 (TT 2:301); *Ultima admonitio ad Ioachimum Westphalum* (1557), CO 9:155, 161, 238–40 (TT 2:364, 372, 478–79); *Optima ineundae concordiae ratio* (1561), OS 2:292–93 (TT 2:575). Calvin thought that the literal interpretation of the *verba* advocated by the Lutherans destroyed the distinctive characteristic

notion that God works through instruments or means.[25] To be sure, he insisted that the primary agency in the sacraments is God's. (Thomas Aquinas had said the same.)[26] But that, Calvin held, does not prevent God from freely using creaturely instruments as he pleases.[27] He asserts tirelessly that if the sign is given, the reality must be given also; or that what is represented is also truly presented. Otherwise, we would be forced into the sacrilegious conclusion that God deceives us.[28]

Calvin met with resistance not only from the Lutherans but from other Reformed theologians as well. Heinrich Bullinger, in particular, thought he kept too close to the papists. It was in part for this reason that Calvin sometimes used a compromise formula. It seems clear enough that he wanted to say that through the eating of the elements a feeding upon Christ's body and blood, or an increase of it, is actually brought about. But he was willing to say that the outward, physical eating indicates an inward, spiritual eating that is occurring *at the same time,* and the "weaker" formula was apparently acceptable to his friend Bullinger.[29] Hence, if we set these two formulas alongside

---

of a sacrament: "Quid enim est sacramentum sine typo vel figura?" (see p. 137, n. 41, above). Further, if there is no *figura,* then it is improper to say that the body is "under," "with," or "in" the bread (*Defensio doctrinae de sacramentis,* OS 2:285 [TT 2:242]; *De vera participatione Christi in coena,* CO 9:473 [TT 2:510]). If, on the other hand, the Lutherans insist on synecdoche, then, Calvin points out, there is no material difference between him and them, only a different choice of figures, in both of which the reality is assumed to be conjoined with the signs (*Defensio doctrinae de sacramentis,* OS 2:287 [TT 2:243]; *De vera participatione Christi in coena,* CO 9:472 [TT 2:509]).

[25]   See n. 33 below.

[26]   Thomas, ST III, Q. 62, a. 1.

[27]   See, e.g., *Inst.* 1559, 4.14.8–9 (2:1283–84). Cf. p. 106 above.

[28]   *Inst.* 1559, 4.17.10 (2:1371). See also, besides the passages cited on p. 137, n. 41, above, Comm. Is. 6.7 (the "live coal" suggests a sacrament to Calvin: CO 36:133); *Catechismus,* Qq. 328, 353, OS 2:134, 140 (TT 2:87, 91); *Defensio doctrinae de sacramentis,* OS 2:264–65 (TT 2:207); *Ultima admonitio ad Westphalum,* CO 9:244 (TT 2:485); *De vera participatione Christi in coena,* CO 9:470–71 (TT 2:507). Note that Calvin sees no fundamental difference of meaning between the words *signum, figura, symbolum,* and *repraesentatio* (CO 9:266, 472; TT 2:209, 509).

[29]   In the 1536 *Institutes* the eucharistic analogy or similitude is expressed as a straightforward *ut . . . ita:* as bread nourishes the life of the body, so Christ's body is the food of our spiritual life. And the nourishing of our spiritual life is said to be continual (OS 1:138; *Institution,* 140–41). This simple comparision is retained in the 1559 *Institutes* (4.17.3, 5 [2:1363, 1365]). Cf. on Baptism (4.15.14 [1314]), where the connection is *tam vere certoque . . . quam certo:* God washes away our sins just as surely as we see our body outwardly cleansed. In his comments on Bullinger's *De sacramentis* (1545), however, Calvin expressed the analogy as a temporal parallel: "Dominus quod signo repraesentat simul efficit" (Calvin to Bullinger, 25 February 1547, CO 12:482). Bullinger objected that the word *simul* in effect ties grace to the sacraments as the papists do (in his *Annotationes* on Calvin's subsequent propositions, CO 7:693). But he did not object

Zwingli's affirmation of the Sacrament as remembrance of a past sacrifice, we need to distinguish within the Reformed camp three conceptions of sacramental signs: symbolic memorialism, symbolic parallelism, and symbolic instrumentalism.[30] In all three the shared component is the notion that a sign or symbol "points to" something else. They differ in that the reality pointed to is variously thought of as a happening in the past, a happening that occurs simultaneously in the present, or a present happening that is actually brought about through the signs. The three ways of looking at the Lord's Supper are by no means mutually exclusive. But without the instrumental language, you do not have a fully Calvinistic doctrine of the Sacrament.

For all the qualifications that no doubt need to be made, it is hard to avoid the conclusion that something portentous was making its appearance in Zwingli's explanation of the sacraments, and that poetry and art had as much cause for alarm as did divinity. As Erich Heller so aptly put it: "And ever since Zwingli the most common response to the reality of symbols has been a shrugging of shoulders, or an edified raising of eyes and brows, or an apologia for poetry, or an aesthetic theory."[31] Ever since Zwingli, in other words, one could no longer be as trustful as the medieval Christian that in handling symbols one of course touched reality. Calvin and Bullinger struggled with this modern predicament, but the theories they came up with

to the analogy itself, and by the time he composed the Second Helvetic Confession (1562; published 1566) he understood the sign and the thing signified in the Eucharist as simultaneous occurrences (as, in fact, Zwingli had come to believe: see p. 112, n. 111, above). The link is provided by the words *intus interim*: the faithful take the bread and the cup and at the same time receive inwardly the flesh and blood of the Lord (chap. 21, CERP, 519). God thus works in the sacraments; sign and thing signified are sacramentally joined (though not so tied together that even unbelievers participate in the grace); the signs are efficacious; God offers the things signified, just as he does *simul* when the word is preached (chap. 19, CERP, 512–16). Clearly, Bullinger came to adopt the *simul* at which he had initially balked. Calvin, for his part, though he assured Bullinger it meant no more than *similiter* (*Responsio ad annotationes Bullingeri* [1549], CO 7:704), continued to use it in a plainly temporal sense, as, e.g., in the added final sentence of *Inst.* 1559, 4.15.14 (2:1314). Where Calvin and Bullinger never agreed was over Calvin's belief that God performs the inward *through* the outward. Nevin seems to reproduce the "Calvinistic doctrine" correctly when he insists that the inward and outward occurrences in the Eucharist "are not simply joined together in time, as the sound of a bell, or the show of a light, may give warning of something with which it stands in no further connection" (*Mystical Presence*, 182). The "occasionalist" view was represented by Hodge (see Gerrish, *Tradition and the Modern World* [1978], 62, 200 n. 31).

[30]   I coined these terms for my study of the Reformed confessions mentioned in n. 19 above.

[31]   Erich Heller, *The Disinherited Mind: Essays in Modern German Literature and Thought* (New York: Farrar, Straus & Cudahy, 1957), 263.

(sacramental, not aesthetic theories, to be sure) actually mirrored the old medieval division between Thomists and Franciscans. Whereas for Thomas a sacrament was an instrumental cause by which God, the principal cause or agent, imparted grace to the soul, Scotus could only understand a sacrament as a sure sign that, by a concomitant divine act, grace was simultaneously being imparted.[32]

Calvin was able, in practice, to adapt either manner of speaking to the evangelical sacraments, and there are scholars who simply identify Calvinist sacramental theology with parallelism. I do not agree with them.[33] But in any case, whether we see Calvin as "Franciscan" (parallelist) or "Thomist" (instrumentalist), it cannot be doubted that for him a sign is the guarantee of a *present* reality. On the words of Paul in 1 Corinthians 10:16, "The bread which we break, is it not a participation in the body of Christ?" he comments:

[32]   See Reinhold Seeberg, *Lehrbuch der Dogmengeschichte*, 3:455–57. Bullinger and his associates expressly branded instrumental language as "Thomistic and scholastic" (Ministers of Zurich to the Ministers of Bern, 17 January 1547, CO 12:471). For two reasons even the weaker, parallelistic language (though not, as far as I know, identified as *Scotist* and scholastic!) posed problems for many Reformed theologians: the temporal link between the inward and outward events might be taken (1) to confine baptismal grace to the moment of administration and (2) to guarantee that unbelieving, as well as believing, communicants receive the body of Christ. Both problems are resolved in the *Consensus Tigurinus* (1549, 1551: OS 2:250–51; TT 2:217–18) in a manner that would have made it easier for Bullinger to accept the *simul* formula.

[33]   François Wendel, for example, asserts that there is an affinity between Calvin's doctrine of the Lord's Supper and Franciscan parallelism (*Calvin* [1963], 344–45). See also Wilhelm Niesel, *Calvins Lehre vom heiligen Abendmahl* (1935), 67–68. I believe I have sufficiently documented my own interpretation—here and in the articles referred to in n. 19 above. It was when studying the exchange between Calvin and Bullinger for the article on the Reformed confessions that I was first struck by the importance of instrumental language in Calvin's theology of the sacraments. In his critique of Bullinger's *De sacramentis* (1545), Calvin not only reaffirmed his view of the sacraments as instruments through which God distributes his grace, but also defended the scholastic expressions that they "confer" and "contain" grace. He made it clear, moreover, that when he said that Christ "exhibits" his body and blood in the Supper, he meant nothing less than "gives his body to be enjoyed" (*fruendum dare*: CO 12:483–88). To be sure, the scholastic language is given a Protestant reinterpretation: grace is contained in the sacraments as Christ is contained in the gospel (col. 484), and the sacraments confer grace as *exercitia fidei* (col. 483). Hence the sharp criticisms of the Schoolmen in *Inst.* 1559, 4.14.14, 17 (2:1289, 1292–93); 15.2 (1304). Calvin, we might say, took more seriously than the Schoolmen themselves the scholastic principle that the sacraments cause grace by the communication of meaning (*significando causant*). Cf. *Secunda defensio contra Westphalum*, CO 9:116–17; TT 2:340–41. Bullinger, by contrast, held tenaciously to the conviction that if the sacraments *signify*, then they do not *confer* (see his annotations on Calvin's propositions, CO 7:695). My reading of the negotiations between Calvin and Bullinger seems to me to be confirmed by the recent studies of Paul Rorem (1988) and Timothy George (1990). See also Jan Rohls, *Theologie reformierter Bekenntnisschriften* (1987), 215–20.

There is no reason to object that this is a figurative expression by which the name of the thing signified is transferred (*deferatur*) to the sign. I certainly admit that the breaking of bread is a symbol, not the thing itself. But, this granted, we will nonetheless duly infer that the thing itself is exhibited by the exhibition of the symbol. Unless anyone wants to call God deceitful, he will not dare to say that an empty symbol is put forward by him. Hence, if by the breaking of bread the Lord truly represents participation in his body, there should be no doubt at all that he truly presents and exhibits (*praestet atque exhibeat*) his body. The rule to be strictly maintained by the devout (*piis*) is this: whenever they see symbols instituted by God, they should assuredly think and be persuaded that there the truth of the thing signified is present. Why would the Lord put the symbol of his body in your hand unless to assure you of a true participation in it? If it is true that a visible sign is shown to us to seal the gift of something invisible, we should accept the symbol of the body and assuredly trust that the body itself is also no less given to us.[34]

So far, the reasons for doubting whether Calvin affirmed the instrumental efficacy of the sacraments have been answered simply by drawing together and amplifying what has already been said in the previous chapters. The fourth reason, however, requires me finally to bring the Calvinist skeleton out of the closet: the Lutherans suspected that Calvin's entire sacramental position was jeopardized, even undermined, by his doctrine of predestination. The doctrine was not at first a controverted issue between Lutherans and Reformed. Little, if anything, that Calvin said on the subject could not be matched with citations from Luther; and when the Lutherans later shrank back from predestination, the Reformed sometimes claimed to be Luther's only true disciples.[35] Nevertheless, in the acrimonious controversy launched by Lutheran critics of the Zurich Consensus Calvin was accused of jeopardizing the Sacrament of Baptism by making its efficacy contingent on predestination, and he correctly perceived that his entire sacramental thinking—including his doctrine of the Lord's Supper—was on the line.[36] If the sacraments effect what they signify only in the elect, sign and reality are not, after all, so joined together that they cannot be separated.[37] The Saxon Visitation Articles of 1592 identified

[34]   *Inst.* 1559, 4.17.10 (2:1370–71).

[35]   See Fredrik Brosché, *Luther on Predestination: The Antinomy and the Unity Between Love and Wrath in Luther's Concept of God*, Studia Doctrinae Christianae Upsaliensia, vol. 18 (Uppsala: Uppsala University, 1978), 100–1, 104; cf. 189–96.

[36]   *Secunda defensio contra Westphalum*, CO 9:118–19; TT 2:343– 44.

[37]   *Inst.* 1559, 4.14.15 (2:1290). As will become clear, I think it is misleading to infer that for Calvin the *Zusammenwirken* of sign and reality is only a "possibility" (Joachim Rogge, *Virtus und Res* [1965], 37, cf. 43).

the apparent contradiction between predestination and sacramental efficacy as one of the reasons why Lutherans need to be on their guard against Calvinists, and the articles expressly discovered the virus of predestination in *both* the Calvinistic sacraments.[38] In the great American debate between John Williamson Nevin and Charles Hodge, the problem resurfaced as an inner-Reformed controversy. Hodge was a predestinarian Calvinist, Nevin a sacramental Calvinist, and their debate may make one wonder if it is possible to be both at once.[39]

The Pavlovian reflexes that the mention of predestination invariably evokes have become a serious obstacle to understanding Calvin's theology; he himself wryly observed that it was as if the petulant human intellect had heard the bugle sound a charge.[40] To hold the petulant intellect in check, I have deliberately kept silent about predestination until now: if you begin with predestination, it becomes virtually impossible to hear Calvin saying anything else. Calvin himself (in the 1559 *Institutes*) did not begin with it: he introduced it in book three, chapter 21, to clinch his case for the unconditional freedom of God's grace: "We will never be clearly persuaded, as we should, that our salvation flows from the fountain of God's free mercy until we come to know his eternal election, which makes God's grace clear by this contrast: that he does not adopt all indiscriminately into the hope of salvation, but gives to some what he denies to others."[41] Free adoption is the citadel of Calvin's faith; double predestination is a defensive outwork, and it has not proved a very effective one. He does not seem to have realized how the proof might place in question what he wanted to prove. Predestination, he supposed, would be the final guarantee of both humility and security. But it has guaranteed neither one, as the later history of Calvinism makes painfully clear: it launched the quest for assurance of election and invited the ultimate form of pride, which is pride of grace. And for those who know what is coming in book three, chapters 21-24 (who does not know?), the double decree is the dark cloud that hangs over the entire work.[42] The "we" for whom

---

[38]   Text and translation in Philip Schaff, *Bibliotheca Symbolica Ecclesiae Universalis: The Creeds of Christendom, with a History and Critical Notes*, 6th ed., ed. David S. Schaff, 3 vols. (New York: Harper and Brothers [1931]), 3:189.

[39]   See Nevin, "Doctrine of the Reformed Church on the Lord's Supper," *Mercersburg Review* 2 (1850):523–24.

[40]   *Inst.* 1559, 3.23.1 (2:947).

[41]   Ibid., 3.21.1 (2:921).

[42]   Predestination, as Barth says, is not the root but the dark background of the answers Calvin gave to every theological question (Karl Barth, "Calvin als Theologe" [1959], 317).

Calvin everywhere speaks are the elect, the fixed number for whom eternal life is foreordained. (If I have seemed presumptuously to identify myself with the "we," I have of course been using a historian's license.) The flaw in Calvin's system is not that he tried to deduce everything from the idea of God's absolute, predestinating will (he did not), but that he invoked the double decree to support his cardinal doctrine of free adoption.

I do not need to give in detail my grounds for deviating from Calvin at this point. (They would have to be strictly exegetical and dogmatic grounds, not the customary expressions of mere distaste or disapproval.) And I will not pause to mention the ways in which Calvin mitigates the harshness of the doctrine of predestination.[43] There is no denying the seriousness of the problem it poses for the entire system, and one may be glad that the two greatest Reformed theologians since Calvin—Schleiermacher and Barth—reaffirmed the importance of the doctrine of election without endorsing Calvin's interpretation of it.[44] The grain of truth in Selbie's judgment on Calvinism must be granted. It is a manifest exaggeration, as must now be clear, to assert that Calvin's "teaching on the sovereignty of God, the Divine decrees, election and a limited atonement leaves no room for the idea of

[43]   I am not referring to the many attempts (from Moses Amyraut on) to prove that Calvin taught universal atonement or a *bona fide* offer of salvation to all. They cannot, in my opinion, be substantiated from the sources; and even if they could, they would do nothing to mitigate the *decretum horribile*, as Calvin called it (*Inst.* 1559, 3.23.7 [2:955]), since no one doubts that for him only the elect will actually be saved anyway. "Unde constat perperam quibuslibet prostitui salutis doctrinam ut efficaciter prosit, quae solis Ecclesiae filiis seorsum reposita esse dicitur" (ibid., 3.22.10 [2:944]). See my essay "'To the Unknown God': Luther and Calvin on the Hiddenness of God" (1973), reprinted in The *Old Protestantism*, chap. 8, especially 143–44, and the discussion on Alexander Schweizer in my *Tradition and the Modern World*, chap. 4, especially 129–32. To the work of Brian G. Armstrong (1969) can now be added (on behalf of universal atonement in Calvin) R. T. Kendall (1979) and, on the other side (for limited atonement), Richard A. Muller (1986) and especially Jonathan H. Rainbow (1990). Whichever way the verdict goes on the extent of the atonement, Calvin certainly taught that God *effectively* wills the salvation of the elect only. I do not share the enthusiasm of some of Calvin's followers for this teaching. However, the (slightly) mitigating factors are that Calvin did not presume to know who were elect (*Inst.* 1559, 4.1.2, 8–9 [2:1013, 1022–24]), and that he therefore considered it the Christian's duty to hope and pray for all (3.20.38 [2:901]). This, he says, is the godly and humane thing to do. He does not seem to have felt that he risked making humans more benevolent than God, who is father only to the members of Christ (Comm. Eph. 4.6, CO 51:192).

[44]   See the comparative study by [James] Daryll Ward, "The Doctrine of Election in the Theologies of Friedrich Schleiermacher and Karl Barth" (Ph.D. diss., University of Chicago, 1989).

Fatherhood save in the most restricted and official sense."[45] But the divine fatherhood *is* restricted.

The pertinent question for the moment, however, is whether the doctrine of predestination negates Calvin's affirmation of sacramental efficacy. The answer, surely, is: no, it does not negate it but limits it. He says repeatedly that a sacrament effects what it signifies only in the elect, and he applies the general rule specifically to each of the two individual sacraments, Baptism and the Supper.[46] As usual, citations from Augustine support his case.[47] Not that the sacraments have *no* effect in the reprobate; rather, like the word (of which they are, after all, visible forms), they carry a judgment with them for those they do not sanctify.[48] But this does not place in doubt God's commitment to the elect: in them, at least, the sacraments are effectual in bringing salvation. The point is perhaps confused in both Augustine and Calvin by association with two other questions: whether God can save the elect only by means of the sacraments, and whether the sacraments are effectual if received unworthily. Calvin's stand on the first question is clear, and it should not be allowed to darken the issue of sacramental efficacy. Of course God's grace is not restricted to the sacraments: justification is no less communicated to us (the elect) by the preaching of the gospel, and Augustine rightly states that there can be invisible sanctification without a visible sign. To assert that God works by means of the sacraments by no means implies that God cannot work without them.[49] Conversely, however, to assert that God can, and does, work without them does not imply that God is not committed to work through them whenever they are received by the elect.

The second question is more difficult: for what happens when the elect, not just the reprobate, receive the Sacrament unworthily? Calvin's solemn admonitions about the right preparation for communion surely imply that even the elect can help or hinder enjoyment of the eucharistic gift.[50] As pastoral commentary on the biblical requirement

---

[45]   W. B. Selbie, *The Fatherhood of God* (London: Duckworth, 1936), 74–75.

[46]   See, e.g., *Inst.* 1559, 4.14.15, 16.15, 17.34 (2:1290–91, 1337, 1410). Cf. Comm. Eph. 5.26 (CO 51:223), where the double principle is affirmed: God may bestow grace without the sacramental sign, and not all who receive the sign are made partakers of the grace (only the elect are).

[47]   *Inst.* 1559, 4.14.15, 17.34, 19.16 (2:1290–91, 1410, 1464).

[48]   Ibid., 3.24.13 (2:980); 4.17.40 (1417). Cf. Comm. Matt. 13.14, 21.45 (CO 45: 360, 598); Comm. Acts 7.54 (CO 48:166).

[49]   *Inst.* 1559, 4.14.14 (2:1290). Cf. p. 107, n. 93, above.

[50]   *Petit traicté de la saincte Cene* (1541), OS 1:511–15 (TT 2:174–79); Comm. 1 Cor. 11.27–29 (CO 49:491–93); *Inst.* 1559, 4.17.40–42 (2:1417–20).

of self-examination (1 Cor. 11:27–29), the counsel given is obvious enough. But does it tacitly admit the possibility that the elect, too, could totally block the proffered grace and sever the bond between sign and reality? I think not. There is a difference in Calvin's mind between absence of faith and weakness of faith. The reprobate have no faith (or only a sham faith), and on them the gentle rain of God's grace falls in vain, as if on a hard rock. The gift is given, but not received. They are unbelievers (*increduli, sine ulla fidei scintilla*), who, though they appear at the celebration, are not the Lord's members and, as Augustine insists, can therefore receive only the sign of the body, not the reality.[51] The elect, on the other hand, have degrees of faith and love. Their indolence may prevent them from receiving as much as they should in the Supper, but they always receive something, and sometimes receive more later as the sacramental seed continues its work.[52] God, we may conclude, keeps faith with them. And if their own faith and love were already perfect, why would God spread the table before them? The best preparation for the holy banquet is their sense of need —their hunger and thirst for the food of their souls.[53]

SACRAMENTAL PRESENCE

Calvin's certainty of the sacramental union between sign and reality in the holy banquet rested, in the final analysis, on his own experience of the mystery. In 1543 he ventured to add to his discussion of the Lord's Supper in the *Institutes* this remarkable confession of his belief that Christ is present in the Sacrament:

[51]   *Inst.* 1559, 4.17.33, 34, 40 (2:1407, 1408–11, 1417–18). On sham or transient faith, see 3.2.11 (1:555–56). For the Lutherans, the objectivity of Christ's bodily presence in the bread meant that even the reprobate receive the body by mouth (*manducatio oralis* entails *manducatio impiorum*). See Calvin's response in the controversial writings: OS 2:277–79, 295 (TT 2:232–34, 578–79); CO 9:88–91, 166, 248, 483–85 (TT 2:302–6, 379, 491, 524–27). A *manducatio impiorum*, in Calvin's eyes, would require an unthinkable separation of Christ from his life-giving Spirit.

[52]   *Consensus Tigurinus*, OS 2:251 (TT 2:218); *Defensio doctrinae de sacramentis*, OS 2:281 (TT 2:237); *Secunda defensio contra Westphalum*, CO 9:117–18 (TT 2:341–42).

[53]   See n. 50 above. Interestingly, Calvin does hold that those who communicate unworthily by reason of some flagrant and unrepented sin, or even by reason of culpable negligence, will be punished in appropriate measure (according to the degree of their unworthiness), though he does not say how. And he goes on to state in as many words that there are some who receive Christ truly in the Supper even though unworthily. They are differentiated, however, from those who are unworthy because they are totally destitute of faith and repentance (Comm. 1 Cor. 11.27, CO 49:491–92).

> Now if anyone asks me how (*de modo*), I will not be ashamed to admit
> that the mystery (*arcanum*) is too sublime for my intelligence to grasp or
> my words to declare: to speak more plainly, I experience rather than
> understand it. Here, then, without any arguing, I embrace the truth of
> God in which I may safely rest content. Christ proclaims that his flesh
> is the food, his blood the drink, of my soul. I offer him my soul to be fed
> with such food. In his sacred supper he bids me take, eat, and drink his
> body and blood under the symbols of bread and wine: I have no doubt
> that he truly proffers them and that I receive them.[54]

Calvin rightly felt that his simple confidence in the efficaciousness of
the signs established a bond of kinship between himself and Martin
Luther. When relations with the Lutherans turned sour, he continued
to insist on this bond and to distance himself, on the other side, from
Zwingli.[55] He had no difficulty with the assertion that when the bread
is proferred in the mystery, the gift of the body is joined with it
(*annexam esse exhibitionem corporis*) because sign and reality are inseparable. Once the notion of a local presence and the "absurdities" that go
with it had been set aside, he gladly accepted whatever could be made
to express the true and substantial communication of the body and
blood that is given under the symbols. For all his sharp criticisms of the
Lutheran arguments, Calvin could still say: "And yet, it is not my
intention to take anything away from the communication of Christ's
body, which I have confessed."[56] The sole difference between the
Lutherans and himself, he thought, concerned the way (the *ratio* or
modus) in which this communication took place.[57]

Now Calvin did not profess to comprehend the way. But he
thought it perfectly legitimate to ask, like the Virgin Mary: "How can
this be?" (Luke 1:34)—not least in order to rule out inadequate
answers. The Lutherans, in his judgment, misstated the question
because they assumed that there must be a local presence of Christ in
the Supper. Their one thorny question was: "How does Christ's body
lie hidden under the bread?" For Calvin himself, on the other hand, the
answer to the question of participation was that the how (*modus*) is

[54]   *Inst.* 1543, CO 1:1010 (cf. *Inst.* 1559, 4.17.32 [2:1403-4]).
[55]   See pp. 139-45 above. Even the brief *Ineundae concordiae ratio* continued to say
in diplomatic language what Calvin had written bluntly in a private letter two decades
earlier: that Zwingli's original opinion on the use of the sacraments was not only wrong
but pernicious (Calvin to Andrew Zebedee, 19 May 1539, CO 10²:346).
[56]   *Inst.* 1559, 4.17.16, 19, 20 (2:1379, 1382, 1384).
[57]   Ibid., 4.17.5, 31 (2:1365, 1403). "Fidem vero nos ista quam enarravimus corporis
participatione non minus laute affluenterque pascimus, quam qui ipsum Christum e
caelo detrahunt" (17.32 [1404]). Cf. *Secunda defensio contra Westphalum*, CO 9:74; TT
2:282.

spiritual; no explanation of a local presence is called for, since there *is* no local presence. The Lutherans retorted that if the eating is spiritual, it cannot be "true and real eating." But Calvin denied the consequence. The "how," he explained, is spiritual because the secret power of the Holy Spirit is the bond of our union with Christ. The body of Christ is subject to the common limits of a human body and cannot be in more than one place at the same time: it is not in the bread but in heaven, separated from ourselves by a great distance. Nevertheless, the Spirit truly unites things separated in space.[58] Calvin describes this remarkable operation in several ways. The Spirit is the chain that links us to Christ, the channel through which Christ is conveyed to us. Thus, we do not drag Christ down from heaven; rather, he pulls us up to himself, and that is how we enjoy his presence. But Calvin can equally well say that Christ does come down to us by the outward symbol and by his Spirit, and in one mixed image he even chides the Lutherans because they do not grasp the manner of descent by which Christ pulls us up to himself.[59] Sometimes, to be sure, the spatial language appears to stand for a mental or cognitive operation: invited by the symbols, we are lifted up to heaven *oculis animisque* ("by our eyes and minds"), and this fits well with the *Sursum corda* of the liturgy. But it cannot possibly be taken to negate everything Calvin says, here and elsewhere, about feeding on the body, which is not a purely mental or cognitive operation.[60]

Calvin assures us, in case we have begun to wonder, that there is nothing absurd, or obscure, or ambiguous in his teaching on the Lord's Supper; it is scriptural and edifying, and he seems puzzled that the world is not eager to accept it. "There is no reason why this opinion should be so odious to the world, or why my defense of it should be forestalled by such prejudice on the part of many people—unless Satan has driven them out of their minds by some terrible spell." Calvin admits (again) that he does not sufficiently comprehend the mystery: he does not want its sublimeness measured by his childishness, but urges his readers to rise much higher than he can lead them. However, he is confident that, as far as it goes, his opinion is right, and he expects every devout heart to approve of it.[61] It does not seem to

[58] *Inst.* 1559, 4.17.25 (2:1392); 17.33 (1405); 17.10, 26 (1370, 1394).

[59] Ibid., 4.17.12 (2:1373); 17.31 (1403); 17.24 (1390); 17.16 (1379).

[60] Ibid., 4.17.18, 36 (2:1381, 1412). On the *Sursum corda* ("Lift up your hearts") see also *De la Cene*, OS 1:522 (TT 2:188); *Ultima admonitio ad Westphalum*, CO 9:213–14 (TT 2:443); *Confession de foy*, CO 9:770 (TT 2:160).

[61] *Inst.* 1559, 4.17.19 (2:1382); 17.7 (1367–68).

176 GRACE AND GRATITUDE

have occurred to him that others might find his language every bit as crass as Luther's more extreme utterances sounded to him. A local presence in heaven is not less problematic than a local presence in the bread and wine; and the fundamental problem, once the warring parties had made their choices, generated others. The Lutheran Joachim Westphal (1510-74), who needed a resurrected body of Christ that was not subject to common human limits, gleefully pointed out that the Lord emerged from a sealed sepulcher and appeared to his disciples when the doors were closed. No ordinary body there! Resourcefully, Calvin answers that the stone probably rolled back, and the walls opened up, to let Christ through. His body cannot have simply penetrated solid matter. And it does not help Westphal's case one bit to point out that on the Emmaus road Christ vanished from the disciples' sight: Christ did not make himself invisible—he disappeared.[62]

Controversy has carried us a long way from the simple analogy: "Our souls are fed by the flesh and blood of Christ just as (*non aliter . . . quam*) bread and wine keep and sustain our bodily life."[63] The difficulty is, of course, that once we move beyond the operational level of knowing when to use these words, the analogy is by no means simple. Calvin appears to have let himself become caught in a logical bind. He has set aside as inadequate or incomplete (we recall) the simpler explanation, that to eat Christ's flesh is to believe in Christ. He wants a *true* partaking of Christ's flesh and is not content to say merely that believing is to the soul what eating is to the body. The eating is not believing but *by* believing. Although the difference in words is small, it is no slight difference, Calvin says, in the thing itself.[64] And yet, he is repelled by any suggestion of an oral partaking. Christ's flesh itself does not enter into us; his body is not conveyed by the mouth to the stomach.[65] Indeed, the body cannot be received in the bread because since the ascension it is in heaven.[66] The notion of a spatial separation between the body of Christ and the eucharistic elements, however, seems bound to exclude not only an *oral* partaking of it but also the *true* partaking that Calvin wants. His attempts to bridge the gap, so to say,

Ibid., 4.17.29 (2:1400).
[63]   Ibid., 4.17.10 (2:1370); cf. 17.1 (1361).
[64]   Ibid., 4.17.5 (2:1365); cf. 17.6 (1366).
[65]   Ibid., 4.17.32 (2:1404); 17.15 (1376–77). Cf. 17.12 (1372– 73), on the forced retraction of Berengarius (1059).
[66]   Ibid., 2.16.14 (1:523); 4.17.12, 18, 26–27, 29 (2:1373, 1381, 1393–95, 1399).

do not convince because they are couched in metaphors that, for the most part, strike his readers as fantastic.

There remains one further metaphor, or cluster of metaphors, that perhaps comes closer to making Calvin's thought intelligible, although his Lutheran critics saw in it, too, a betrayal of the Real Presence. Sometimes Calvin suggests, not that Christ descends to us or that we ascend to him, and not that the Spirit is the chain or channel linking his body to believers, but rather that the body exercises a powerful force or influence on believers—in other words, that it acts upon them—and that this is the meaning of the "communication" we receive from him. In a passage that goes back to the first edition of the *Institutes*, Calvin writes:

> Although he has taken his flesh away from us and has ascended in the body into heaven, nevertheless he sits at the Father's right hand—that is, rules in the Father's power and majesty and glory. This rule (*regnum*) is not at all limited by location in space or circumscribed by dimensions. Christ exercises his power (*virtutem*) wherever he pleases, in heaven or on earth. He shows himself present in power and strength (*potentia et virtute*) and is always present to his own, breathing his life into them. He lives in them, sustains them, strengthens them, keeps them safe (*incolumes*)—just as if present in the body.[67]

By themselves, these words say nothing about the relation of Christ's power and strength to his body. But in 1539 Calvin added immediately after this passage: "In short, he feeds them with his body, bestows the communion of the body upon them by the power (*virtute*) of his Spirit." And before the same passage he inserted the words: "If we are lifted up to heaven by our eyes and minds, to seek Christ there in the glory of his kingdom (*regni*), then under the symbol of bread we will feed on his body." Framed carefully as it is between these two additions, the meaning of the passage cited is clear: to feed upon Christ's flesh, or to have communion with his body, is nothing other than to be brought under the sway of the vital power that Christ wields from the right hand of the Father.

The idea of a vital power that comes from Christ in heaven is, of course, just as much quasi-physical as the images of the chain and the channel, and it was also in 1539 that Calvin furnished it with what is perhaps the most suitable illustration from nature: the rays that radiate from the sun. He reiterates his point that Christ's body, being finite (like all human bodies), is contained in heaven until he returns

---

[67]   Ibid., 4.17.18 (2:1381).

as judge. We are not to drag it back under the corruptible elements, or to imagine it everywhere present. But neither do we need to. "For if we see that the sun, by shining on the earth with its rays, in a sense casts its substance on it, to generate, nurture, and give growth to her offspring, why should the radiance of Christ's Spirit be any less able to impart to us the communion of his body and blood?"[68] Particularly interesting here is the word "substance," which had become a code word in the eucharistic debates—like the Nicene *homoousios* in the trinitarian debates.

Unfortunately, the way Calvin used "substance" and its cognates was, to say the least, confusing. In the 1536 *Institutes* he expressly denied that the actual substance of Christ's body is given in the Lord's Supper.[69] Further, his tendency was to employ various circumlocutions for what he took "eating Christ's body" to mean: he speaks of "receiving life from the body," of "the power of the body," and so on.[70] And

---

[68]   Ibid., 4.17.12 (2:1373). Cf. *Defensio doctrinae de sacramentis*, OS 2:284 (TT 2:240); *Secunda defensio contra Westphalum*, CO 9:72; TT 2:279. Calvin's other two favorite images—the root and the branches, the head and its members— likewise picture a vital energy (the "sap," the "vigor") emanating from Christ to the faithful (see, e.g., *Ineundae concordiae ratio*, OS 2:292; TT 2:575).

[69]   *Inst.* 1536, OS 1:142–43; *Institution*, 145–46. *Substantia corporis* here refers to the *verum et naturale corpus* as distinct from the benefits Christ procured in his body: "substance," we might say, means the actual, space-occupying *material* of the body. It is a quite different usage when Calvin says that Jesus Christ himself is the *substantia sacramentorum*: i.e., the essential content or *essence* of the sacraments. See, e.g., *De la Cene*, OS 1:507 (TT 2:169); *Inst.* 1559, 4.14.16 (2:1291), 17.11 (1372). It is the former use of *substantia* that concerns us here, and, as Kilian McDonnell points out, Calvin takes the term in an empirical, rather than (like Thomas) a metaphysical, sense (*John Calvin, the Church, and the Eucharist* [1967], 238). In one place, Calvin seems to use the expression *substantialiter pasci* much as we speak of "eating a substantial meal." He insists that even before Christ's flesh was created, it exercised its *vis* in the Old Testament patriarchs, but we (Christians) feed on it substantially in the sense (apparently) of receiving more. They, too, received the "substance" of the sacraments, which is Christ (*Ultima admonitio ad Westphalum*, CO 9:176–77; TT 2:393–94). Cf. the expression *substantialis communicatio* in *De vera participatione Christi in coena*, CO 9:489; TT 2:533. It is, of course, yet another use of the term *substantia* when Calvin says that in the Supper we become "one substance" with Christ (e.g., in Comm. 1 Cor. 11.24, CO 49:487).

[70]   The controversial writings against Westphal and Heshusius abound in such circumlocutions, intended, Calvin insists, simply to make clear the mode of Christ's presence, or the mode of communion with him. Instead of "the flesh of Christ," we find, for instance, "the *vigor* of his flesh" (CO 9:72; TT 2:279); "*life* from his flesh" (77–78/287), or "from the substance of his [or the] flesh" (81/293, 182/401, 467/502, 470/506), or "from the substance of his body" (466/501); and (most interesting!) "the mystical and incomprehensible *operation* of the flesh" (509/560). Similarly, in place of the allegedly simple affirmation that Christ's body is really present, we find his presence ascribed to his "grace and power" (*virtus*: 170/384), "the immense power (*virtus*) of his Spirit" (487/531), and so on. Small wonder if Heshusius found Calvin's language slippery (478/518) and dubbed the Calvinists "Energists" (466/501–2): i.e., those who hold that only the *virtus* of Christ's body is present in the Supper.

yet, when challenged by his tough-minded Lutheran adversary Joachim Westphal, he indignantly asserted twenty years after his first *Institutes* that, in his view, our souls do feed in the Lord's Supper on the actual substance of Christ's flesh. Ought Calvin to have admitted to Westphal that he had had second thoughts about the Eucharist, however much the admission would have gone against the grain of his confident disposition? Perhaps so. Instead, the denial that the substance of Christ's body is given in the Supper was quietly dropped from later editions.[71] Still, the analogy of the sun's rays suggests that in Calvin's mind to receive the substance of Christ's body is to receive its power. The two ways of speaking are not exclusive but synonymous, or may be so construed. The word "substance" is disqualified only if it means, as Calvin thought it meant to his critics, physical mass—extension. The presence of the body is its presence in power and efficacy (*virtute, efficacia*). And this, as Calvin had affirmed in the very first edition of the *Institutes*, is the presence that the nature (*ratio*) of a sacrament demands.[72] On the strength of this affirmation, we must surely say that

---

[71]   *Secunda defensio contra Westphalum*, CO 9:70; TT 2:277. Note that what Calvin here affirms is not what he denied in 1536 (n. 69 above): he still repudiates the "substantial *presence* that Westphal imagines," which entails the "fiction of a transfusion" of Christ's substance into the communicants, but he certainly confesses that their "souls are *fed* by the substance of Christ's flesh" (my emphases). A case can perhaps be made for Calvin's consistency. Still, that he dropped the passage in question (from the first edition of the *Institutes*) at least indicates second thoughts about how he had expressed himself (see CO 1:1009–10; *Inst.* 1559, 4.17.18 [2:1381]): granted that the mode of communion is not carnal, he did not want to imply that the substance of the body is not *given*. Neither did he wish to provide evidence for those who accused him of reducing the eucharistic gift to the *beneficia Christi* (as the selfsame passage in the 1536 *Institutes* implies).

[72]   *Inst.* 1536, OS 1:143; *Institution*, 146. Cf. the parallels in the later editions (cited in the previous note), where the efficacious presence of the body is detached from talk about the presence of the *beneficia*. Two further passages help to clarify Calvin's meaning. (1) In his Commentary on 1 Corinthians 11:24 he explained the *modus* of participation in Christ's body, concluding that the body is really—that is, truly—given to us in the Supper, and that our souls are fed with the substance of the body. He then added, in a subsequent edition of the commentary: " vel, quod idem valet, vim ex Christi carne vivificam in nos per spiritum diffundi" (CO 49:487). It could not be said more plainly that "feeding on the substance" and "receiving power from the flesh" were, for Calvin, one and the same thing, and that they presupposed a real or true giving of the body of Christ. (2) One of Calvin's best, if still overcomplicated, statements on the problem word *substantia* appears in his *Ineundae concordiae ratio*, in which he makes clear where (so to say) the adjectival form *substantialis* belongs, and where it does not belong. What takes place in the Supper is not a *substantialis unio*, a union of two substances (corruptible bread and the flesh of Christ), but a *sacramentalis coniunctio* of them. Similarly, there is no *substantialis praesentia*, or presence of the actual substance of Christ's body on earth, as in the days of his earthly ministry; but there certainly is a *substantialis societas*, a faith–union with him by which we feed *substantialiter* on his flesh, just as the *substantialis vigor* flows from the head to the members. Union with Christ is

Calvin believed in a *sacramental* presence of the body of Christ in the Eucharist; it followed from his conviction that the sacramental signs do not deceive.

The eminent German philosopher Gottfried Wilhelm Leibniz (1646-1716), who took an irenic interest in the relations between Roman Catholics, Lutherans, and Reformed, suggested that Calvin (when he was true to his own best insight) was moving toward a fresh conception of the substance of Christ's body precisely as its force or power, so that the substance is present, albeit in a nondimensional way, wherever its power is applied. This conception, Leibniz believed, held out the best prospect for harmony between the two Protestant confessions.[73] The learned historian of the Eucharist August Ebrard (1818-88), who drew attention to Leibniz's verdict, agreed: he thought that it was the merit of Calvin to have shown the compatibility between a real union with the body of Christ (Luther) and the material circumscription of the body (Zwingli).[74] He may have been right. But whether

---

"substantial," not because his substance is tranfused into us (just as bread is digested), but because the vital power we receive is *from* the substance: it is an *abstractum aliquid a substantia* (CO 9:520–22; TT 2:576–78). Cf. the expressions *substantialis communicatio* and *substantialiter participes* (CO 9:486, 509; TT 2:529, 560). *Abstractum*, as Gollwitzer rightly says, was "an unfortunate expression" (*Coena Domini* [1937], 121–22), which did not convey Calvin's belief that Christ himself is the eucharistic gift.

[73]   Leibniz, *Pensées sur la religion et la morale*, 2d ed. (Paris: Nyon, 1803), 106. Unfortunately, I have not been able to obtain this source, quoted by August Ebrard in *Das Dogma vom heiligen Abendmahl* (1845–46), 2:413–14. But I have seen a later edition of the *Pensées* (2 vols., Brussels: Société Nationale pour la Propagation des Bons Livres, 1838), in which the quotation appears on p. 322 of volume 1 and is identified as an extract from a letter to Fabricius.

[74]   Ebrard, *Das Dogma vom heiligen Abendmahl*, 2:413. Ebrard argued that Calvin understood the Sacrament as an *actus in actu* rather than an *extensum in extenso:* that is, as a divine act in a liturgical act rather than a heavenly substance in an earthly substance (ibid., 2:459). This, I think, is correct (though I would prefer to say *actus per actum!*). It is confirmed by the places in which Calvin identifies the signs with the eucharistic actions, not the elements—with eating and drinking, not with bread and wine (see p. 13, n. 55, above)—albeit he does not do so consistently. Perhaps the expression that best captures his eucharistic doctrine is not so much "real presence" as "true communion" (see p. 8, n. 26; for the word "true" see n. 72 above and p. 138, n. 42). The important thing is that we partake of Christ's flesh, the very substance of his body (*De la Cene*, OS 1:529 [TT 2:197]; *Confession de foy*, CO 9:770–71 [TT 2:161]). This *vera participatio* is what Calvin was contending for in his doctrine of the Lord's Supper (*Secunda defensio contra Westphalum*, CO 9:47; TT 2:248). His argument in the controversial writings is that communion (or partaking, or giving) is possible without presence—i.e., without a local presence of the body. "Quod inter opiniones reiectitias alicubi posui, Christi corpus realiter et substantialiter adesse in coena, minime cum vera et reali communicatione pugnat" (ibid., CO 9:73 [TT 2: 281]; cf. CO 9:80, 472, 475–78 [TT 2:291, 509–10, 514–19]). He can say this because "mysticam et incomprehensibilem carnis *operationem* non prohibet

Calvin would have welcomed philosophical support from Leibniz or anyone else is hard to say. In those days reason was a temptress, and Calvin was hurt when Westphal accused him of being so addicted to human reason that he allowed no more to the power of God than the order of nature permits.

Calvin replied, in effect, that his eucharistic theory was no more reasonable than his adversary's: he by no means subjected the mystery to the laws of nature. "Have we learned, pray, from physics that Christ feeds our souls from heaven with his flesh, as our bodies are nourished by bread and wine? . . . Anyone who has tasted our doctrine will be seized by amazement at God's secret power."[75] But he saw nothing absurd in (so to say) a remote presence—that is, a presence in power and efficacy—and the commendation of a Christian philosopher might not have been unwelcome to him.[76] What must strike those who have yielded more than he did to the siren voice of reason, however, is where exactly he locates the strain upon our credulity. "There is nothing more incredible," he says, "than that things separated and removed from each other by the entire space between heaven and earth should not only be linked across such a great distance, but so united that souls receive nourishment from the flesh of Christ."[77] For Calvin the "miracle," as he himself calls it, is the bridging of the gap between heaven and earth. His credulity was not at all tested by the presupposition of this miracle: that the body of Christ is in fact confined in heaven. Most of his readers, I suspect, if they do not judge

---

absentia localis" (my emphasis: CO 9:509; TT 2:560). But he can also say that drawing life from Christ's flesh is a kind of presence (*praesentiae species:* CO 9:76 [TT 2:286]; cf. CO 9:505 [TT 2:554]), so that it would clearly be a mistake to suppose he wanted to substitute communion for presence. As he puts it in one place, the argument was not about every kind of absence, but only local absence (CO 9:487; TT 2:531); in other words, it was only about the mode of presence (CO 9:472; TT 2:510). The whole Christ, God and Man, is present everywhere in one mode of presence; "locally," however, his body is in heaven. In support of this distinction, Calvin invokes the scholastic formula *totus non totum,* but without giving it the elucidation it surely needs (CO 9:223, 246, 475–76; TT 2:457, 487–88, 514–15; cf. *Inst.* 1559, 4.17.30 [2:1403]).

[75]   *Inst.* 1559, 4.17.24 (2:1390). On reason and philosophy in the controversial writings, see CO 9:79, 167, 212–13, 235, 469, 474, 513–14; TT 2:289, 379–80, 442, 473, 505, 512–13 (three kinds of reason), 566.

[76]   Calvin believed, of course, that his view of the *modus* was warranted by Scripture, but his proofs are not very specific. "Pro multis tamen unus locus sufficiet. Paulus enim ad Rom. cap. octavo [Rom. 8:9–11], Christum non aliter in nobis quam per Spiritum suum habitare disserit " (*Inst.* 1559, 4.17.12 [2:1373]).

[77]   Ibid., 4.17.24 (2:1390).

the presupposition to be mistaken, will find it far too strange to be taken for granted.[78]

THE ECCLESIAL BODY

Our review of the difficulties in Calvin's theology of the Lord's Supper has led us finally to a difficulty that he himself does not seem to have

---

[78]   Much more would be required than I can attempt here if a just verdict is to be given on the bitter exchange between Calvin and Westphal. For now, I must be content to add a brief interim comment to this section of my concluding chapter. Hermann Sasse thought the controversy proved only that "there is no via media between 'est' and 'significat'"; in his view, "it was a tragic error for Calvin to believe that he had found the solution" to the eucharistic impasse (*This is My Body: Luther's Contention for the Real Presence in the Sacrament of the Altar* [Minneapolis, MN: Augsburg Publishing House, 1959], 326). But this cannot be the last word, because it so plainly rests in part on the continuing failure of many of Calvin's Lutheran critics to grasp his understanding of signs as instruments (see ibid., 327– 29). For their part, on the other hand, the Calvinists have just as persistently failed to recognize that what most of Calvin's Lutheran opponents wanted was neither an enclosing of Christ's body in the bread nor a carnal ("Capernaitic": see John 6:52, 59) eating of it. As Calvin rightly admonished Bullinger, not everyone who affirms a real eating affirms a carnal eating (Calvin to Bullinger, 25 February 1547, CO 12:482). At least three points should be noted. (1) Luther himself, at any rate, even when he endorsed Berengarius's recantation (1059), denied that Christ's body is chewed like meat: what one does to the bread is attributed to the body by virtue of the sacramental union (*Vom Abendmahl Christi, Bekenntnis*, WA 26.442.29–443.7; LW 37:300–1). The body is not torn in pieces as wolves devour a lamb; Christ did not say at the Last Supper, "Peter, you eat my finger; Andrew, you eat my nose," etc. (*Kurzes Bekenntnis vom heiligen Sakrament* [1544], WA 54.145.7–30; LW 38:292–93). It is not surprising that some Lutherans interpret the distribution of the body "in, with, and under" the bread to mean "nothing else than simultaneity" (Werner Elert, *The Structure of Lutheranism*, vol. 1: *The Theology and Philosophy of Life of Lutheranism Especially in the Sixteenth and Seventeenth Centuries*, trans. Walter A. Hansen [St. Louis, MO: Concordia Publishing House, 1962], 305; the German original has *die Gleichzeitigkeit*). (2) Further, when Heshusius said that by the communication of properties ubiquity is ascribed *in concreto* to the whole person of Christ, Calvin answered that this was his own doctrine exactly. For Calvin, however, it followed that the presence of the God-Man did not require his body to leave heaven, and this Calvin takes to be the sense of the dictum "Totus sed non totum" (*De vera participatione Christi in coena*, CO 9:475–76; TT 2:514– 15). The reason why the flesh of Christ can be said to dwell essentially in believers even apart from the Supper is precisely because they have the presence of his divinity (ibid., CO 9:509– 10; TT 2:560). (3) Finally, I quote without further comment an interesting question put by Alexander Barclay: "And does Luther not approach the 'dynamical' view of Calvin in some places? In a well-known illustration he speaks of light which comes from one sun, and which illuminates innumerable places at the same time. He speaks of the mirror which, when smashed in a thousand pieces, will show in each piece the same image; of the voice of the preacher which may be heard by four or five thousand people. Are we not led to the conclusion that with Luther it is not really a question of the substance but of the presence of an activity of the substance?" (*The Protestant Doctrine of the Lord's Supper* [1927], 252–53).

felt at all. There are no sufficient reasons for doubting that he believed both in the efficacy of sacramental signs and in the sacramental presence of the body of Christ, albeit he did not affirm either one in the manner of the Roman Catholics or the Lutherans. But his confident belief that Christ's body is located in heaven remains puzzling. Inextricably bound up with this belief is, of course, the question: How are we to understand all the sixteenth-century talk about the ascended or glorified body? Luther, Zwingli, and Calvin speak as though everyone knows what the expression "glorified body" denotes, the main question being where it is—in the bread, or in heaven.[79] Calvin's assertion that it must share the properties common to all human bodies, and must therefore be confined in the place to which it ascended, is by no means a readily dispensable feature of his doctrine; it is the cornerstone of his argument against the Lutherans.[80] Still, the purpose of the assertion must not be misunderstood. Its function is not to inform us of the exact location of the body (a question he dismisses), but to show that the mode of its presence cannot be what it was in the days of Christ's earthly life.[81] And the affirmation that Christ's bodily presence is now mediated by the secret power of his Spirit must not be divorced from another affirmation: that Christ is present in the church, which *is* his body.

When the three reformers spoke of the glorified body of Christ, their thoughts diverged; when they turned to the ecclesial body, their thoughts were in some respects similar. Partly in reaction against Zwinglian talk of signs and symbols, Luther resisted any suggestion that the words "This is my body" contain a figure of speech.[82] But he

[79] For Luther, of course, Christ's body can nowhere be strictly absent, but in the Eucharist Christ binds his body and blood through the word, so that they are received corporeally (*Sermon von dem Sakrament des Leibes und Blutes Christi, wider die Schwärmgeister* [1526], WA 19.492.19–493.8; LW 36:342–43).

[80] "Si inter dotes glorificati corporis numeratur, invisibili modo omnia implere: corpoream substantiam aboleri palam est, nec discrimen ullum relinqui deitatis et humanae naturae" (*Inst.* 1559, 4.17.29 [2:1398–99]).

[81] Ibid., 4.17.26 (2:1394). Christ dwells *extra mundum*, and his body has been carried *supra coelos:* this is the point, not where heaven, the magnificent palace of God, is (*Secunda defensio contra Westphalum*, CO 9:79–80; TT 2:290). The right hand of God is everywhere (Comm. Eph. 1.20, CO 51:158; cf. *De vera participatione Christi in coena*, CO 9:507–8 [TT 2:558–59]). Heaven, by contrast, seems to be a place, even though you would not find its location in a scientific cosmology (*Consensus Tigurinus*, art. 25, OS 2:253; TT 2:220). Yet even here, in this last passage, the point is simply that we are as far distant from the body of Christ as heaven from earth. Calvin knew perfectly well that to speak of a "place beyond the world" was to employ conventional or popular language (Comm. Eph. 4.10, CO 51:195).

[82] *Vom Abendmahl Christi, Bekenntnis*, WA 26.391–400; LW 37:262–68.

freely acknowledged that a figure is present in Paul's reference to the one eucharistic loaf: "Because there is one bread, we who are many are one body, for we all partake of the one bread" (1 Cor. 10:17). The important thing, in Luther's view, is not to put the figure or symbol in the wrong place. In his very first eucharistic treatise, *The Blessed Sacrament of the Holy and True Body of Christ* (1519), it was the ecclesial— or, as he says, the "spiritual"—body that chiefly interested him. There, he does start from the Augustinian contrast between the external, visible sign and the internal, spiritual significance: the sign in the Eucharist is eating and drinking, and the significance is communion or fellowship—incorporation with Christ and the saints. For we are all one loaf, ground together out of many grains. In this treatise Luther has not yet renounced transubstantiation, but he mentions the transformation of the bread and wine into Christ's natural body and blood less for its own sake than as an analogue to *our* transformation into Christ's spiritual body, which is the church. It is precisely in or by the Sacrament that we, in ourselves a collection of individuals, are changed into one spiritual body. And Luther states expressly: "It is more needful that you discern the spiritual than the natural body of Christ."[83]

This remarkable understanding of the "blessed Sacrament" never disappears from Luther's subsequent writings, but it yields first place to other thoughts. Part of it falls aside as the Roman doctrine of transubstantiation is cast off, and the analogue is of no further use. More important, the symbolism of the one loaf is overshadowed by Luther's discovery of the testament motif and by the demands of polemic against the "fanatics."[84] And yet, whether or not Luther realized it, Zwingli shared his early interest in the ecclesial body. Had the idea of an ecumenical theology been better cultivated in those acrimonious times, the rival parties might have begun at Marburg by listing the ecclesial body among the "things believed in common." It was argued by Julius Schweizer that the Zurich liturgy (1525) implied a kind of Reformed doctrine of transubstantiation: Zwingli wanted to convey the idea of a congregation transformed in the liturgy of the word into the true body of Christ, which then offers itself as an oblation to God. My own view is that this interpretation of Zwingli's liturgy, however attractive, has been pressed too strongly. The idea of an ecclesial transubstantiation has been read into Zwingli, and with-

---

[83]   *Ein Sermon von dem hochwürdigen Sakrament des heiligen wahren Leichnams Christi und von den Brüderschaften* (1519); quotation from WA 2.751.13 (LW 35:62).
[84]   See pp. 146–47 above; also my "Discerning the Body," 391–93.

out due acknowledgment that it was explicitly present in the early Luther. But there can be no doubt that the ecclesial body, quite apart from any notion of a collective transubstantiation, was a strong concern in Zwingli's reflections on the Eucharist.[85]

Calvin, it is true, thought that the Swiss contribution to the eucharistic debate of the 1520s had been purely negative. With his colleague Oecolampadius, Zwingli had rightly protested against the medieval idolatry of a carnal presence of Christ's body in the bread, but he was so engrossed in the critical task that, according to Calvin, he forgot to show the presence of Christ that *should* be believed.[86] There is no doubt something in this estimate of Zwingli. Indeed, the importance of his critique of sacramentalism ought not to be belittled. He perceived in the sacramental thinking of Rome—and even of Wittenberg—another way of salvation, in competition with the Reformation's *sola fide* (salvation only through faith in the gospel), and he had a horror of anything that smacked of placing God at human disposal through the performance of wonder-working rituals.[87] Nevertheless, there was a positive side to his eucharistic theology, too, and Calvin seems in fact to have quietly taken it over in his own reflections on the Lord's Supper. Zwingli made a serious attempt to understand the actual setting of the Eucharist in the life of the early church. He noted in particular the situation at Corinth, where the division of the church into cliques betrayed itself even at table fellowship, which should have culminated in the Lord's Supper; for the have-nots went hungry, while the haves ate their fill and got drunk (1 Cor. 11:17–22). Zwingli drew what is surely the right conclusion: Paul's warning about the failure of the Corinthians to "discern the body" (v. 29) was directed to Christians who had no sense of the church, which is the body of Christ. "Do this in remembrance of me" (vv. 24-25) suggested to Zwingli not a private devotional exercise but a corporate celebration, which would be violated by the formation of separate groups or parties. His entire

---

[85]   Julius Schweizer, *Reformierte Abendmahlsgestaltung in der Schau Zwinglis* (Basel: Friedrich Reinhardt, 1954). For a critique of Schweizer's argument (and the similar argument of Jaques Courvoisier), see my articles referred to in n. 19 above.

[86]   See p. 141 above.

[87]   " So mūß 'sin fleisch essen' und 'in inn vertruwen' ein ding sin, oder aber es wärind zwen weg zur säligheit" (*Eine klare Unterrichtung vom Nachtmahl Christi* [1526], SW 4:817; LCC 24:205). "Illi enim tribuunt sacramentis, quasi alligata sit eis divina virtus, ut, ubicunque adhibeantur, operentur; hoc enim rem illis auget, ut qui omnia dei dona venalia habent, immo deum ipsum longe carius quam Judas vendunt" (*De convitiis Eccii*, SW 6, 3:272; LWZ 2:118).

liturgy was designed to convey the sense of a common meal celebrated, as an act of thanksgiving, by a single congregation.[88]

Usually, Calvin's criticisms of Zwingli and his friends do not mention them by name. But in one unguarded moment he expressly called Zwingli's opinion on the use of the sacraments "false and pernicious."[89] The trouble was, in Calvin's eyes, that Zwingli reduced the sacraments to acts by which we *attest* our faith, whereas they are first and foremost acts of God to *strengthen* our faith.[90] And yet Calvin's harsh verdict should not make us overlook the fact that even what he himself identifies as the primary use of the Supper has at least one point in common with the Zwinglian view: it affirms that the Lord's Supper is a genuine meal, a holy banquet. And, as we have seen, Calvin never denied a secondary place to Zwingli's view of a sacrament as a confession of faith. Hence, while he held the Supper itself to be a gift, he included in the celebration both the church's grateful remembrance of Christ's death and the call to unity in the body as well:

> For the Lord so communicates his body to us there [in the Supper] that he is made completely one with us and we with him. Since he has but one body of which he makes us all partakers, it is necessary that all of us also be made one body by such participation. The bread exhibited in the Sacrament represents this unity: as it is made of many grains so mixed together that one cannot be distinguished from another, so we too should be joined and bound together by such agreement of mind that no dissent or division should come between us.[91]

Besides Paul in 1 Corinthians 10:16–17, Calvin, as usual, invokes in his support the name of Augustine, who called the Sacrament the "bond of love" (*caritatis vinculum*).

---

[88]   *De vera et falsa religione commentarius* (1525), SW 3:801–3 (LWZ 3:231–33); *Aktion oder Brauch des Nachtmahls* (1525), SW 4:1–24. Zwingli understood κοινωνία in 1 Cor. 10:16 to mean "community" (*die gemeind*): the Eucharist signifies that the Christians at Corinth are one body, which is the church of Christ (*Vom Nachtmahl*, SW 4:860; LCC 24:237). Sometimes he takes τὸ σῶμα in 1 Cor. 11:29 to mean the historical body of Christ, which he gave up to death (ibid., SW 4:851; LCC 24:231). Elsewhere, he suggests that partaking of the sacraments without faith dishonors the body of Christ in the double sense of both the historical and the ecclesial body (*Fidei expositio*, CERP, 48–49, 53; LCC 24:259–60, 265). See also *Ad Matthaeum Alberum de coena dominica epistola* (1524), SW 3:347–49 (ZW 2:140–42), and *Amica exegesis, id est: expositio eucharistiae negocii ad Martinum Lutherum* (1527), SW 5:635–45 (ZW 2:289–97).

[89]   Cited in n. 55 above.

[90]   See pp. 8-9 above. Calvin could equally well assert the principle that a sacrament is not a human work but a work of God against "the papists" (Comm. Gal. 5.3, CO 50:245).

[91]   *Inst.* 1559, 4.17.38 (2:1414–15). Cf. Comm. 1 Cor. 10.16 (CO 49:464), from which my epigraph for this chapter is taken.

Calvin's point in this passage is that Christ makes us not simply *one* body, but *his* body. Hence the Sacrament impresses upon us that an injury done to one of "the brethren" is an injury done to Christ in him; conversely, that we cannot love Christ unless we love him in them.[92] The main warrant for this line of thought comes, of course, a little further on in Paul's First Letter to the Corinthians—not in chapter ten, but in chapter twelve. In his commentary on 1 Corinthians 12:12, Calvin asserts that Christians are "the spiritual and mystical (*arcanum*) body of Christ," and he notes with particular interest that in one phrase, "so it is with Christ," Paul actually uses the name "Christ" for the church. (Paul does not say, as we might expect, "Just as the body is one and has many members . . . *so it is with the church*," but "so it is *with Christ*.")[93] Elsewhere, Calvin acknowledges that the image of the ecclesial body in this text differs from the image of Christ as head of the body in Ephesians and Colossians. But he takes this divergence in his stride and simply remarks that the unity of the head and members is so great that the name "Christ" sometimes includes the whole body.[94] The metaphor of the head suggests to him that the life of the body flows from Christ as the tree draws sap from the root;[95] but because the church *is* the body, Calvin does not hesitate to speak of Christ as actually being and living in us. Not until we are one with him is Christ complete, for the church is "the fullness of him who fills all in all" (Eph. 1:23).[96] As the soul quickens the body, he imparts life to his members.[97] Once, his body was confined within the walls of Jerusalem; now it is extended far and wide,[98] and he wants to be recognized in his members.[99]

This striking imagery of an "ecclesial presence" of Christ, as we may call it, is a fundamental theme in Calvin's theology. Engrafting

[92]   *Inst.* 1559, 4.17.38 (2:1415). I stress this perhaps rather obvious point, not only because it does not become explicit until Calvin moves beyond the words I have cited, but also because he twice says (a little surprisingly) "*our* body."

[93]   Comm. 1 Cor. 12.12, CO 49:501.

[94]   Comm. Col. 1.24, CO 52:93. Calvin takes the text ("in my flesh I complete what is lacking in Christ's afflictions for the sake of his body, that is, the church") to mean: "Quemadmodum ergo semel passus est in se Christus, ita quotidie patitur in membris suis."

[95]   Comm. Eph. 4.16, CO 51:203.

[96]   Comm. Eph. 1.23, CO 51:159–60.

[97]   Comm. Gal. 2.20, CO 50:199.

[98]   Comm. Acts 8.1, CO 48:173. By the body confined to Jerusalem Calvin means here not the body of the historical Jesus, but the first Christian community (as the text suggests).

[99]   Comm. 1 Cor. 12.12, CO 49:501.

into Christ coincides so completely with entrance into the church that, when he writes of the body of Christ, it is not always possible to tell whether he means the glorified or the ecclesial body.[100] One cannot, of course, ignore his perplexing assertions about the glorified body, or simply reduce the presence of Christ (as he sees it) to an ecclesial presence. For, in the first place, Calvin, like Luther, believed that only through participation in the glorified body could anyone be incorporated into the ecclesial body;[101] and, in the second place, he feared that the resurrection hope of Christians would be weak and fragile if human flesh had not been truly raised in Christ and had not entered heaven.[102] Nevertheless, if one is interested not only in Calvin but also in the doctrines Calvin thought about, it is worth noting that something like his favorite metaphor of the sun's rays reappeared in later Protestant thinking about Christ and the church quite apart from any speculation on the glorified body of Christ.

In an important essay on "Schleiermacher and the Church," Ernst Troeltsch maintained that for Schleiermacher the sociological idea of a "community" meant in general an "organic radiation from some strong nodal point in the development of life," and that Schleiermacher then defined the distinctively Christian community by the particular religious content of Christianity and by the connection of this content with the figure of Christ.[103] Here, the "point" from which the spiritual force radiates is located in history, not in heaven: it is the historical, not the glorified, humanity of the Redeemer. Schleiermacher was convinced that the only adequate way to think of the believer's relationship with the Redeemer is to see it as mediated through the living

---

[100]   Ronald S. Wallace, *Calvin's Doctrine of the Word and Sacrament* (1953), 154–55.

[101]   This is clearly how Calvin read 1 Cor. 10:16 (CO 49:464). The *verum* ("it is true") in the passage cited as my epigraph is concessive, as is his admission that the unity of believers among themselves is properly termed κοινωνία (cf. Zwingli, n. 88 above). Calvin goes on to insist that in this text the κοινωνία intended is the *societas quae nobis est cum Christi sanguine* (not, that is, *per Christi sanguinem*). "Atqui unde, obsecro, illa inter nos κοινωνία, nisi quia sumus Christo coadunati hac lege, ut caro simus de carne eius et ossa ex ossibus eius? Incorporari enim (ut ita loquar) nos Christo oportet primum, ut inter nos uniamur." Cf. Comm. Eph. 5.30 (CO 51:225): we grow into one body by the communication of his substance. The same point was made by Luther in his *Von Anbeten des Sakraments des heiligen Leichnams Christi* (1523), WA 11.440.34–441.3; LW 36:286–87.

[102]   *Inst.* 1559, 4.17.29 (2:1400). Cf. *Ultima admonitio ad Westphalum*, CO 9:174; TT 2:390–91.

[103]   Troeltsch, "Schleiermacher und die Kirche," in Troeltsch et al., *Schleiermacher der Philosoph des Glaubens*, Moderne Philosophie, no. 6 (Berlin–Schöneberg: Buchverlag der "Hilfe," 1910), 29–32.

historical community that the Redeemer brought into being, and which is called his "body." The redeeming activity of Christ is the establishment of a new life common to him and to us (original in him and in us derived): to be redeemed, individuals must therefore enter the sphere of Christ's historical efficacy, which means the church. The term Schleiermacher chooses to define this manner of ecclesial communion with Christ is "mystical"—a term he admits to be vague, but which he thinks is nonetheless justified to denote an experience that can be grasped only from the inside. And, he says, his exposition rests entirely on the inner experience of the believer and seeks only to describe and elucidate it.[104] If Schleiermacher succeeded in construing the believer's experience correctly, then we might say that what the communicant is aware of in the Eucharist is the manner in which the historical body of Christ continues to work in and upon the ecclesial body.

Such a manner of thinking is clearly not foreign to Calvin, although it does not give the whole of his conception of Christ's bodily presence. In the *Geneva Catechism* he wrote that the one effect of the work of Christ is that there should be a church; and in his commentary on 1 Corinthians 10:16 he found a part—albeit not the whole—of Paul's meaning in the fact that the sacrificial death of Christ establishes a community, which is the body symbolized by the one eucharistic bread.[105] The community, in his thinking, transcends the individuals who belong to it: in one image, it is their "mother," by whose hands God holds out the spiritual food of the soul; in another, it is the true body of the living Christ himself, its members "incorporated" through the sacramental word and efficacious signs.[106] Calvin had no need to choose between a glorified body in heaven and an ecclesial body on earth. But if the enduring value of his strange talk about Christ's life-

---

[104]   Friedrich Schleiermacher, *Der christliche Glaube nach den Grundsätzen der evangelischen Kirche im Zusammenhange dargestellt*, 7th ed., based on the 2d ed. of 1830–31, ed. Martin Redeker, 2 vols. (Berlin: Walter de Gruyter, 1960), § 100.2–3, § 101.3–4. For such a conception of Christ's mystical presence one might perhaps even appropriate the scholastic *totus non totum* (see nn. 74, 78, above), since the distance that separates believers from Christ's historical body by no means detracts from the presence of the whole person in the ecclesial body.

[105]   *Catechismus*, OS 2:89 (TT 2:50); Comm. 1 Cor. 10.16 (see n. 101 above).

[106]   *Inst.* 1559, 4.1.1, 4–5 (2:1012, 1016–17). Cf. Comm. Eph. 4.12 (CO 51:199): "Et certe ecclesia communis est piorum omnium mater." Josef Bohatec (1937) drew attention to Calvin's use of "organic" images in speaking of the church, and I think that Harro Höpfl (1982) is much too quick in dismissing Bohatec's contribution. For a general study of Calvin's doctrine of the church see Benjamin Charles Milner, Jr. (1970).

giving flesh is not to be missed, it may be more needful for a later generation to discern the ecclesial body of Christ.

It is not at all surprising that stalwart Reformed divines have sometimes been not merely puzzled but offended by Calvin's talk about the communciation of Christ's life-giving flesh. They may choose to reject it as a perilous intrusion into Reformed theology and insist that Christ's body is life-giving only because it was crucified. But in so doing they should note that Calvin's view of the Lord's Supper was bound up with a total conception of what it means to be saved and of how the historical deed of Christ reaches out to the present. It is impossible to read Calvin's ideas on Baptism and the Eucharist in their own historical context and not to notice that they were developed in part as a warning against what he took to be another peril: a mentality that reduces sacred signs to mere reminders, communion with Christ to beliefs about Christ, and the living body of the church to an association of likeminded individuals. Only a careful study of later Reformed history can show which has turned out to be the greater of the two perils. But this much, I think, can fairly be said in conclusion: even if the Calvinists have the greatest difficulty in expressing what exactly that something *more* is that they experience in the holy banquet, ecumenical theology will always have need of them to throw their weight on Calvin's side of the Reformed boat.

BIBLIOGRAPHY

I. SOURCES AND TRANSLATIONS

Proof texts for recurring themes in Calvin could have been extended well beyond the quotations and references I have given. It will, I hope, be more useful to list here, in chronological order, the main writings of Calvin on which my interpretations rest. With the general reader in mind, I give each title (sometimes abbreviated) in English, and wherever I can I note, along with the edition I have used, an accessible English translation. But no attempt is made to include all the existing editions and translations.

Calvin's commentaries, published in English by the Calvin Translation Society (Edinburgh, 1844–56), have been reprinted in twenty-two volumes (Grand Rapids, MI: Baker Book House, 1981). There is no need to cite the volumes individually. His *consilia*, mostly undated, are translated by Mary Beaty and Benjamin W. Farley as *Calvin's Ecclesiastical Advice* (Louisville, KY: Westminster/John Knox Press, 1991). Unfortunately, none of the letters I have mentioned appears in the selection, *Letters of John Calvin*, edited by Jules Bonnet and translated by David Constable and M.R. Gilchrist in four volumes (vols. 1–2, Edinburgh: T. Constable, 1855; vols. 3–4, Philadelphia, PA: Presbyterian Board of Publications, 1855–58), now available again in *Selected Works of John Calvin: Tracts and Letters*, edited by Henry Beveridge and Jules Bonnet (7 vols., Grand Rapids, MI: Baker Book House, 1983), volumes 4–7.

Calvin's Commentary on Seneca's De Clementia, 1532. Edited with introduction, translation, and notes by Ford Lewis Battles and André Malan Hugo. Renaissance Text Series, vol. 3. Leiden: E.J. Brill, 1969.
"Preface to Olivétan's New Testament," 1535 (1543). CO 9:791– 822. LCC 23:58–73.
Institution of The Christian Religion, 1536. OS 1:11–283. Translated by Ford Lewis Battles. Atlanta, GA: John Knox Press, 1975. The revised edition of this translation bears the more familiar title, *Institutes of the Christian Religion,* and has a different pagination. Grand Rapids, MI: Wm. B. Eerdmans

191

Publishing Co. in collaboration with the H. H. Meeter Center for Calvin Studies, 1986.

Instruction in Faith, 1537. OS 1:378–417. Translated by Paul T. Fuhrmann. Philadelphia, PA: Westminster Press, 1949.

The Genevan Confession, 1537. OS 1:418–26. LCC 22:25–33. Calvin was probably coauthor of the confession with Farel.

Confession of Faith Concerning the Eucharist [1537]. OS 1: 433– 36. LCC 22:167–69. Coauthored by Calvin with Farel and Viret.

Letter to Andrew Zebedee, 19 May 1539. CO 10²:344–47 (no. 171).

Institutes of the Christian Religion, 1539. CO 1:253–1152. A collated text of the Latin editions published between the first (1536) and the last (1559).

Reply to Cardinal Sadolet's Letter, 1539. OS 1:437–89. TT 1:23– 68.

Commentary on Romans, 1540. CO 49:1–292.

Short Treatise on the Holy Supper of Our Lord Jesus Christ, 1541. OS 1:499–530. TT 2:163–98.

Institutes of the Christian Religion, 1541 (French). *Institution de la religion chrestienne*. Edited by Jacques Pannier. 4 vols. Paris: Société Les Belles Lettres, 1936–39.

Forms of Prayer for the Church, 1542. OS 2:1–58. TT 2:100–28. The companion "Essay on the Lord's Supper," not translated in TT, will be found in *Calvin's Ecclesiastical Advice*, 165–70.

Institutes of the Christian Religion, 1543. CO 1:253–1152.

A Humble Exhortation to the Most Invincible Emperor Charles V, 1544. CO 6:453–534. TT 1:121–234. Commonly referred to as *The Necessity of Reforming the Church*.

Treatise Against Anabaptists, 1544. CO 7:45–142. *Treatises Against the Anabaptists and Against the Libertines*. Translated and edited by Benjamin Wirt Farley. Grand Rapids, MI: Baker Book House, 1982.

Catechism of the Church of Geneva, 1545. OS 2:59–157. TT 2: 33–94.

Commentary on 1 Corinthians, 1546. CO 49:293–574.

Letter to Henrich Bullinger, 25 February 1547. CO 12:480–89 (no. 880).

Acts of the Council of Trent with the Antidote, 1547. CO 7:365– 506. TT 3:17–188.

Commentary on 2 Corinthians, 1548. CO 50:1–156.

Commentaries on Galatians, Ephesians, Philippians, and Colossians, 1548. CO 50:157–268 (Galatians), 51:137–240 (Ephesians), 52:1–76 (Philippians), 52:77–132 (Colossians).

Commentaries on 1 and 2 Timothy, 1548. CO 52:241–336 (1 Timothy), 337–96 (2 Timothy).

Commentary on Hebrews, 1549. CO 55:1–198.

Concerning Scandals, 1550. OS 2:159–240. Translated by John W. Fraser. Grand Rapids, MI: Wm. B. Eerdmans Publishing Co., 1978.

Commentary on Titus, 1550. CO 52:397–436.

Mutual Consent as to the Sacraments [Consensus Tigurinus], 1551. OS 2:241–58. TT 2:199–204, 212–20. The consensus was concluded in 1549, but not published until 1551. With the Articles of Agreement, both OS and TT include Calvin's letter to the Zurich pastors (1 August 1549) and their response (30 August 1549), but none of the preliminary exchanges between Calvin and Bullinger (for which see CO 7:693–716).

Commentary on Isaiah, 1551. CO 36–37:455.

Commentary on 1 John [the Catholic Epistles], 1551. CO 55:293– 376.

Commentary on John, 1553. CO 47:1–458.

Letter to John Marbach, 25 August 1554. CO 15:211–14 (no. 1998).

Commentary on Acts, 1552–54. CO 48:1–574.

Commentary on Genesis, 1554. CO 23:1–622.

Defense of the Sound and Orthodox Doctrine Concerning the Sacraments, 1555. OS
    2:259–87. TT 2:204–44. The *Defense* is included in TT under the heading
    "Mutual Consent as to the Sacraments": Calvin's preface is on pp. 204–12
    (letter to the pastors of Zurich, 24 November 1554), and the defense itself
    on pp. 221–44 ("Exposition of the Heads of Agreement," i.e., of the
    Consensus Tigurinus). This, of course, is the "first defense" implied in the
    title of the "second defense" against Westphal (1556).

Letter to Peter Martyr Vermigli, 8 August 1555. CO 15:722–25 (no. 2266).

Sermons on Deuteronomy [1555–56]. CO 25:573–29:232.

*Second Defense of the Pious and Orthodox Faith Concerning the Sacraments, in
    Answer to the Calumnies of Joachim Westphal*, 1556. CO 9:41–120. TT 2:245–
    345.

Last Admonition to Joachim Westphal, 1557. CO 9:137–252. TT 2:346–494.

Commentary on Psalms, 1557. CO 31–32:442.

Institutes of the Christian Religion, 1559. CO 2. Edited by John T. McNeill and
    translated by Ford Lewis Battles. 2 vols. LCC 20–21. Philadelphia, PA:
    Westminster Press, 1960. *Inst.* 1559 is cited by book, chapter, and section,
    followed in parentheses by the volume and page in the LCC translation.

Commentary on Micah [the Minor Prophets], 1559. CO 43:281–434.

The French [Gallican] Confession of Faith, 1559. OS 2:297–324. Emily O. Butler's
    translation is reproduced with introduction and notes (including a
    discussion of Calvin's role in the authorship of the confession) in B. A.
    Gerrish, ed., *The Faith of Christendom*, 126–63. Cleveland and New York:
    World Publishing Company (Meridian Books), 1963.

Institutes of the Christian Religion, 1560 (French). Jean Calvin, *Institution de la
    religion chrestienne*. Edited by Jean-Daniel Benoit. 5 vols. Bibliothèque des
    Textes Philosophiques. Paris: Librairie Philosophique J. Vrin. 1957–63.

*Clear Explanation of Sound Doctrine Concerning the True Partaking of the Flesh and
    Blood of Christ in the Holy Supper, in Order to Dissipate the Mists of Tileman
    Heshusius*, 1561. CO 9:457–518. TT 2:495–572.

*The Best Method of Obtaining Concord, Provided the Truth Be Sought Without
    Contention*, 1561. OS 2:291–95. TT 2:573–79.

Commentary [Lectures] on Daniel, 1561. CO 40:517–41:304.

Confession of Faith in Name of the Reformed Churches of France, 1562. CO 9:753–
    72. TT 2:137–62.

Sermons from Job, 1563. CO 33–35:414. Translated by Leroy Nixon. Grand
    Rapids, MI: Wm. B. Eerdmans Publishing Company, 1952. Nixon selects
    only twenty of the original 159 sermons, not including the one referred to
    in chapter six.

II. SELECTED SECONDARY LITERATURE ON CALVIN

The following list gives the full publication data for studies of Calvin mentioned
in the chapters and notes and for one or two other pertinent items. There are
several excellent Calvin bibliographies in which more exhaustive guides to

194 GRACE AND GRATITUDE

the secondary literature are readily available. The CO bibliography (1900) has
been reprinted: Alfred Erichson, *Bibliographia Calviniana* (Nieuwkoop: B. De
Graaf, 1960). It was supplemented by Wilhelm Niesel, *Calvin-Bibliographie
1901–1959* (Munich: Chr. Kaiser Verlag, 1961), and D[ionysius] Kempff, *A
Bibliography of Calviniana 1959–1974*, Studies in Medieval and Reformation
Thought, vol. 15 (Leiden: E. J. Brill, 1975). These two volumes are in turn
supplemented annually by the very comprehensive bibliographies of Peter
De Klerk in the *Calvin Theological Journal*.

Alting von Geusau, L. G. M. *Die Lehre von der Kindertaufe bei Calvin, gesehen im
Rahmen seiner Sakraments- und Tauftheologie: Synthese oder Ordnungsfehler?*
Bilthoven: H. Nelissen, 1963.
Armstrong, Brian G. *Calvinism and the Amyraut Heresy: Protestant Scholasticism
and Humanism in Seventeenth-Century France*. Madison: University of
Wisconsin Press, 1969.
Babelotzky, Gerd. *Platonische Bilder und Gedankengänge in Calvins Lehre vom
Menschen*. Veröffentlichungen des Instituts für Europäische Geschichte
Mainz, vol. 83. Wiesbaden: Franz Steiner, 1977.
Barclay, Alexander. *The Protestant Doctrine of the Lord's Supper: A Study in the
Eucharistic Teaching of Luther, Zwingli, and Calvin*. Glasgow: Jackson, Wylie
& Co., 1927.
Barth, Karl. "Calvin als Theologe." *Reformatio* 8 (1959):317–18.
Battenhouse, Roy W. "The Doctrine of Man in Calvin and Renaissance
Platonism." *Journal of the History of Ideas* 9 (1948):447–71.
Bauke, Hermann. *Die Probleme der Theologie Calvins*. Leipzig: J. C. Hinrichs,
1922.
Beckmann, Joachim. *Vom Sakrament bei Calvin: Die Sakramentslehre Calvins in
ihren Beziehungen zu Augustin*. Tübingen: J. C. B. Mohr (Paul Siebeck), 1926.
Bizer, Ernst. *Studien zur Geschichte des Abendmahlsstreits im 16. Jahrhundert*.
Beiträge zur Förderung christlicher Theologie, 2d series, vol. 46, 1940.
Reprint, Darmstadt: Wissenschaftliche Buchgesellschaft, 1962.
Bizer, Ernst, and Walter Kreck. *Die Abendmahlslehre in den reformatorischen
Bekenntnisschriften*. Theologische Existenz heute, new series, no. 47. Munich:
Chr. Kaiser Verlag, 1955.
Blaser, Klauspeter. *Calvins Lehre von den drei Ämtern Christi*. Theologische
Studien, vol. 105. Zurich: EVZ-Verlag, 1970.
Bohatec, Josef. *Calvins Lehre von Staat und Kirche mit besonderer Berücksichtigung
des Organismusgedankens*. Untersuchungen zur deutschen Staats- und
Rechtsgeschichte, vol. 147, 1937. Reprint, Aalen: Scientia, 1961.
Boisset, Jean. *Sagesse et sainteté dans la pensée de Jean Calvin: Essai sur l'humanisme
du réformateur français*. Bibliothèque de l'École des Hautes Études, Section
des Sciences Religieuses, vol. 71. Paris: Presses Universitaires de France,
1959.
Bouwsma, William J. *John Calvin: A Sixteenth-Century Portrait*. New York:
Oxford University Press, 1988.
———————————. "The Quest for the Historical Calvin." *Archive for
Reformation History* 77 (1986):47–57.
———————————. "The Spirituality of John Calvin." In *Christian Spirituality:
High Middle Ages and Reformation*, edited by Jill Raitt, in collaboration with
Bernard McGinn and John Meyendorff, 318–33. World Spirituality: An

Encyclopedic History of the Religious Quest, vol. 17. New York: Crossroad, 1987.

Brunner, Peter. *Vom Glauben bei Calvin, dargestellt auf Grund der Institutio, des Catechismus Genevensis und unter Heranziehung exegetischer und homiletischer Schriften.* Tübingen: J. C. B. Mohr (Paul Siebeck), 1925.

Cadier, Jean. *La Doctrine calviniste de la Sainte Cène.* Études théologiques et religieuses, vol. 26. Montpellier: Faculté de théologie protestante, 1951.

Dankbaar, Willem Frederik. *De sacramentsleer van Calvijn.* Amsterdam: H. J. Paris, 1941.

Dee, Simon Pieter. *Het geloofsbegrip van Calvijn.* Kampen: J. H. Kok, 1918.

Douglass, Jane Dempsey. "Calvin's Use of Metaphorical Language for God: God as Enemy and God as Mother." *Archive for Reformation History* 77 (1986):126–40.

Doumergue, É[mile]. *Jean Calvin: Les hommes et les choses de son temps* Vol. 4. *La Pensée religieuse de Calvin.* Lausanne: Georges Bridel, 1910.

Dowey, Edward A., Jr. *The Knowledge of God in Calvin's Theology.* New York: Columbia University Press, 1952. The second printing (1965) has the same pagination except in the new preface and the supplementary bibliography.

——————————. "The Structure of Calvin's Theological Thought as Influenced by the Two-Fold Knowledge of God." In Wilhelm H. Neuser, ed. (see below), 135–48.

Duffield, G[ervase] E., ed. *John Calvin.* Courtenay Studies in Reformation Theology, vol. 1. Grand Rapids, MI: Wm. B. Eerdmans, 1966.

Ebrard, [Johannes Heinrich] August. *Das Dogma vom heiligen Abendmahl und seine Geschichte.* 2 vols. Frankfurt am Main: Heinrich Zimmer, 1845–46.

Engel, Mary Potter. *John Calvin's Perspectival Anthropology.* American Academy of Religion Academy Series, no. 52. Atlanta, GA: Scholars Press, 1988.

Evans, G[illian] R. "Calvin on Signs: An Augustinian Dilemma." *Renaissance Studies* 3 (1989):35–45.

Fischer, Danièle. "Calvin et la Confession d'Augsbourg." In Wilhelm H. Neuser, ed. (see below), pp. 245–71.

Fitzer, Joseph. "The Augustinian Roots of Calvin's Eucharistic Thought." *Augustinian Studies* 7 (1976):69–98.

Forstman, H. Jackson. *Word and Spirit: Calvin's Doctrine of Biblical Authority.* Stanford, CA: Stanford University Press, 1962.

Gäbler, Ulrich. "Das Zustandekommen des Consensus Tigurinus im Jahre 1549." *Theologische Literaturzeitung* 104 (1979):321–32.

Ganoczy, Alexandre. *The Young Calvin.* Translated from the French (1966) by David Foxgrover and Wade Provo. Philadelphia: Westminster Press, 1987.

Ganoczy, Alexandre, and Stefan Scheld. *Herrschaft—Tugend—Vorsehung: Hermeneutische Deutung und Veröffentlichung handschriftlicher Annotationen Calvins zu sieben Senecatragödien und der Pharsalia Lucans.* Veröffentlichungen des Instituts für Europäische Geschichte Mainz, vol. 105. Wiesbaden: Franz Steiner, 1982.

George, Timothy. "John Calvin and the Agreement of Zurich." In Timothy George, ed. (see below), 42–58.

——————————, ed. *John Calvin and the Church: A Prism of Reform.* Louisville, KY: Westminster/John Knox Press, 1990.

Gerrish, B[rian] A[lbert]. "Atonement and 'Saving Faith.'" *Theology Today* 17 (1960–61):181–91.

—————————. "Discerning the Body: Sign and Reality in Luther's Controversy with the Swiss." *Journal of Religion* 68 (1988):377–95.

—————————. "Do We 'Offer Christ' in the Lord's Supper?" *McCormick Speaking* 13 (1959):15–20.

—————————. "From Calvin to Schleiermacher: The Theme and the Shape of Christian Dogmatics." In *Internationaler Schleiermacher-Kongress Berlin 1984*, edited by Kurt-Victor Selge, 1033–51. Schleiermacher-Archiv, vol. 1. Berlin: Walter de Gruyter, 1985.

—————————. *The Old Protestantism and the New: Essays on the Reformation Heritage.* Chicago: University of Chicago Press; Edinburgh: T. & T. Clark, 1982.

—————————, ed. in collaboration with Robert Benedetto. *Reformatio Perennis: Essays on Calvin and the Reformation in Honor of Ford Lewis Battles.* Pittsburgh Theological Monograph Series, no. 32. Pittsburgh, PA: Pickwick Press, 1981.

—————————. "The Reformers' Theology of Worship." *McCormick Quarterly* 14 (1961): 21–29.

—————————. *Tradition and the Modern World: Reformed Theology in the Nineteenth Century.* Chicago: University of Chicago Press, 1978.

Gollwitzer, Helmut. *Coena Domini: Die altlutherische Abendmahlslehre in ihrer Auseinandersetzung mit dem Calvinismus dargestellt an der lutherischen Frühorthodoxie.* Munich: Chr. Kaiser Verlag, 1937.

Grass, Hans. *Die Abendmahlslehre bei Luther und Calvin: Eine Kritische Untersuchung.* Beiträge zur Förderung christlicher Theologie, second series, vol. 47. Gütersloh: C. Bertelsmann, 1954.

Grislis, Egil. "Calvin's Doctrine of Baptism" *Church History* 31 (1962):46–65.

—————————. "Calvin's Use of Cicero in the *Institutes* I, 1–5: A Case Study in Theological Method." *Archive for Reformation History* 62 (1971):5–37.

Hall, Charles A. M. *With the Spirit's Sword: The Drama of Spiritual Warfare in the Theology of John Calvin.* Basel Studies of Theology, no. 3. Richmond, VA: John Knox Press, 1968.

Hartvelt, G[errit] P. *Verum corpus: Een studie over een centraal hoofdstuk uit de avondmaalsleer van Calvijn.* Delft: W. D. Meinema, 1960.

Hodge, Charles. "Doctrine of the Reformed Church on the Lord's Supper." *Princeton Review* 20 (1848):227–78.

Höpfl, Harro. *The Christian Polity of John Calvin.* Cambridge: Cambridge University Press, 1982.

Jansen, John Frederick. *Calvin's Doctrine of the Work of Christ,* London: James Clarke & Co., 1956.

Kendall, R. T. *Calvin and English Calvinism to 1649.* Oxford Theological Monographs. Oxford: Oxford University Press, 1979.

Kolfhaus, Wilhelm. *Christusgemeinschaft bei Johannes Calvin.* Beiträge zur Geschichte und Lehre der reformierten Kirche, vol. 3. Neukirchen: Buchandlung des Erziehungsvereins, 1939.

Koopmans, Jan. *Das altkirchliche Dogma in der Reformation.* Translated from the Dutch (1938) by H. Quistorp. Beiträge zur evangelischen Theologie, vol. 22. Munich: Chr. Kaiser Verlag, 1955.

Krusche, Werner. *Das Wirken des Heiligen Geistes nach Calvin.* Forschungen zur Kirchen- und Dogmengeschichte, vol. 7. Göttingen: Vandenhoeck & Ruprecht, 1957.

Lane, A. N. S. "Calvin's Sources of St. Bernard." *Archive for Reformation History* 67 (1976):253–83.

Leith, John H. "Calvin's Doctrine of the Proclamation of the Word and its Significance for Today." In Timothy George, ed. (see above), 206–29.

McDonnell, Kilian. *John Calvin, the Church, and the Eucharist.* Princeton, NJ: Princeton University Press, 1967.

McLelland, Joseph C. "Meta-Zwingli or anti–Zwingli? Bullinger and Calvin in Eucharistic Concord." In *Huldrych Zwingli, 1484–1531: A Legacy of Radical Reform,* edited by E[dward] J. Furcha, 179–95. Papers from the 1984 International Zwingli Symposium, McGill University. ARC Supplement, no. 2. Montreal: Faculty of Religious Studies, McGill University, 1985.

McNeill, John T. "The Significance of the Word of God for Calvin." *Church History* 28 (1959):131–46.

Meyer, John R. [Boniface]. "Calvin's Eucharistic Doctrine: 1536–39." *Journal of Ecumenical Studies* 4 (1967):47–65.

——————. "Mysterium Fidei and the Later Calvin." *Scottish Journal of Theology* 25 (1972):392–411.

——————. "Sacramental Theology in the *Institutes* of John Calvin." *American Benedictine Review* 15 (1964):360–80.

Milner, Benjamin Charles, Jr. *Calvin's Doctrine of the Church.* Studies in the History of Christian Thought, vol. 5. Leiden: E. J. Brill, 1970.

Moltmann, Jürgen, ed. *Calvin-Studien 1959.* Neukirchen: Neukirchener Verlag, 1960.

Mülhaupt, Erwin. *Die Predigt Calvins: Ihre Geschichte, ihre Form und ihre religiösen Grundgedanken.* Arbeiten zur Kirchengeschichte, no. 18. Berlin: Walter de Gruyter, 1931.

Muller, Richard A. *Christ and the Decree: Christology and Predestination in Reformed Theology from Calvin to Perkins.* Studies in Historical Theology, vol. 2. Durham, NC: Labyrinth Prss, 1986.

Neuser, Wilhelm H., ed. *Calvinus ecclesiae Genevensis custos: Die Referate des Internationalen Kongresses für Calvinforschung, 1982.* Frankfurt am Main: Peter Lang, 1984.

Nevin, John W. *The Mystical Presence: A Vindication of the Reformed or Calvinistic Doctrine of the Holy Eucharist.* Philadelphia: J. B. Lippincott & Co., 1846. Reproduced, but with a different pagination, in John W. Nevin, *The Mystical Presence and Other Writings on the Eucharist,* edited by Bard Thompson and George H. Bricker, Lancaster Series on the Mercersburg Theology, vol. 4. Philadelphia and Boston: United Church Press, 1966.

Niesel, Wilhelm. *Calvins Lehre vom Abendmahl im Lichte seiner letzten Antwort an Westphal.* Forschungen zur Geschichte und Lehre des Protestantismus, 3d series, vol. 3. Munich: Chr. Kaiser Verlag, 1930. The second edition (1935) was unaltered except for the new preface.

——————. *Die Theologie Calvins.* Munich: Chr. Kaiser Verlag, 1938. Translated by Harold Knight as *The Theology of Calvin.* London: Lutterworth Press, 1956.

Nijenhuis, W[illem]. *Calvinus oecumenicus: Calvijn en de eenheid der kerk in het licht van zijn briefwisseling.* Kerkhistorische studien, vol. 8. 'S-Gravenhage: Martinus Nijhoff, 1959.

——————. *Ecclesia reformata: Studies on the Reformation.* Kerkhistorische bijdragen, vol. 3. Leiden: E. J. Brill, 1972. The chapter entitled "Calvin's

Attitude Towards the Symbols of the Early Church During the Conflict with Caroli" was first published in 1960.

Parker, T[homas] H. L. *The Doctrine of the Knowledge of God: A Study in the Theology of Calvin*. Edinburgh: Oliver & Boyd, 1952. The American printing, *Calvin's Doctrine of the Knowledge of God* (Grand Rapids, MI: Wm. B. Eerdmans, 1959), though identified as "revised edition," was unchanged except for the addition of an appendix on Dowey's book (see above). The second Edinburgh edition (Oliver & Boyd, 1969) took the title of the American printing.

——————————. *The Oracles of God: An Introduction to the Preaching of John Calvin*. London: Lutterworth Press, 1947.

Partee, Charles. *Calvin and Classical Philosophy*. Studies in the History of Christian Thought, vol. 14. Leiden: E. J. Brill, 1977.

Peterson, Robert A. *Calvin's Doctrine of the Atonement*. Phillipsburg, NJ: Presbyterian and Reformed Publishing Co., 1983.

Pruett, Gordon E. "A Protestant Doctrine of the Eucharistic Presence." *Calvin Theological Journal* 10 (1975):142–74.

Rainbow, Jonathan H. *The Will of God and the Cross: An Historical and Theological Study of John Calvin's Doctrine of Limited Redemption*. Pickwick Theological Monograph Series, vol. 22. Allison Park, PA: Pickwick Publications, 1990.

Raitt, Jill. "Calvin's Use of Bernard of Clairvaux." *Archive for Reformation History* 72 (1981):98–121.

——————————. *The Eucharistic Theology of Theodore Beza: Development of the Reformed Doctrine*. AAR Studies in Religion, no. 4. Chambersburg, PA: American Academy of Religion, 1972.

——————————. "Roman Catholic New Wine in Reformed Old Bottles? The Conversion of the Elements in the Eucharistic Doctrines of Theodore Beza and Edward Schillebeeckx." *Journal of Ecumenical Studies* 8 (1971):581–604.

——————————. "Three Inter-related Principles in Calvin's Unique Doctrine of Infant Baptism." *Sixteenth-Century Journal* 11 (1980):51–61.

Reuter, Karl. *Das Grundverständnis der Theologie Calvins unter Einbeziehung ihrer geschichtlichen Abhängigkeiten*, vol. 1. Beiträge zur Geschichte und Lehre der reformierten Kirche, vol. 15. Neukirchen-Vluyn: Neukirchener Verlag (Verlag des Erziehungsvereins), 1963.

Richard, Lucien Joseph. *The Spirituality of John Calvin*. Atlanta, GA: John Knox Press, 1974.

Ritschl, Otto. *Die reformierte Theologie des 16. und des 17. Jahrhunderts in ihrer Entstehung und Entwicklung. Dogmengeschichte des Protestantismus*, vol. 3. Göttingen: Vandenhoeck & Ruprecht, 1926.

Rogge, Joachim. *Virtus und Res: Um die Abendmahlswirklichkeit bei Calvin*. Arbeiten zur Theologie, first series, vol. 18. Stuttgart: Calwer Verlag, 1965.

Rohls, Jan. *Theologie reformierter Bekenntnisschriften: Von Zürich bis Barmen*. UTB für Wissenschaft: Uni-Taschenbücher 1453. Göttingen: Vandenhoeck & Ruprecht, 1987.

Rorem, Paul. *Calvin and Bullinger on the Lord's Supper*. Alcuin GROW Liturgical Studies, no. 12. Bramcote, Notts.: Grove Books, 1989. First published as two articles in the *Lutheran Quarterly* (1988).

Rotondò, Antonio. *Calvin and the Italian Anti-Trinitarians*. Trans. John and Anne Tedeschi. Reformation Essays and Studies, no. 2. St. Louis, MO: Foundation for Reformation Research, 1968.

Saxer, Ernst. "'Siegel' und 'Versiegeln' in der calvinisch–reformierten Sakramentstheologie des 16. Jahrhunderts." *Zwingliana* 14 (1974–78):397–430.

Schreiner, Susan E. *The Theater of His Glory: Nature and the Natural Order in the Thought of John Calvin.* Studies in Historical Theology, vol. 3. Durham, NC: Labyrinth Press, 1991.

Schümmer, Léopold. *Le Ministère pastoral dans l'Institution Chrétienne de Calvin à la lumière du troisième sacrement.* Veröffentlichungen des Instituts für Europäische Geschichte Mainz, vol. 39. Wiesbaden: Franz Steiner, 1965.

Shepherd, Victor A. *The Nature and Function of Faith in the Theology of John Calvin.* NABPR Dissertation Series, no. 2. Macon, GA: Mercer University Press, 1983.

Smits, Luchesius. *Saint Augustin dans l'oeuvre de Jean Calvin.* 2 vols. Assen: Van Gorcum & Co., 1957–58.

Stauffer, Richard. "Un Calvin méconnu: Le prédicateur de Genève." *Bulletin de la Société de l'histoire du protestantisme français* 123 (1977):184–203.

Stuermann, Walter E. *A Critical Study of Calvin's Concept of Faith.* Tulsa, OK (printed at Ann Arbor, MI: Edwards Brothers), 1952.

Tamburello, Dennis E. "Christ and Mystical Union: A Comparative Study of the Theologies of Bernard of Clairvaux and John Calvin." Ph.D. diss., University of Chicago, 1990.

Torrance, T[homas] F. *Calvin's Doctrine of Man.* London: Lutterworth Press, 1949.

——————————. "Calvins Lehre von der Taufe." In Jürgen Moltmann, ed. (see above), 95–129.

Tylenda, Joseph N. "Calvin and Christ's Presence in the Supper— True or Real." *Scottish Journal of Theology* 27 (1974):65–75.

——————————. "Calvin's Understanding of the Communication of Properties." *Westminster Theological Journal* 38 (1975–76):54–65.

——————————. "The Calvin–Westphal Exchange: The Genesis of Calvin's Treatises against Westphal." *Calvin Theological Journal* 9 (1974):182–209.

——————————. "Christ the Mediator: Calvin versus Stancaro." *Calvin Theological Journal* 8 (1973):5–16.

——————————. "The Controversy on Christ the Mediator: Calvin's Second Reply to Stancaro." *Calvin Theological Journal* 8 (1973):131–57.

——————————. "The Ecumenical Intention of Calvin's Early Eucharistic Teaching." In *Reformatio Perennis,* edited by B. A. Gerrish (see above), 24–47.

——————————. "A Eucharistic Sacrifice in Calvin's Theology?" *Theological Studies* 37 (1976):456–66. Also published as "Calvin on the Relationship between Christ's Cross and the Lord's Supper: The Supper as Eucharistic Sacrifice," in *Renaissance, Reformation, Resurgence,* edited by Peter DeKlerk, 113–26. Grand Rapids, MI: Calvin Theological Seminary, 1976.

——————————. "The Warning That Went Unheeded: John Calvin on Giorgio Biandrata." *Calvin Theological Journal* 12 (1977):24–62.

Van Buren, Paul. *Christ in Our Place: The Substitutionary Character of Calvin's Doctrine of Reconciliation.* Edinburgh: Oliver & Boyd, 1957.

Walker, G. S. M. "The Lord's Supper in the Theology and Practice of Calvin." In G. E. Duffield, ed. (see above), 131–48.

Wallace, Ronald S. *Calvin's Doctrine of the Christian Life.* Grand Rapids, MI:

Wm. B. Eerdmans, 1959.

—————————. *Calvin's Doctrine of the Word and Sacrament.* Edinburgh:
Oliver & Boyd, 1953.

Warfield, Benjamin B. [1909a]. "Calvin's Doctrine of God." *Princeton Theological
Review* 7 (1909):381–436. Reprinted in Warfield, *Calvin and Calvinism* (New
York: Oxford University Press, 1931), and Warfield, *Calvin and Augustine*
(Philadelphia: Presbyterian and Reformed Publishing Co., 1956).

—————————. [1909b]. "Calvin's Doctrine of the Trinity." *Princeton
Theological Review* 7 (1909):553–652.

Wencelius, Léon. *L'Esthétique de Calvin.* Paris: Société d'Édition "Les Belles
Lettres," 1937.

Wendel, François. *Calvin: The Origins and Development of His Religious Thought.*
Translated from the French (1950) by Philip Mairet. London: Collins, 1963.

Wernle, Paul. *Calvin. Der evangelische Glaube nach den Hauptschriften der
Reformatoren,* vol. 3. Tübingen: J. C. B. Mohr (Paul Siebeck), 1919.

Willis, E[dward] David. *Calvin's Catholic Christology: The Function of the So-
Called Extra Calvinisticum in Calvin's Theology.* Studies in Medieval and
Reformation Thought, vol. 2. Leiden: E. J. Brill, 1966.

—————————. "Calvin's Use of *substantia.*" In Wilhelm H. Neuser, ed.
(see above), 289–301.

—————————. "The Influence of Laelius Socinus on Calvin's Doctrines of
the Merits of Christ and the Assurance of Faith." In *Italian Reformation
Studies in Honor of Laelius Socinus,* edited by John A. Tedeschi, 231–41.
Firenze: Felice LeMonnier, 1965.

Wilterdink, Garret A. *Tyrant or Father? A Study of Calvin's Doctrine of God.* 2
vols. Scholastic Monograph Series. Bristol, IN: Wyndham Hall Press, 1985.

Zachman, Randall C. "The Testimony of the Conscience in the Theology of
Martin Luther and John Calvin: A Comparative Study." Ph.D. diss.,
University of Chicago, 1990.

INDEX

on Baptism, 124
on Lord's Supper, 10, 173-74
on mass, 146 n.65
on sacraments, 12, 105, 133 n.27
Institutes of the Christian Religion
    1559, 10, 16, 18, 24-27, 44-45, 83,
    91 n.15, 170
on Baptism, 109, 116, 120 n.137
on Christ, 53, 56, 84
on faith, 63, 66
on Lord's Supper, 21, 125-26, 142,
    144, 154 n.84, 166 n.29
on mass, 145, 146 n.65
on sacraments, 12, 102-5, 113-14
Institutes of the Christian Religion
    1560, 97
Institution, words of, 51, 137 n.41,
    142, 165, 182 n.78, 183
Instruction in Faith, 110 n.103

Jansen, J.F., 55 n.16
Jesus., 38, 56 n.16, 59, 67, 92, 130
    See also Christ.
John the Baptist, 110 n.105, 118
Judas, 154 n.84
Justification, 56 n.17, 60, 70 n.83, 93,
    96, 98, 106, 139, 172
and faith, 62 n.47, 72 n.93, 85 n.144,
    134 n.29
and freedom, 101
and union with Christ, 56 n.17

Kendall, R.T., 171 n.43
Keys, 83
Knowledge, 63 nn.50, 51; 64-68
of God, 18, 19 n.84, 25-26, 63-64, 67-
    68
of humanity, 18, 25, 41
Kolfhaus, W., 62 n.47
Koopmans, J., 53 n.10
Krusche, W., 72 n.93

Lactantius, 39 n.81
Lane, A.N.S., 96 n.43
Language, 25, 51
accommodated, 53
eucharistic, 6, 12
gender inclusive, 30 n.37, 61 n.38,
    88 n.3, 89 n.9
Latitudinarians, 1, 22

Law, 65-66, 78-79, 98, 101
Leibnitz, G.W., 180-81
Leith, J., 76 n.106
Lieberg, H., 104 n.77
Locher, G.W., 145 n.64
Lord's Supper, 2-3, 13, 19-21, 48
    n.128, 109, 126, 131-34, 137, 139,
    147-49, 158, 162, 163 n.16,
    168 n.33, 184, 190
and Baptism, 110 n.102, 124-25, 134
    n.30
and Christ. *See* Christ: and Lord's
    Supper
corporate character, 150-51
efficacy of, 9, 127, 133, 162, 163 n.16
and faith, 74, 126-27, 136, 138-39
frequency of, 125, 151 n.77, 159 n.6
as gift, 19-20, 135-139, 144-45, 149-
    51, 156
and gratitude, 19-20, 156
Luther on. *See* Luther: on Lord's
    Supper
Lutherans on. *See* Lutherans,
    Lutheranism: on Lord's Supper
modus (manner of eating), 74, 130-
    31, 135, 138 n.42, 142 n.57, 144,
    160, 174-76, 178 n.70, 182 n.78
as mystery, 135 n.32, 173, 175, 181
as offering, 126-27, 136 n.34
as pledge, 124, 127, 133
and predestination, 169, 172
and promise, 126-27, 148, 164
Real Presence in, 9-10, 13, 19, 54,
    126, 160, 164, 173 n.51, 177, 180
    n.74
reception of, 125, 138, 143, 173
    nn.51, 53
as sacrifice, 126, 146 n.65, 152-56
and signs, 19, 137, 140-41, 144
and Spirit, 131, 137-38, 175
use of, 13, 125-27, 144
and word, 131-32, 139
Zwingli on. *See* Zwingli: on Lord's
    Supper
See also Institution, words of; Mass;
    Sacraments
Love, 64, 92, 126
Luther, M, 2, 6-7, 31, 33, 35, 37, 46
    n.114, 93, 97, 141, 143 n.61, 156
    n.91, 183 n.79